HOLIDAY HOME COOKING

FAVORITE RECIPES

FROM THE

Members of the Cooking & Crafts Club

Text Complied & Edited by Frances McCullough

COOKING & CRAFTS CLUB · NEW YORK

HOLIDAY HOME COOKING

The publisher wishes to acknowledge the following for permission to reprint the recipes listed. Every effort has been made to identify the copyright owners of each recipe. We apologize to those we have been unable to locate.

Mexican Corn Soup from *The Cuisines of Mexico* by Diana Kennedy. Copyright © 1972 by Diana Kennedy. Reprinted by permission of Harper & Row, Publishers, Inc. Mulligatawny from *Classic Indian Cooking* by Julie Sahni. Copyright © 1980 by Julie Sahni. By permission of William Morrow & Company. Baked Parsnips with Apples and Oranges from the *Victory Garden Cookbook,* by Marian Morash. Copyright © 1982 by Marian Morash and WGBH Educational Foundation. Reprinted by permission of Alfred A. Knopf, Inc. Sweet Potatoes with Apples and Chestnuts courtesy *Gourmet.* Copyright © 1982 by The Condé Nast Publications, Inc. Old-Fashioned Corn Fritters copyright © 1979, New York News, Inc. Reprinted with permission. Stuffed Crown Roast of Pork from *Southern Living 1980 Annual Recipes.* Copyright 1980 by Oxmoor House, Inc. Reproduced by permission. Jewish Apple Cake from the *Sweet Energy Cookbook.* Reprinted by permission of Sweet Energy, P.O. Box G, Essex Center, VT 05451. Rich Chocolate Cheesecake from *Southern Living 1981 Annual Recipes.* Copyright 1981 by Oxmoor House, Inc. Reproduced by permission. Speculaas from the *Ulster County Extension Home Economics Program "Tercentennial Cookbook."* Ice Box Cookies from *Let's Cook! A Book for Junior Cooks,* Copyright © 1936, 1942 by Bernice Budlong. French Doughnuts reprinted by permission of *The Daily Gleaner,* Fredericton, New Brunswick.

Book-of-the-Month Records® offers a wide range of opera, classical and jazz recordings. For information and catalog write to BOMR, Dept. 901, Camp Hill, PA 17012.

DESIGNED BY JOEL AVIROM

Library of Congress Cataloging-in-Publication Data

Holiday home cooking.

Includes index.
1. Holiday cookery.   I. McCullough, Frances Monson,
1939–   . II. Cooking and Crafts Club (Book-of-the-Month Club)
TX739.H653 1986   641.5′68   86-20773

ACKNOWLEDGMENTS

This book literally could not have been put together without the help of our dedicated tester-cooks at Peter Kump's New York Cooking School. Peter himself made the entire project possible, and Gaynor Grant, who coordinated the testing, saw to it that the whole process went more or less smoothly and managed to remain unfussed when everything went completely crazy. Our first-rate testers were Diane Hayes, Karen McCleary Metz, Betsy Schultz, Barbara Lind, Donna Gelb, Lorna DeVries, Richard Simpson, Mark Feldman, Dan Wollner, Anne Barry, Toya Tsuya, Anita Jacobsen, Deborah Sayre Lahm, Jane Kilbourne, and Sarah Ross. Special thanks go to Prudence Hilburn, our dessert expert, whose constant enthusiasm and vigilant professionalism contributed a great deal to this book.

We've relied enormously on the invaluable services of our extraordinary copy editor, Elaine Chubb. If these recipes read as smoothly as we hope they do, the credit is hers alone.

CONTENTS

INTRODUCTION

When we first decided to ask our members to send in their favorite holiday recipes, we had no idea what we'd get back in the mail. We were thinking of those great cookbooks put together by church groups or women's clubs, with their unique recipes that never turn up in big cookbooks. Of course, it's always the local element that holds these books together, and we were attempting something a lot more ambitious: a cookbook for all of North America. All we knew was that our members consistently buy the best cookbooks we can find, and that seemed like a great recommendation for their favorite recipes.

What I feel, looking over these recipes now that the book is done, is enormous pride in North America's home cooks. This, to me, is real food, food that means something. It's food that has stood the test of being made dozens and dozens of times, or hundreds and hundreds of times, in some cases. The recipes have been preserved on scraps of paper, clipped from newspapers now decades old, treasured in obscure cookbooks temporarily lost to the mice in the attic but discovered in time to save the best recipes. Or a recipe has been found among a grandmother's papers, tucked into her savings book where it was sure to be found; or given to a foreigner who took it back home and gave it to an admiring American overseas who brought it back home and gave it to someone from another state. Most of all, it's grandmother's cooking; we had submissions from a number of professional chefs, but very few of them measured up to the best from our home cooks.

In all, we got over three thousand recipes, and they're still trickling in as we go to press. You'll notice right away that the book is heavily balanced toward sweets. In case anyone was ever in doubt, what Americans and Canadians think of right away when they think of the holidays is baking. And rightly so: it seemed to us the very best recipes, as a category, were the sweet ones. In part, that may be because the centerpiece of a feast is usually some extraordinary display of protein: a standing rib roast, for instance, or a turkey, a leg of lamb, a goose, maybe even a suckling pig. And although we did get some excellent main-course recipes, they were the exception.

We also discovered the particular foods people really love. The first position on the list goes to the classic American holiday dishes, made with native ingredients: pumpkin pie, turkey, sweet potato dishes, baked beans, coleslaw, barbecue, cranberries, blueberries, fruitcakes, shortbread, pecans, plum puddings, and, in first place, sugar cookies, with cheesecake as runner-up. There were dozens on dozens of pickles, and the recipes were outstanding. And there was a special fondness for seafood, especially for Christmas Eve. Sometimes it was difficult to tell whether a dish itself was terrific or the emotions surrounding it simply transformed it. There were a lot of everyday recipes from the Depression that people really adored, for instance, but nearly always the real enthusiasm was for a much-missed grandmother or aunt who originally made the dish. It was moving to see how loyal people were to these particular dishes, how proud they were to be keeping the traditions alive in the mouths of the newest generation. And, of course, often these dishes were splendid.

The only way to find out, though, was to test them, and for that we engaged Peter Kump's New York Cooking School. Choosing among the thousands of recipes was a nearly impossible task. We set up all sorts of criteria, but still it couldn't be made into a truly scientific project. Anyone whose recipe wasn't chosen should realize that we're very fallible and that the only truly important judges are the ones at your table. In the end, what mattered to us most was the single question: Would you want to make this dish again? A hearty "Yes!" sent the recipe straight into the book.

Aside from the great hand-me-down recipes, which come from all over the world, there are some truly unusual recipes here: the fish-smoking method from Finland, done in a fireplace; the thirteenth-century Baghdad dessert; the Arctic salmon cooked in a dishwasher; and the Quebec turkey covered in a mustard crust, for starters. You can probably bring the Aleut Fish Pie to a potluck supper without fear of its being duplicated, and the Christmas Beef will certainly be on no other menu but yours.

As you'll see, we've interpreted the word "holiday" very broadly. There are not just the traditional holidays; we also thought about the times you have a full house for several days and want to have something really good and unusual but not hard to prepare, since your energies should go elsewhere. We assume you want to fuss a bit for the grand occasions and turn out a spectacular Yule Log, for instance—but also have a great breakfast ready without much effort.

We've had a very good time cooking these dishes, and we can guarantee that each of them tastes terrific to someone out there and some one of us. We hope you have the same sense of discovery and pleasure in this book and that some of these recipes will become your own favorites.

Frances McCullough

HOLIDAY HOME COOKING

Appetizers

FRIED BLACK-EYED PEAS

◆◆◆◆◆◆◆◆◆◆◆◆◆◆◆◆◆◆◆◆◆◆◆◆◆◆◆◆◆◆◆◆◆◆◆

Mrs. David Butler Jackson, Mississippi A superlative recipe given
◆◆◆◆◆◆◆◆◆◆◆◆◆◆◆◆◆◆◆◆◆◆◆◆◆◆◆◆◆◆◆◆◆ to Mrs. Butler's mother in
1949 by an octogenarian friend. Mrs. Butler advises serving these in summer,
accompanied by Bloody Marys frozen to a slush, or on New Year's Day (for
good luck) with homemade onion soup. But she thinks perhaps they're best
with very cold martinis.

½ pound black-eyed peas
2 cloves garlic, chopped
1 jalapeño pepper, chopped
1 teaspoon salt
*1¼ teaspoons freshly
ground black pepper*
*½ cup peanut oil (more
if necessary)*

Serves 4 to 6.

Soak the peas in 3 quarts hot water overnight. Next morning, slip the skins off the peas, drain, and pat dry with paper towels. (If you become impatient with the skins, you can leave them on, but the result will be slightly cruder.)

Place in the bowl of a food processor or blender with the garlic, jalapeño pepper, salt, and black pepper. Process until the peas are ground and will hold together.

Spoon out about a tablespoon of the pea mixture and form it into a thin patty about 1 inch in diameter. Repeat until the pea mixture is used up.

Heat the peanut oil and fry the patties in a skillet over medium heat in batches on both sides until they are golden brown, about 5 minutes to a side. Drain on paper towels. May be served hot or cold. Unused mixture keeps virtually indefinitely in refrigerator.

LEEKS WITH PROSCIUTTO GRATINÉ

◆◆◆◆◆◆◆◆◆◆◆◆◆◆◆◆◆◆◆◆◆◆◆◆◆◆◆◆◆◆◆◆

Rebecca Purro   New York, New York   A really superb appetizer that's
◆◆◆◆◆◆◆◆◆◆◆◆◆◆◆◆◆◆◆◆◆◆◆◆◆◆◆◆◆◆◆◆ also on the hearty side—it
would be a delicious contribution to a buffet table.

8 medium leeks

8 slices prosciutto or ham

3 tablespoons unsalted
  butter

3 tablespoons all-purpose
  flour, sifted

3 cups strong chicken
  stock, heated

1 cup grated Gruyère
  cheese

⅓ cup plain bread crumbs

Serves 4 as an appetizer.

Trim the leeks, split them lengthwise through the green part only, and wash them thoroughly. Put them in a saucepan with enough water to cover completely and bring to a boil. Reduce heat and simmer until tender, about 10 minutes.

Drain and cool the leeks. When you can handle them, wrap each leek in a slice of prosciutto and place side by side in a buttered shallow baking dish.

Preheat oven to 375° F.

Meanwhile, make a roux by combining the butter and flour in a medium saucepan. Cook for a few minutes, stirring, over medium heat until all the flour is absorbed and the mixture is light and foamy. Add the chicken stock—it should be very hot—to the roux and continue cooking over medium heat until the sauce thickens.

Pour the sauce over the leeks, sprinkle the cheese and bread crumbs evenly over the top, and bake uncovered until brown and bubbly, about 15 to 20 minutes.

SPINACH BALLS

◆◆◆◆◆◆◆◆◆◆◆◆◆◆◆◆◆◆◆◆◆◆◆◆◆◆◆◆◆◆

Judith Thorn   New York, New York   Don't pass these by if you don't
◆◆◆◆◆◆◆◆◆◆◆◆◆◆◆◆◆◆◆◆◆◆◆◆◆◆◆◆ like recipes that use convenience
foods—we don't either, but these little appetizers are truly delicious, so good
that Judith Thorn is besieged with requests for the recipe every time she
serves them. Children can easily put this recipe together—but warn them that
the sauce is very pungent.

2 (10-ounce) packages
 frozen spinach,
 defrosted and squeezed
 dry

2 cups herbed stuffing mix

1 cup freshly grated
 Parmesan cheese

8 tablespoons butter,
 melted

4 scallions, chopped,
 including some green

3 eggs, beaten

Dash of nutmeg,
 preferably freshly grated

SAUCE
(Allow 4 hours for
 marinating)

½ cup dry mustard

½ cup dry white wine

¼ cup honey

Serves 20 as an appetizer.

Mix all of the ingredients for the spinach balls together,
form into 1-inch balls, and refrigerate for at least 30
minutes. (They can also be frozen at this point.)

Prepare sauce by mixing all ingredients. Let sit 4 hours.

If spinach balls have been frozen, bring them to room
temperature. Preheat oven to 350° F. Put the spinach balls
on an ungreased cookie sheet and bake 10 minutes.

To serve, stick a toothpick into each spinach ball and let
guests dip them into the sauce.

ESCARGOTS PROSCIUTTO

◆◆◆◆◆◆◆◆◆◆◆◆◆◆◆◆◆◆◆◆◆◆◆◆◆◆◆◆

Donal Weaving   Tulsa, Oklahoma An unusual way of preparing snails,
◆◆◆◆◆◆◆◆◆◆◆◆◆◆◆◆◆◆◆◆◆◆◆◆◆◆◆◆ particularly suitable for a cocktail
party. Donal Weaving is an executive chef at a country club, one of the very
few professional chefs whose recipes matched the best of our home cooks'.

1 (24-count) can French
    snails

24 paper-thin slices
    prosciutto

1⅓ sticks butter

1 teaspoon minced garlic

1 teaspoon freshly
    squeezed lemon juice

1 teaspoon dry white wine

Freshly ground white
    pepper to taste

1 teaspoon minced fresh
    parsley

*Serves 8 to 10 as an
    appetizer.*

Rinse and drain the snails. Roll each snail in a slice of prosciutto and secure with a small round toothpick. Arrange neatly in a chafing dish in which you'll serve them. Warm the snails in the chafing dish over low heat just before serving.

Make the butter sauce just prior to serving. In a small saucepan, melt the butter with the garlic. Bring to a boil (it will foam up). Allow to boil for about 30 seconds, then remove from the heat and beat with a wire whisk. While beating, gradually add the lemon juice, wine, pepper, and parsley. Pour over the snails in the chafing dish.

SCALLOPED OYSTERS

◆◆◆◆◆◆◆◆◆◆◆◆◆◆◆◆◆◆◆◆◆◆◆◆◆◆◆◆◆◆◆◆◆◆◆◆◆

Mary Proctor   Weaverville, North Carolina Oysters seem to loom

◆◆◆◆◆◆◆◆◆◆◆◆◆◆◆◆◆◆◆◆◆◆◆◆◆◆◆◆◆◆◆◆◆ large as favorite holiday fare, especially for intimate occasions such as Christmas Eve. This plain but classic preparation is very satisfying.

1 quart oysters, shucked

2 cups crushed saltine crackers

Butter

Salt and freshly ground black pepper to taste

1 egg

½ cup milk

Serves 4 to 6.

Preheat oven to 350° F.

Drain the oysters, reserving the liquor. Alternate layers of cracker crumbs and oysters in a buttered casserole, dotting each layer with butter and sprinkling with salt and pepper, until all ingredients are used.

Beat the egg with the milk and reserved oyster liquor. Pour over casserole. Bake uncovered for 30 minutes.

CAVIAR PIE

◆◆◆◆◆◆◆◆◆◆◆◆◆◆◆◆◆◆◆◆◆◆◆◆◆◆◆

Nancy O'Hara   Lititz, Pennsylvania This voluptuous pie has been
◆◆◆◆◆◆◆◆◆◆◆◆◆◆◆◆◆◆◆◆◆◆◆◆◆◆ served at both Nancy O'Hara's
daughters' weddings, where half the guests begged for the recipe. You can use
several types of caviar if you want a more elaborate presentation—black
lumpfish, red, and golden. Serve with an assortment of crackers.

6 hard-cooked eggs

3 tablespoons mayonnaise

*1½ bunches scallions,
chopped fine, including
some green*

*⅔ cup sour cream, at
room temperature*

*1 (8-ounce) package
cream cheese, softened
to room temperature*

*1 (3-ounce) jar caviar,
well drained*

*Lemon slices and parsley
sprigs for garnish*

Serves 20.

Oil an 8-inch springform pan thoroughly.

Grate the eggs and mix with the mayonnaise. Pat down evenly in the pan.

Sprinkle the scallions on top of the egg layer. Blend the sour cream and cream cheese and spread carefully on top of the scallions. Cover with plastic wrap and chill for 24 hours.

Just before serving, remove the sides of the pan and place the pie on a decorative platter. Sprinkle the caviar evenly on top and garnish with lemon slices and parsley.

ANCHOVY RONDELLES

◆◆◆◆◆◆◆◆◆◆◆◆◆◆◆◆◆◆◆◆◆◆◆◆◆◆◆◆◆◆◆◆◆◆◆

John Nuttall   Vancouver, British Columbia There seems to be a
◆◆◆◆◆◆◆◆◆◆◆◆◆◆◆◆◆◆◆◆◆◆◆◆◆◆◆◆◆◆◆◆◆◆ growing passion in North
America for anchovies—these delectable little morsels should further the cause.

12 slices white bread

Olive oil

6 tablespoons unsalted butter, softened to room temperature

1 (2-ounce) can anchovy fillets plus additional slivers for garnish

Dash of Burgess Genuine Original Anchovy Sauce (optional)

1 (2-ounce) jar red lumpfish caviar, or beluga

Serves 3 to 6.

Using a cookie cutter with a serrated edge, about 3 inches in diameter, cut out 12 circles of bread. Brush the circles on one side with olive oil. Toast them in the broiler, oiled side up, until they are golden.

Preheat oven to 325° F. Thoroughly blend the butter and anchovy fillets. If you can find the imported English anchovy sauce, a dash will enrich the anchovy butter. Spread the anchovy butter on the untoasted side of half the bread circles. Cover with the other 6 circles, toasted side up, heat the rondelles gently in the oven, and garnish with slivers of anchovy fillets and a dab of caviar just before serving.

HOME-SMOKED FISH

◆◆◆◆◆◆◆◆◆◆◆◆◆◆◆◆◆◆◆◆◆◆◆

Shelagh Robinson   Bath, Ontario   When Shelagh Robinson's family lived
◆◆◆◆◆◆◆◆◆◆◆◆◆◆◆◆◆◆◆◆◆◆◆   in Finland years ago, their cook used
to smoke whitefish in the dining room fireplace. Now they use his method to
smoke trout, either in their fireplace in winter or on the barbecue in summer.
It's a slightly messy but very rewarding operation.

*Trout, cleaned and rinsed
    with lemon juice and
    water*

Salt

*Butter, softened to room
    temperature*

*Serves 1 for each fish
    smoked.*

Begin with very fresh trout, sprinkle it with salt, and leave it covered in the refrigerator for 1 hour.

Put a walnut-sized lump of butter inside each fish and smear the outside with softened butter. Wrap each fish separately in buttered brown paper, using a piece large enough to cover the fish twice. Fold in the ends of the paper.

Wrap each fish bundle in about 4 double pages of newspaper. Place directly on well-burned (to the white stage) charcoal. Turn once during smoking. Fish are usually done when the newspaper has burned away. Serve hot or cold.

CLAMS CASINO À LA VARRATI

◆◆◆◆◆◆◆◆◆◆◆◆◆◆◆◆◆◆◆◆◆◆◆◆◆◆

Greg Varrati   Anchorage, Alaska As a young boy growing up on Long
◆◆◆◆◆◆◆◆◆◆◆◆◆◆◆◆◆◆◆◆◆◆◆◆◆ Island, Greg Varrati used to be sent
out into the Great South Bay to tread up clams, which his mother would serve
as appetizers at her dinner parties. Now that he lives in Alaska, he's been
experimenting with his mother's basic recipe, and we agree that he has it down
right. The clams can be prepared several hours ahead of time, then covered
and refrigerated until broiling and serving.

*3 dozen littleneck or
cherrystone clams*

*1 cup fresh tomato sauce,
or canned Italian
tomatoes chopped and
cooked lightly in 1
tablespoon of olive oil*

3 cloves garlic, minced

Tabasco sauce

*Freshly squeezed lemon
juice*

*½ cup bread crumbs,
preferably homemade
from good Italian bread*

*¼ pound sliced bacon, cut
into ½-inch pieces*

Serves 6 as an appetizer.

Thoroughly scrub clams before opening. Dispose of any
clam that is not tightly shut or that has a cracked shell.
Using a strong, thin-bladed knife or a clam knife, open
each clam, discard half the shell, and loosen clam from
remaining half shell. Place the clams on the half shell in a
baking dish.

Preheat broiler.

Top each clam with a teaspoon (or less, depending on the
size of the clam) of tomato sauce, 2 or 3 pieces of chopped
garlic, 2 dashes of Tabasco, and 2 drops of lemon juice.
Sprinkle with bread crumbs and place a piece of bacon on
top of each clam.

Place under preheated broiler and broil until bacon is crisp,
about 6 minutes. Serve immediately with crusty bread.

CLAMS BORDELAISE

◆◆◆◆◆◆◆◆◆◆◆◆◆◆◆◆◆◆◆◆◆◆◆◆◆◆◆◆◆

Jeanne Boyle   Hewitt, New Jersey A very tasty clam dish that works
◆◆◆◆◆◆◆◆◆◆◆◆◆◆◆◆◆◆◆◆◆◆◆◆◆◆◆◆◆ as either an appetizer or the centerpiece of a light supper. The recipe evolved from one of Pierre Franey's.
Mrs. Boyle suggests it as an appetizer for the Fourth of July—it would also do
nicely for Bastille Day (July 14).

8 tablespoons butter

1 medium onion, chopped

2 cloves garlic, minced

*⅓ cup chopped fresh
  parsley*

*1 (13¾-ounce) can
  chicken broth*

1 cup dry white wine

½ cup uncooked rice

*2 dozen well-scrubbed
  clams*

**Serves 4 as an appetizer,
  2 for light supper.**

In a large kettle, melt the butter and add the onion, garlic, and parsley. Cook and stir until the onion is soft. Add the chicken broth, wine, and rice. Bring to a boil, reduce heat, cover, and simmer 15 minutes.

Add clams, cover, and simmer 5 to 10 minutes, until clams pop open. Discard any clams that do not open. Ladle into bowls.

ANNIE'S PICKLED SHRIMP

◆◆◆◆◆◆◆◆◆◆◆◆◆◆◆◆◆◆◆◆◆◆◆◆

Linda Gay   Houston, Texas We think these tasty shrimp would be
◆◆◆◆◆◆◆◆◆◆◆◆◆◆◆◆◆◆◆◆◆◆◆ particularly delicious served with homemade mayonnaise with minced jalapeño or *serrano* peppers added. A little extra
Tabasco on the side is also a good idea.

*¼ cup mixed pickling
  spices*

*4 stalks celery, leaves
  attached*

2½ pounds fresh shrimp

*1 medium onion, sliced
  thin*

8 bay leaves

*1¼ cups vegetable oil,
  including some olive oil*

¾ cup white vinegar

2½ teaspoons celery seeds

2 teaspoons salt

Tabasco sauce

Serves 8 to 10.

Bring enough water to cover the shrimp to a boil in a
large pot. Add the mixed pickling spices and celery to
the pot and boil 5 minutes to season the water. Add
the shrimp. When the water comes back to the boil and the
shrimp are pink, remove and drain them. When they are cool
enough to handle, shell and devein them.

Arrange the shrimp in a shallow glass dish in alternating
layers with the onion slices and bay leaves.

Combine the remaining ingredients and pour over the shrimp.
Cover and place in the refrigerator for 24 hours before
serving. Serve with toothpicks or on small plates. This dish
will keep for at least a week, refrigerated and tightly covered.

TOSTADAS WITH SUN-DRIED TOMATOES, GOAT CHEESE, AND THYME

◆◆◆◆◆◆◆◆◆◆◆◆◆◆◆◆◆◆◆◆◆◆◆◆◆◆◆◆◆◆◆◆

Anita Roberts   Pound Ridge, New York Anita Roberts was longing
◆◆◆◆◆◆◆◆◆◆◆◆◆◆◆◆◆◆◆◆◆◆◆◆◆◆◆◆◆◆ for tostadas one day but
didn't have the traditional ingredients on hand. She improvised and came up
with this version, halfway between a tostada and an elegant pizza. Try hard to
get fresh thyme leaves—they really do make a difference.

1 (10-ounce) jar sun-
    dried tomatoes, cut in
    slivers, oil reserved

8 large flour tortillas

½ pound goat cheese
    (Bûche, Biquou, or
    Montrachet), crumbled

½ pound mozzarella,
    coarsely shredded

3–4 tablespoons finely
    chopped jalapeño
    peppers, fresh or
    canned

3–4 tablespoons fresh
    thyme leaves or 1
    tablespoon dried thyme

Freshly ground black
    pepper to taste

Serves 8 as an appetizer.

Preheat oven to 400° F. Brush the oil from the tomatoes onto one side of the tortillas. Place on a baking sheet, oiled side up, and bake for 5 to 7 minutes, or until lightly browned and crisp. Remove from the oven.

Toss together the goat cheese and mozzarella and divide among the tortillas, covering the surfaces with cheese. Scatter the tomatoes and jalapeño peppers over the cheese. Sprinkle with thyme leaves and season with black pepper. Sprinkle any additional reserved oil over each tortilla.

Return the tortillas to the oven until the cheeses are melted and bubbling. Serve whole or cut into quarters.

ANCHOVY BREAD

◆◆◆◆◆◆◆◆◆◆◆◆◆◆◆◆◆◆◆◆◆◆◆◆◆◆◆◆◆

Robert Rapone   Fort Wayne, Indiana   You have to love anchovies to
◆◆◆◆◆◆◆◆◆◆◆◆◆◆◆◆◆◆◆◆◆◆◆◆◆◆◆   appreciate this bread, which
will feed one Italian, according to Mr. Rapone, or three to four regular people.
We liked it best the next day, toasted. It would be a splendid contribution to
an antipasto platter. A few extra strips of anchovies laid on top before baking
would add to its charm.

*1 loaf homemade bread
   dough or frozen white
   bread dough*

*1 (2-ounce) can flat
   anchovy fillets, oil
   reserved, plus more if
   desired*

*7–8 tablespoons tomato
   sauce*

*Freshly ground black
   pepper*

Olive oil

*Makes 1 loaf; serves 6
   to 8.*

If using frozen dough, thaw it, let rise, and punch down. If
using freshly made dough, bring it through the first rise.
Roll out to a 12 × 18-inch rectangle.

Cut the anchovy fillets into very small pieces. Sprinkle on
top of the dough. Combine the oil from the anchovy can and
5 tablespoons of the tomato sauce. Pour on the surface of
the dough and distribute evenly with your fingers. Season
lightly with black pepper.

Oil a baking sheet with the olive oil. Roll up the dough
lengthwise as for a jelly roll. Place on the baking sheet in a
horseshoe shape. With your fingers, spread 2 to 3 tablespoons
more sauce to cover the roll.

Cover with plastic wrap and allow to rise until doubled in
bulk.

Preheat oven to 350° F. Decorate loaf with additional anchovy
strips if desired. Bake for 45 minutes, or until medium brown.
Cool on a wire rack.

ANCHOVY MAYONNAISE

◆◆◆◆◆◆◆◆◆◆◆◆◆◆◆◆◆◆◆◆◆◆◆◆◆◆◆◆◆◆◆

Marilyn Medini Mount Kisco, New York This excellent recipe has
◆◆◆◆◆◆◆◆◆◆◆◆◆◆◆◆◆◆◆◆◆◆◆◆◆◆◆◆◆ been passed down from a
great-grandmother. People who dislike anchovies intensely have eaten this dip
at Mrs. Medini's house and raved over it, unable to guess what might be in it.
This makes a delicious dip for fresh vegetables and is also excellent with poached
fish or as a spread on sandwiches.

*12–14 anchovy fillets
(1 [2-ounce] can)*

2 cloves garlic, chopped

*¼ cup chopped fresh
parsley*

*¼ cup chopped fresh basil
leaves*

*1 tablespoon Dijon
mustard*

*1 teaspoon capers,
drained*

*2 cups mayonnaise,
preferably homemade*

*Makes slightly over 2
cups.*

Place the anchovies, garlic, parsley, basil, mustard, and capers in a blender or food processor, and puree.

Combine the puree with the mayonnaise. Allow the mixture to stand for a few hours before serving so that the flavors blend.

GOAT CHEESE WITH GARLIC AND HERBS

◆◆◆◆◆◆◆◆◆◆◆◆◆◆◆◆◆◆◆◆◆◆◆◆◆

Sibley Gillis   Cockeysville, Maryland   Sibley Gillis serves this delect-
◆◆◆◆◆◆◆◆◆◆◆◆◆◆◆◆◆◆◆◆◆◆   able cheese as a light side dish
for New Year's Day lunch. She also puts 6 to 8 slices in decorative glass jars
for Christmas presents. Another possibility is to heat the cheese briefly under
the broiler and serve it over a salad of spinach or sharp greens—such as
watercress and radicchio—mixing it in as you toss the salad.

*1 (11-ounce) log
    Montrachet cheese*

1 cup olive oil

*4 large cloves garlic,
    chopped coarsely*

*1 tablespoon snipped
    chives or chopped
    shallots*

*1½ teaspoons fresh thyme
    leaves or ½ teaspoon
    dried thyme*

*1½ teaspoons fresh basil
    leaves*

1 teaspoon dried rosemary

1 bay leaf, crumbled

*Freshly ground black
    pepper to taste*

Serves 4 to 6.

Slice the cheese into ½-inch disks and place them in a wide-mouthed glass jar.

Combine the rest of the ingredients and pour over the cheese to cover it completely. Allow to sit at room temperature for 3 to 4 days. Serve at room temperature with green salad and French bread.

WISCONSIN THREE-CHEESE BALL

◆◆◆◆◆◆◆◆◆◆◆◆◆◆◆◆◆◆◆◆◆◆◆◆◆◆◆◆◆◆◆◆

Paula Collins   Eau Claire, Wisconsin   Wisconsin is famous not only for
◆◆◆◆◆◆◆◆◆◆◆◆◆◆◆◆◆◆◆◆◆◆◆◆◆◆◆◆◆◆   its cheese but also for its horseradish. Here three cheeses are set off by the pungency of horseradish and the
sweetness of the pecans. Serve with crackers or toast.

*11 ounces cream cheese,
  softened to room
  temperature*

*4 ounces blue cheese,
  crumbled*

*1½ cups shredded sharp
  Cheddar cheese*

¼ cup minced onion

*1 tablespoon
  Worcestershire sauce*

2 tablespoons milk

2 tablespoons mayonnaise

*1 cup pecans, finely
  chopped*

Serves 20.

Place the cheeses in a mixer bowl. Add the rest of the ingredients except the pecans and blend on low speed, scraping sides and bottom of bowl occasionally. Beat on medium speed until fluffy. Cover the bowl and chill overnight.

Shape the mixture into a ball, roll the ball in the pecans, and chill for 2 hours, until firm.

PUMPKIN SEED DIP

◆◆◆◆◆◆◆◆◆◆◆◆◆◆◆◆◆◆◆◆◆◆◆◆◆

Jim Fobel New York, New York This earthy, unusual dip of Mayan
◆◆◆◆◆◆◆◆◆◆◆◆◆◆◆◆◆◆◆◆◆◆◆◆ inspiration goes beautifully with corn
chips, crisp-fried tortillas, cold cooked shrimp, or raw vegetables. It has a
haunting rustic flavor.

*1½ cups (8 ounces)
hulled, unsalted
pumpkin seeds*

3 tablespoons olive oil

1 clove garlic, minced

¾–1 cup chicken broth

*¼ cup freshly squeezed
lime or lemon juice*

*1 hot chili pepper, finely
chopped (or hot sauce
to taste)*

1 teaspoon salt

*¼ teaspoon freshly ground
black pepper*

*1 small sprig of parsley
for a garnish*

*1 small red hot chili
pepper for garnish*

Makes 2 cups.

Toast the pumpkin seeds in a small, ungreased skillet over moderate heat until they start to pop and turn golden, about 2 to 3 minutes. Cool slightly, place in a blender or food processor, and set aside.

Heat the olive oil in a small skillet over moderate heat. Add the garlic and sauté about 30 seconds, or until it just starts to color. Pour over the reserved pumpkin seeds. Add ¾ cup chicken broth, the lime juice, chopped chili pepper, salt, and black pepper. Puree, stopping occasionally to scrape down the sides. If the dip is too thick, add more chicken broth until it reaches a moderately thick consistency.

Transfer the mixture to a serving bowl and chill, covered. Stir, and garnish with parsley and a chili pepper.

BLUE CHEESE MOUSSE

◆◆◆◆◆◆◆◆◆◆◆◆◆◆◆◆◆◆◆◆◆◆◆◆◆◆◆◆◆◆◆◆◆◆◆

Bertram Heckel   San Juan, Puerto Rico   A very rich and very savory
◆◆◆◆◆◆◆◆◆◆◆◆◆◆◆◆◆◆◆◆◆◆◆◆◆◆◆◆◆◆ mousse—a little goes a long
way. It makes an unusual contribution to a buffet table, and it can be dressed
up to look gorgeous.

*2 cups cottage cheese
(large- or small-curd)*

2 cups sour cream

5 ounces blue cheese

*2 envelopes unflavored
gelatin*

½ cup milk, chilled

1 cup chopped pecans

*1 cup heavy cream,
whipped*

*Salt and freshly ground
black pepper to taste*

*Green food coloring
(optional)*

*Sliced cucumbers for
garnish (optional)*

Serves 12 to 20.

Grease a 2-quart mold and set aside.

In a blender or food processor, blend the cottage
cheese, sour cream, and blue cheese.

Soften the gelatin in the cold milk, then place the mixture in
the top of a double boiler over simmering water until the
gelatin is dissolved. Remove from the double boiler and add
to the cheese mixture. Add the nuts and fold in the whipped
cream.

Season lightly with salt and pepper to taste, and add a few
drops green food coloring if desired.

Pour the mousse into the prepared mold and let it set,
covered with plastic wrap, for at least 4 hours in the
refrigerator. Unmold onto a large platter and garnish with
the sliced cucumbers, if using.

SANTA FE PECANS

◆◆◆◆◆◆◆◆◆◆◆◆◆◆◆◆◆◆◆◆◆◆◆◆◆◆◆◆◆

Sibley Gillis   Cockeysville, Maryland These are very addictive spiced
◆◆◆◆◆◆◆◆◆◆◆◆◆◆◆◆◆◆◆◆◆◆◆◆◆◆◆ nuts, which go particularly well
with chilled beer.

*6 tablespoons unsalted
   butter*

3 tablespoons chili powder

*½ teaspoon cayenne
   pepper*

*Shake of crushed red
   pepper flakes*

*½ teaspoon cinnamon
   (optional)*

1½ teaspoons salt

1 pound pecans

Makes 1 pound pecans.

Preheat oven to 325° F..

Melt the butter in a skillet over low heat. Add the seasonings, stirring well. Toss in the pecans, turning to coat well. Put this mixture in a jelly roll pan, smoothing the pecans out into a single layer. Toast in the oven for 15 minutes.

Drain the pecans on paper towels and store in an airtight container. The nuts will keep several weeks.

CAREY'S DEVILED EGGS

◆◆◆◆◆◆◆◆◆◆◆◆◆◆◆◆◆◆◆◆◆◆◆◆◆◆◆

Carey Moss   Arlington, Virginia Sweetly piquant, spicy, a little different from the classic, these deviled eggs are both tasty and attractive.

6 eggs

2 tablespoons mayonnaise

2 teaspoons prepared mustard with horseradish

1½ teaspoons sugar (optional)

2 tablespoons sweet pickle relish

¼ teaspoon sweet pickle vinegar

½ teaspoon garlic salt

Pinch of celery seed

Pinch of freshly ground black pepper

Pinch of nutmeg, preferably freshly grated

Green olives, sliced, for garnish

Paprika for garnish

Serves 6.

Hard-cook the eggs and remove shells. Slice the eggs in half and separate yolks from whites. Mash the yolks until creamy. Add the mayonnaise, mustard, sugar (if using), pickle relish and relish vinegar, garlic salt, celery seed, pepper, and nutmeg. Mix well.

Stuff the whites with the yolk mixture, either with a spoon or piping through a pastry bag. Garnish with the green olives and paprika.

Soups

EASTER BORSCHT

Maria Piergies-Ptacin   Battle Creek, Michigan   Red beet borscht not only is a favorite among our contributors, but also has a very honored place in traditional Polish cooking. Maria Piergies-Ptacin, who is at work on a Polish cookbook, had the best recipe. She says there are two versions of this vibrant red soup: Christmas Eve borscht, made quickly with meatless stock, and Easter borscht, a more festive version made with meat stock. It's served in cups with an enticing variety of additions: hard-cooked egg wedges, beans, stuffed crepes, boiled young potatoes with dill, cheese straws, noodles, or savory morsels called Little Ears. Although substitutions can of course be made, the soup is at its best only when soup stock made from scratch and sour beet juice are included.

4–5 medium beets

6 cups Soup Stock (see recipe below)

1½ cloves garlic, pressed

1 bay leaf

2 whole allspice

2 tablespoons marjoram

1½ tablespoons sugar

3 whole peppercorns

Juice of 1½ lemons

2 tablespoons snipped fresh dill

1 tablespoon chopped fresh Italian parsley

¼ teaspoon freshly ground black pepper

1½ teaspoons salt (reduce if using salted stock)

Preheat oven to 350° F. Wash and trim the beets, and place in a 1-quart ovenproof dish. Wrap dish in foil and bake for 45 minutes. Cool; peel and grate beets.

Heat the stock to near boiling and add the beets, garlic, bay leaf, allspice, marjoram, sugar, peppercorns, and juice of 1 lemon. Cook for 30 minutes, simmering gently, and let stand for 15 minutes. Strain liquid.

1 cup Sour Beet Juice
(optional; see recipe
below)

Serves 6.

SOUP STOCK

1½ pounds beef bones
2 large onions, quartered
½ chicken, cut up
2 carrots
1 stalk celery
1 small leek, well cleaned
and sliced
1 parsley root or parsnip
1 small celeriac root
¼ head savoy cabbage,
sliced
1 kohlrabi, sliced
(optional)
1 egg white, lightly
beaten, for clarifying
stock

Makes 2 quarts.

SOUR BEET JUICE

1½ pounds (about 4
large) beets, washed,
peeled, and sliced
4 cups boiled warm water
2 cloves garlic, chopped
¼ slice whole wheat or rye
bread, broken up

Makes about 6 cups juice.

Add the rest of the lemon juice with the dill, parsley, ground pepper, salt, and sour beet juice. Serve hot.

Preheat oven to 525° F. Place the beef bones in a roasting pan with the quartered onions and roast for 45 minutes. Meat should be brown and onions almost scorched. After roasting pour 1 cup hot water into roasting pan, let stand for a few minutes, and put bones and liquid in a 5–6-quart pot.

Add 6 cups water, the chicken, and sliced vegetables. Simmer gently for 1½ hours.

Just before finishing simmering, add the egg white, stirring well, and bring to a boil. Pour stock through a sieve lined with a wet tea towel or double layer of cheesecloth.

To skim the fat, refrigerate stock until the fat solidifies on top.

Stock will keep in refrigerator 3 days, and in freezer for several months.

Place beets in a glass or glazed dish. Cover with the water; add the garlic and bread to accelerate fermenting process. Keep in a warm place. After 3 to 4 days, carefully skim off foam, strain, and store in tightly covered jars or bottles in a cold, dark place. The juice will keep up to 3 months.

MEXICAN CORN SOUP

◆◆◆◆◆◆◆◆◆◆◆◆◆◆◆◆◆◆◆◆◆◆◆◆◆◆◆◆◆◆◆

Darryl Pinckney   New York, New York An unusual, delicate, deeply

◆◆◆◆◆◆◆◆◆◆◆◆◆◆◆◆◆◆◆◆◆◆◆◆◆◆◆◆◆◆ satisfying soup that could be
the basis of a light lunch or a restorative after a brisk fall or winter walk. It's
even better made a day ahead and thinned with a little milk before serving.
The source is *The Cuisines of Mexico* by that extraordinary expert on Mexican
cooking, Diana Kennedy.

*4 cups corn (5 ears' worth
or 1½ pounds frozen
corn, measured frozen)*

4 tablespoons butter

3½ cups milk

½ teaspoon salt

*3 tablespoons fresh chile
poblano or canned
peeled green chilies,
diced*

*6 tablespoons crumbled
cream cheese or
Boursault*

*6 small tortillas, cut in
small squares and fried
crisp*

Serves 6.

Blend the corn with 1 cup water on high speed until smooth. Puree in a food mill. Melt the butter, add the corn puree, and cook over medium heat 5 minutes, stirring constantly. Add the milk and salt and bring the mixture to a boil. Lower the heat and let the soup simmer 15 minutes, stirring frequently.

To serve: Put ½ tablespoon chili and 1 tablespoon cheese in each bowl and pour the hot soup over. Garnish with crisp tortilla squares.

MULLIGATAWNY

◆◆◆◆◆◆◆◆◆◆◆◆◆◆◆◆◆◆◆◆◆◆◆◆◆◆◆◆◆◆◆◆◆◆◆◆

Dinah PoKempner   Princeton, New Jersey This is a truly outstand-

◆◆◆◆◆◆◆◆◆◆◆◆◆◆◆◆◆◆◆◆◆◆◆◆◆◆◆◆◆◆◆◆◆◆◆◆ ing soup—delicate, fra-

grant, and soul-satisfying. It's elegant enough to serve with a standing rib roast, and yet it's easy to make. The source is *Classic Indian Cooking* by Julie Sahni, who discovered it in a restaurant in Frankfurt, Germany, of all places.

3 cups cooked vegetables (onions, carrots, parsnips, and mushrooms)

6 cups homemade meat broth or canned chicken broth

1 teaspoon finely chopped garlic

1 sprig fresh coriander

¼ teaspoon freshly ground black pepper

2 tablespoons clarified butter

½ cup finely chopped onion

4 teaspoons curry powder (without fennel; check ingredients)

3 tablespoons flour

½ cup heavy cream

Coarse salt

2 tablespoons finely minced fresh coriander leaves

Serves 6.

Put the vegetables in a deep, heavy, pot with the broth, garlic, sprig of coriander, and pepper. Bring to a boil over medium heat. Reduce heat and simmer covered for 45 minutes, or until vegetables are soft. Turn off heat and let cool.

Puree the soup in a blender or food processor and then pass it through a fine sieve to give it a velvety texture. Return the soup to the pan and bring to a gentle simmer.

Put the clarified butter and onion in a small frying pan over medium-high heat. Fry the onion until it turns caramel color—this will take about 10 minutes—stirring constantly. Add the curry powder and flour and cook for 1 minute, stirring constantly, and remove from heat. Add the curried onion to the soup, stirring to prevent lumping. Simmer 2 minutes, or until soup is thickened. Remove from heat.

The soup can be made ahead to this point. Cover and set aside; it can be refrigerated up to 3 days.

To serve: Stir in cream, salt to taste, and minced coriander. Simmer until warmed through.

AUTUMN SQUASH SOUP

◆◆◆◆◆◆◆◆◆◆◆◆◆◆◆◆◆◆◆◆◆◆◆◆◆◆◆◆◆

Deborah Tuosto   Watsonville, California It's hard to imagine a more
◆◆◆◆◆◆◆◆◆◆◆◆◆◆◆◆◆◆◆◆◆◆◆◆◆◆◆   impressive soup presenta-
tion than this, served in a pumpkin shell. The fall vegetables make a savory
combination. The soup only improves if you make it a day ahead.

¼ cup vegetable oil

4 medium onions, chopped

2 teaspoons fresh thyme leaves or 1 teaspoon dried thyme

½ teaspoon nutmeg, preferably freshly grated

1 pound rutabagas, peeled and diced

2 pounds thin-skinned potatoes, peeled and cubed

16 cups (about 7 pounds) squash (banana, pumpkin, acorn, or Hubbard), peeled and cubed

3½ quarts chicken broth

1 large pumpkin shell (about 6-quart capacity), cleaned and seeded

Makes 6 quarts soup; serves 12 to 16.

In a 10-quart kettle over medium-high heat, combine the oil, onions, thyme, and nutmeg. Stir frequently until the onions are limp, about 15 minutes.

Add the rutabagas, potatoes, and squash; cook, stirring occasionally, until the vegetables begin to soften, about 30 minutes. Pour in the chicken broth, cover, and bring to a boil over high heat. Reduce the heat and simmer until the squash mashes easily, about 1½ hours.

In a blender or food processor, a portion at a time, whirl the vegetables and broth until smooth. (At this point you can cool and refrigerate the soup overnight.)

Return the soup to the kettle and bring to a boil, stirring often; keep warm.

About 30 minutes before serving, heat the pumpkin shell by pouring boiling water into it and letting it stand 20 minutes or longer, until the shell feels warm. Drain the shell and add the hot soup.

KOPROVA (POTATO SOUP WITH DILL)

◆◆◆◆◆◆◆◆◆◆◆◆◆◆◆◆◆◆◆◆◆◆◆◆◆◆◆◆

Rochelle Bray   Lincoln, Nebraska   This intriguing soup comes from
◆◆◆◆◆◆◆◆◆◆◆◆◆◆◆◆◆◆◆◆◆◆◆◆◆   Czechoslovakia, where it's actually
pronounced "kaprovka." It's very simple to make and would be good on a cold
winter evening. We liked it best with a touch of vinegar. It may also be served
chilled.

6 medium potatoes, peeled

2 teaspoons salt

*3 tablespoons snipped
fresh dill*

2 tablespoons flour

1½ cups sour cream

*1 tablespoon white vinegar
(optional)*

Serves 6.

Boil the potatoes in 6 cups water with the salt for about 30 minutes, or until done. Remove the potatoes with a spoon.

Add the dillweed to the potato water and boil 5 minutes.

Mix the flour with ½ cup water. Off the heat, add the flour mixture to the dill mixture while stirring. Return the pan to the heat and boil 3 minutes, stirring constantly.

Off the heat, stir in the sour cream. Either dice the potatoes or put them through a food mill; return the potatoes to the soup. Add the vinegar, if desired.

TUGBOAT CHOWDER

◆◆◆◆◆◆◆◆◆◆◆◆◆◆◆◆◆◆◆◆◆◆◆◆◆◆◆◆◆◆◆

Herb Radley   Sacramento, California A hearty, satisfying soup that
◆◆◆◆◆◆◆◆◆◆◆◆◆◆◆◆◆◆◆◆◆◆◆◆◆◆ makes an informal meal when
served with spinach salad and a baguette. The recipe is Herb Radley's invention.

4 slices bacon, diced

5 large potatoes, peeled
and diced

Salt and freshly ground
black pepper to taste

½ pound fresh
mushrooms, stems
removed and caps
quartered

2 (6½-ounce) cans
chopped clams with
liquid

1 (6½-ounce) can crab
meat, broken up

½ pound fresh shrimp,
peeled and deveined,
cooked just until they
color, liquid reserved

1½ cups half-and-half

2 tablespoons chopped
fresh Italian parsley

1½ tablespoons
cornstarch, mixed with
¼ cup cold water

Serves 4 to 6.

In a large soup kettle, cook the bacon until slightly brown but not crisp. Add the potatoes and enough water to slightly cover them, with salt and pepper to taste. Cook over medium heat until potatoes are almost tender, about 25 minutes. Then add the mushrooms and continue cooking for another 5 to 10 minutes.

Add the clams, crab meat, and shrimp with all their juices and reserved liquid. Still over medium heat, allow the chowder to come to a boil, and cook for another 5 minutes. Then add the half-and-half and parsley.

When the chowder begins bubbling, slowly add the cornstarch mixture while stirring until desired thickness is reached. Serve hot.

JELLIED CONSOMMÉ MADRILÈNE

◆◆◆◆◆◆◆◆◆◆◆◆◆◆◆◆◆◆◆◆◆◆◆◆◆◆◆◆◆◆◆◆◆◆◆◆

Susan Robyn   Hawthorne, New Jersey *Madrilène* always seems like
◆◆◆◆◆◆◆◆◆◆◆◆◆◆◆◆◆◆◆◆◆◆◆◆◆◆◆◆◆◆◆◆ the height of elegance at the
beginning of a meal—it's perfect in the summer, and even in the winter it
strikes a light, refreshing note that would be welcome at the festive table as
well.

*4 cups beef or chicken
    broth*

2 cups canned tomatoes

1 medium onion, sliced

½ cup sliced carrots

2 whole cloves

1 stalk celery, diced

3 whole peppercorns

*1 egg white, lightly
    beaten, to clarify broth*

*1 envelope unflavored
    gelatin*

½ cup cold stock or water

*Lemon slices for a
    garnish*

Serves 6 to 8.

Combine all ingredients except the gelatin in a medium
saucepan and simmer covered for 1 hour. Add the egg
white and bring the soup to a boil. Strain through a thin
cloth to get the soup as clear as possible.

Soften the gelatin in ½ cup cold stock or water for 5 minutes,
then add to the hot soup. Stir until dissolved. Chill until set.
Beat with a fork and garnish with lemon slices before serving.

CHILLED CUCUMBER SOUP

◆◆◆◆◆◆◆◆◆◆◆◆◆◆◆◆◆◆◆◆◆◆◆◆◆◆◆◆◆◆◆◆◆

Norma Marshall   Brooklyn, New York There are some famous ver-
◆◆◆◆◆◆◆◆◆◆◆◆◆◆◆◆◆◆◆◆◆◆◆◆◆◆◆ sions of this soup: one of them
is M. F. K. Fisher's, made with shrimp; another has raisins and walnuts in it.
This is a plainer one, very easy to put together, and absolutely superb. It's
nearly impossible to guess what's in it if you don't know.

*2 cucumbers, peeled, if
    skins are waxed, and
    grated*

1 onion, grated

*1 tablespoon Dijon
    mustard*

1 cup sour cream

Pinch of salt

½ teaspoon sugar

1 quart buttermilk

Serves 4 to 6.

Mix the cucumbers, onion, mustard, sour cream, salt,
and sugar together and stir thoroughly. Add the
buttermilk last, and chill for several hours before
serving.

CHILLED PEACH SOUP

◆◆◆◆◆◆◆◆◆◆◆◆◆◆◆◆◆◆◆◆◆◆◆◆◆◆◆◆◆◆◆◆◆◆◆

Ruth Ann Lederer   Toms River, New Jersey A lovely cool, fruity
◆◆◆◆◆◆◆◆◆◆◆◆◆◆◆◆◆◆◆◆◆◆◆◆◆◆◆◆◆◆◆ soup for the summer.
Make this only when the peaches are perfectly ripe and in season. If you can
find some cardamom buds to grind freshly, it will make a tremendous difference
to the taste of your soup.

*3½ cups sliced fresh
   peaches*

1½ cups Chablis

¼ cup sugar

1 (3-inch) stick cinnamon

*½ teaspoon ground
   cardamom, preferably
   freshly ground*

½ teaspoon vanilla extract

½ cup heavy cream

*Chopped peaches, sliced
   lemon, or mint sprigs
   (optional, for garnish)*

Serves 6.

In a saucepan, combine the sliced peaches, wine, 1½ cups water, sugar, and cinnamon stick. Bring to a boil. Simmer 30 minutes and remove the cinnamon stick.

Add to the soup the cardamom and the vanilla. Transfer the soup to a blender and process briefly, until the peaches are smoothly mixed into the soup. Add the cream.

Chill at least 2 hours and serve garnished with chopped peaches, sliced lemon, or a mint sprig.

FRUIT SOUP

◆◆◆◆◆◆◆◆◆◆◆◆◆◆◆◆◆◆◆◆◆◆◆◆◆◆◆◆◆◆◆◆

Linda Schwerin   Aurora, Colorado   This Scandinavian fruit soup is

◆◆◆◆◆◆◆◆◆◆◆◆◆◆◆◆◆◆◆◆◆◆◆◆◆◆◆◆◆ truly delicious, easy to make, and endlessly versatile. It's wonderful for a first course before a hearty dinner but also fine for a light dessert or even, with yogurt, for breakfast.

1 (3-inch) stick cinnamon

4 cups mixed dried fruits, such as apricots, prunes, and currants

1 tablespoon cornstarch

¼ cup quick-cooking tapioca

¼ cup sugar, or to taste

1 tablespoon freshly squeezed lemon juice

Serves 8 to 10.

Combine 2 quarts water, cinnamon, and fruit. Boil 5 minutes. Add a little water to the cornstarch to make a thin paste. Add with the tapioca to the fruit mixture and cook for 10 minutes.

Stir in the sugar and continue cooking for 3 minutes more. Add the lemon juice, remove the cinnamon stick, and serve hot.

Salads

CURRIED CHICKEN SALAD

◆◆◆◆◆◆◆◆◆◆◆◆◆◆◆◆◆◆◆◆◆◆◆◆◆◆◆◆◆◆◆◆◆◆◆

Sandra Schifferle   West Point, New York   A good choice for the buf-
◆◆◆◆◆◆◆◆◆◆◆◆◆◆◆◆◆◆◆◆◆◆◆◆◆◆◆◆◆◆◆◆◆ fet table, this interesting
salad would be especially welcome on a warm day.

¼ cup mayonnaise

½ cup plain yogurt

Juice of 1 lemon

1 stalk celery, diced

*2 scallions, sliced thin,
including some green*

½ cup minced fresh chives

1 tart apple, diced

*½ cup dried currants,
soaked for 15 minutes
in warm water*

*½ cup diced mixed dried
fruit or dried apricots*

*2 cups cubed cooked
chicken*

*2 tablespoons packaged or
homemade Garam
Masala (see recipe
below)*

*¼–½ teaspoon crushed
red pepper flakes*

*2 cups uncooked
macaroni*

*Salt and freshly ground
black pepper to taste*

Serves 4 to 6.

In a large mixing bowl, combine the mayonnaise, yogurt, and lemon juice. Add the celery, scallions, chives, apple, drained currants, dried fruit, chicken, garam masala, and red pepper flakes. Mix well.

Cook the macaroni to the al dente stage, drain, and cool before adding to the mixture in the bowl. Mix well. Add salt and pepper to taste.

Chill overnight. If the salad appears dry the next day, moisten it with additional yogurt.

GARAM MASALA

4 tablespoons coriander
    seeds

2 tablespoons cumin seeds

1 tablespoon whole black
    peppercorns

2 teaspoons ground
    cardamom

4 (3-inch) sticks
    cinnamon

1 teaspoon whole cloves

1 teaspoon nutmeg,
    preferably freshly grated

Combine the spices in a frying pan and roast until the spices smell fragrant. Cool, then put in a blender and blend to a fine powder. Store in an airtight glass jar.

LABOR DAY PICNIC SALAD

◆◆◆◆◆◆◆◆◆◆◆◆◆◆◆◆◆◆◆◆◆◆◆◆◆◆◆◆◆◆◆

Rebecca Purro New York, New York A delicious, hearty main-course
◆◆◆◆◆◆◆◆◆◆◆◆◆◆◆◆◆◆◆◆◆◆◆◆◆◆◆ salad that can be made well
ahead of time. Don't think of this just for summer; it would also be an excellent
addition to a winter buffet table.

*3 pounds new potatoes,
    boiled, quartered, and
    unpeeled*

*1 pound Polish kielbasa,
    sliced diagonally*

*¼ cup chopped drained
    capers*

½ cup julienned pimientos

*1 cucumber, peeled and
    thinly sliced*

*1 bunch scallions,
    diagonally sliced,
    including some green*

1 egg plus 1 egg yolk

1 teaspoon dry mustard

*1 teaspoon freshly
    squeezed lemon juice*

*¼ teaspoon red wine
    vinegar*

*1½ cups mixture of olive
    oil and light salad oil*

*2 tablespoons Dijon
    mustard*

*Salt and freshly ground
    black pepper to taste*

Serves 6.

Put the potatoes, kielbasa, capers, pimientos, cucumber, and scallions in a large bowl.

In a blender or food processor fitted with the metal blade, add the egg and egg yolk, dry mustard, lemon juice, and vinegar and process 10 seconds. Add the oil very slowly in a steady stream, with the machine running. Fold in the Dijon mustard and adjust salt and pepper to taste.

Pour the dressing over the salad ingredients and toss well.

LIME GELATIN SALAD

Lynn Stallworth   Brooklyn, New York Gelatin salads can be wonderfully light, especially as part of a buffet or a heavy holiday meal. This one has the additional virtue of not being sweet.

2 medium firm ripe
   cucumbers

1 teaspoon salt

1 tablespoon vegetable oil

2 (3-ounce) packages lime
   gelatin dessert

2 (8-ounce) packages
   cream cheese, cut into
   ½-inch bits

2 tablespoons strained
   freshly squeezed lime
   juice

2 teaspoons
   Worcestershire sauce

¼ teaspoon Tabasco sauce

¼ cup finely chopped
   onion

¼ cup finely snipped fresh
   dill

Serves 6 to 8.

Peel the cucumbers and slice them in half lengthwise. Scoop out the seeds and then dice the cucumbers. Place the dice in a sieve set over a bowl, add the salt, and toss around with a spoon to coat the dice evenly. Set aside to drain for at least 30 minutes, then pat dry with paper towels.

Meanwhile, spread the oil evenly over a 6-cup mold. Turn the mold upside down on paper towels and let the excess oil drain out.

Place the gelatin dessert in a bowl, pour in 3 cups boiling water, and mix well. Put the cream cheese in a large bowl and, with an electric mixer, beat until light and fluffy. While beating, pour in the gelatin mixture in a slow thin stream, and when it's thoroughly incorporated, add the lime juice, Worcestershire, and Tabasco.

Set the bowl in a larger bowl filled with crushed ice or ice cubes and cold water. Stir with a metal spoon until the gelatin mixture thickens enough to flow sluggishly off the spoon. Stir in the cucumber dice, onion, and dill.

Pour the gelatin mixture into the prepared mold, cover with plastic wrap, and refrigerate for 4 hours, or until salad is firm to the touch.

To unmold, run a thin knife around the sides of the mold and dip the bottom briefly into hot water. Refrigerate until ready to serve.

TOMATO ASPIC

◆◆◆◆◆◆◆◆◆◆◆◆◆◆◆◆◆◆◆◆◆◆◆◆◆◆◆◆

Sheri Huser   Salmo, British Columbia Tomato aspic seems to have
been left behind in the dust as
a chic dish. Still, it seems to us there's nothing so refreshing on a hot, sultry
day as a tremblingly cold tomato aspic, with perhaps a seafood salad. On the
other hand, Sheri Huser's grandmother wouldn't think of serving a turkey
without it, and here is her recipe.

1 envelope unflavored
  gelatin

1½ cups tomato juice

¼ teaspoon sugar

½ bay leaf

2 whole cloves

1–2 tablespoons white
  vinegar

Onion salt

Celery salt

2 scallions, chopped

1 stalk celery, chopped

Serves 4.

G rease a 2-cup jelly mold and set aside. Soften the gelatin
in ¼ cup cold water.

Over medium heat, heat the tomato juice, sugar, bay
leaf, and cloves until warm. Add the softened gelatin and stir
over heat until dissolved.

Remove the bay leaf and cloves. Add the vinegar and spices
to taste. Remove from heat. Stir in the scallions and celery.

Pour into jelly mold and chill until set, about 4 hours.

STRAWBERRY SALAD

◆◆◆◆◆◆◆◆◆◆◆◆◆◆◆◆◆◆◆◆◆◆◆◆◆◆◆◆◆◆◆◆

Dorothy Dorrance   Clum's Corners, New York This gelatin salad is
◆◆◆◆◆◆◆◆◆◆◆◆◆◆◆◆◆◆◆◆◆◆◆◆◆◆◆◆◆◆◆ quite sweet, quite
rich, and quite addictive. Children adore it, but even fancy eaters can't leave it
alone. It seems to work as well for winter holidays as summer ones.

*1 (3-ounce) package wild
cherry gelatin dessert*

*1 (10-ounce) package
frozen strawberries,
thawed and drained*

*1 (3-ounce) package
lemon gelatin dessert*

*1 small (8-ounce) can
crushed pineapple,
drained, juice reserved*

*1 (3-ounce) package
cream cheese, softened
to room temperature*

1 cup heavy cream

Serves 12.

Oil a ring mold and set aside.

Pour 1 cup boiling water over the cherry gelatin dessert and stir to dissolve. Add the thawed strawberries. Put the mixture in the refrigerator, and when it begins to thicken, pour it into the prepared mold.

Dissolve lemon gelatin dessert in 1 cup boiling water. Add enough water to the juice from the pineapple to make 1 scant cup. Add to the gelatin.

With a fork, mash the cream cheese and pineapple together and add to the lemon gelatin.

Whip the cream and fold into the lemon gelatin mixture. Pour the mixture into the prepared mold over the cherry gelatin and let thicken in refrigerator.

To unmold, run a thin knife around the sides of the mold and dip the bottom briefly into hot water. Refrigerate until ready to serve.

MANDARIN ORANGE SALAD

◆◆◆◆◆◆◆◆◆◆◆◆◆◆◆◆◆◆◆◆◆◆◆◆◆◆◆◆◆◆◆◆◆

Susan Menetrey   Fort Sam Houston, Texas   A lovely salad that can

◆◆◆◆◆◆◆◆◆◆◆◆◆◆◆◆◆◆◆◆◆◆◆◆◆◆◆◆◆◆◆◆◆   be made virtually any
time of year. When fresh clementines are in season, use three fresh ones, in
sections, instead of the canned mandarin oranges.

*1 (11-ounce) can
    mandarin orange
    sections, chilled and
    drained*

*1 head Bibb lettuce,
    separated*

*12 leaves spinach, torn
    into small pieces*

2 scallions, sliced

*1 avocado, peeled, pitted,
    and sliced*

½ cup pecans, toasted

¼ cup safflower oil

*3 tablespoons white wine
    vinegar*

*Salt and freshly ground
    black pepper to taste*

Serves 4.

Toss all ingredients together to coat evenly with dressing.
Serve immediately.

REUNION TOMATO SALAD

◆◆◆◆◆◆◆◆◆◆◆◆◆◆◆◆◆◆◆◆◆◆◆◆◆

Billie Steele   Jefferson, Texas This recipe has been in Mrs. Steele's
◆◆◆◆◆◆◆◆◆◆◆◆◆◆◆◆◆◆◆◆◆◆◆◆◆ husband's family for over seventy years,
and it's always served at the family reunion in the summer, when the tomatoes
are at their best. It's especially good made with fresh thyme.

6 cups chopped garden
    tomatoes

1 cup chopped green
    pepper

1 cup chopped scallion

½ cup red wine vinegar

½ cup sugar (optional)

Salt and freshly ground
    black pepper to taste

1 teaspoon fresh thyme
    leaves or ¼ teaspoon
    dried thyme

Serves 10 to 12.

Mix all ingredients together and serve. Surprisingly, this salad can be kept in the refrigerator overnight, and it won't be too soggy the next day. But give it a good shake before serving.

RAW MUSHROOM SALAD

Clare Urion   Dover, Massachusetts   A superb, fresh-tasting light salad. It's perfect for summer picnics or as a light accent on the buffet table during the winter holidays.

1–1½ pounds
   mushrooms, stems
   removed

6 tablespoons olive oil

2 tablespoons freshly
   squeezed lemon juice

Freshly ground black
   pepper to taste

½ clove garlic, crushed

½ teaspoon salt, or to
   taste

1 teaspoon chopped fresh
   parsley

1 teaspoon chopped fresh
   chives

Serves 4.

Wipe the mushrooms with a damp paper towel and slice them into a bowl. Add the oil, lemon juice, pepper, and garlic. Marinate for 1 hour and drain. Season with salt to taste and garnish with the parsley and chives.

SERBIAN SALAD

◆◆◆◆◆◆◆◆◆◆◆◆◆◆◆◆◆◆◆◆◆◆◆◆

Disa Mouat   Decatur, Georgia   This recipe comes from a Yugoslavian
◆◆◆◆◆◆◆◆◆◆◆◆◆◆◆◆◆◆◆◆◆◆◆◆ exchange student who was in Disa
Mouat's high school years ago. It should be made only with first-class vine-
ripened tomatoes, so it's perfect for the Fourth of July or Labor Day. It's not
a mistake that there's no dressing—the tomato juice and feta cheese combine
to make a delicious dressing. If this seems too plain, add fresh herbs—basil,
chives, thyme—and a little olive oil to taste.

10 ripe tomatoes
2 large green peppers
1 bunch scallions
Salt and freshly ground
    black pepper to taste
½ pound feta cheese,
    preferably imported

Serves 8.

Cut the tomatoes into bite-sized wedges and put in a
large bowl. Core and seed the green peppers and cut
them into bite-size pieces. Clean the scallions, slice
them crosswise, and add them to the tomatoes.

Sprinkle with salt and pepper to taste. Crumble the feta
cheese and add to the vegetables. Mix well. Serve the salad
at room temperature on the day it's made.

ITALIAN SALAD

◆◆◆◆◆◆◆◆◆◆◆◆◆◆◆◆◆◆◆◆◆◆◆◆◆◆

Jeanne Boyle   Hewitt, New Jersey A hearty salad that's a good item
◆◆◆◆◆◆◆◆◆◆◆◆◆◆◆◆◆◆◆◆◆◆◆◆◆ for the buffet. The idea here is to
marinate the ingredients in the separate elements of the dressing—the cheese
bathed in oil and herbs, and the spicy meats enlivened by the vinegar.

¼ pound pepperoni

¼ pound Genoa salami

⅓ cup red wine vinegar

*½ pound mozzarella
cheese, cubed*

*⅔ cup extra virgin olive
oil*

*Handful of fresh basil
leaves*

*1 large head romaine
lettuce*

*Salt and freshly ground
black pepper to taste*

Serves 4 to 6.

Cut the pepperoni and salami into julienne slices and put
them in a small bowl; cover with the vinegar. Marinate
for several hours, turning from time to time.

Put the mozzarella in a small bowl and cover with the olive
oil. Tear the basil leaves into small pieces and sprinkle over
the cheese. Stir well and leave to marinate for several hours,
turning from time to time.

Tear the romaine leaves into a salad bowl and add the drained
meats and cheese, reserving the marinades. Combine the
reserved vinegar and oil and whisk together. Pour dressing
over salad and toss; taste for salt and pepper before serving.

GURKENSALAT

◆◆◆◆◆◆◆◆◆◆◆◆◆◆◆◆◆◆◆◆◆◆◆◆◆◆◆◆◆◆◆◆◆◆◆◆

Sabrina Charbonneau   New York, New York A cucumber salad from

◆◆◆◆◆◆◆◆◆◆◆◆◆◆◆◆◆◆◆◆◆◆◆◆◆◆◆◆◆◆◆ the old country—tasty

and tangy, it goes well with a spread of cold meats.

*2 large cucumbers, peeled,
if skins are waxed, and
sliced thin*

½ cup sour cream

*2 tablespoons white
vinegar*

*¾ teaspoon Dijon
mustard*

*Salt and freshly ground
black pepper to taste*

Pinch of sugar (optional)

*¼ teaspoon Worcestershire
sauce*

1 small onion, minced

*2 tablespoons chopped
chives*

Serves 4 to 6.

Mix all ingredients together, chill briefly, and serve.

SAUERKRAUT SALAD

◆◆◆◆◆◆◆◆◆◆◆◆◆◆◆◆◆◆◆◆◆◆◆◆◆◆◆◆◆◆◆

R. Pawelko Creston, British Columbia This is a salad with a little
◆◆◆◆◆◆◆◆◆◆◆◆◆◆◆◆◆◆◆◆◆◆◆◆◆◆◆◆◆ bite, unusual and very good—
assuming, of course, that you're fond of sauerkraut.

1 pound sauerkraut,
  rinsed and drained

½ cup sliced celery

½ cup sliced radishes

2 tablespoons chopped
  Italian parsley

1 small onion, sliced

2 tablespoons safflower oil

1 tablespoon white vinegar

¼ teaspoon freshly ground
  black pepper

1 teaspoon salt

Serves 4 to 6.

Toss all ingredients together and serve.

LESLIE NEWMAN'S COLESLAW

◆◆◆◆◆◆◆◆◆◆◆◆◆◆◆◆◆◆◆◆◆◆◆◆◆◆

Janet Bailey   Santa Fe, New Mexico Leslie Newman is a screenwriter
◆◆◆◆◆◆◆◆◆◆◆◆◆◆◆◆◆◆◆◆◆◆◆◆ and famous cook who lives in
New York City. This recipe appeared in *Esquire* a few years ago and has been
a favorite in the Bailey household ever since. It's a zippy, New Orleans–style
slaw that's easily made in the food processor. It will keep for days, and the
flavor only improves.

*2 pounds green cabbage,
  cored and shredded*

*1 (4-ounce) turnip, peeled
  and shredded*

*2 carrots, peeled and
  shredded*

⅔ cup minced red onion

4 radishes, chopped

*4 tablespoons minced
  parsley*

*4 tablespoons finely
  snipped fresh dill*

1 teaspoon sugar

½ cup cider vinegar

*¼ teaspoon freshly ground
  black pepper*

⅛ teaspoon white pepper

*¼–½ teaspoon crushed
  red pepper flakes*

¾ cup mayonnaise

Salt to taste

Serves 10 to 12.

Put all the vegetables and herbs together in a large bowl. Whisk the sugar into the vinegar and add the spices, then the mayonnaise. Mix thoroughly, taste for salt, and refrigerate until ready to serve.

RED CABBAGE SALAD

◆◆◆◆◆◆◆◆◆◆◆◆◆◆◆◆◆◆◆◆◆◆◆◆◆◆◆◆◆◆◆◆◆◆◆◆

Charlotte St. Germain Fort Worth, Texas A tasty salad that is really
◆◆◆◆◆◆◆◆◆◆◆◆◆◆◆◆◆◆◆◆◆◆◆◆◆◆◆◆◆◆◆ more like a coleslaw—
particularly good with pork and barbecue.

3 cups chopped red
   cabbage

⅓ cup chopped scallion

⅓ cup chopped green
   pepper

¼ cup chopped pimiento

¼ cup chopped celery

Salt and freshly ground
   black pepper to taste

¼ cup apple cider vinegar

2 tablespoons sugar
   (optional)

2 tablespoons bacon
   grease, slightly cooled

Serves 6 to 8.

Toss all the vegetables together with the salt, pepper, vinegar, and sugar, if using. Chill for 1 hour or longer. Just before serving, add the bacon grease and toss well.

OLD-FASHIONED COOKED DRESSING

Dorothy Dorrance   Clum's Corners, New York   This excellent boiled dressing makes a wonderful potato salad: just add cubed cooked potatoes, chopped hard-cooked eggs, chopped onion, celery seed, and salt and pepper. Mrs. Dorrance's mother-in-law, who came from Pennsylvania, always made this dressing for potato salad. It's a real classic, subtle and delicious.

6 tablespoons all-purpose flour (more if necessary)

6 tablespoons sugar

3 eggs, beaten

¾ teaspoon salt, or more to taste

½ cup white vinegar

1 level teaspoon dry mustard

Makes about 1 pint.

Mix all ingredients with 1½ cups water and put in the top of a double boiler. Cook over medium heat, stirring frequently. You want a thick, creamy sauce, and it may be necessary to add a little more flour to reach the right consistency.

If making potato salad, pour warm sauce directly onto boiled, cubed potatoes. Otherwise, store dressing in refrigerator—it will keep at least a week—until ready to use for coleslaw, potato salad or seafood or chicken salad.

Side Dishes

GRANDMA'S GRAND TURKEY STUFFING

◆◆◆◆◆◆◆◆◆◆◆◆◆◆◆◆◆◆◆◆◆◆◆◆◆◆◆

Gloria King   Etobicoke, Ontario A very unusual stuffing recipe that
◆◆◆◆◆◆◆◆◆◆◆◆◆◆◆◆◆◆◆◆◆◆◆◆◆ should be served in a somewhat un-
traditional holiday meal. Gloria King's grandmother used to make this stuffing
at the turn of the century in South America; when she moved to England, the
recipe went with her. Now her granddaughter makes it three times a year in
Canada, so it's a well-traveled recipe. It would be as delicious with other poultry
as it is with turkey.

*1 pound sirloin steak,
    trimmed of all fat*

2 tablespoons olive oil

1 onion, minced

1 clove garlic, minced

*2 tomatoes, skinned,
    seeded, and chopped*

*2 hard-cooked eggs,
    chopped*

2 tablespoons raisins

*2 tablespoons coarsely
    chopped walnuts*

*2 tablespoons coarsely
    chopped almonds*

*6 large green olives, pitted
    and chopped*

*Salt and freshly ground
    black pepper to taste*

*2–3 tablespoons fresh
    bread crumbs*

*Makes enough stuffing for
    a 12- to 14-pound
    turkey.*

Put the meat through the coarse disk of a meat grinder or cut into cubes and chop coarsely in a food processor.

Heat the olive oil in a large skillet and sauté the onion and garlic over medium heat until the onion is translucent. Add the steak and sauté until no longer pink.

Add the tomatoes, hard-cooked eggs, raisins, walnuts, almonds, olives, salt and pepper, and enough bread crumbs to bind the mixture together.

Sauté until thoroughly heated, but be careful not to cook fully, as the stuffing will continue to cook inside the bird.

Allow the mixture to cool and the flavors to develop, preferably overnight, in the refrigerator, before stuffing the bird.

ROY'S DRESSING

◆◆◆◆◆◆◆◆◆◆◆◆◆◆◆◆◆◆◆◆◆◆◆◆◆◆◆◆

Peggy Whiter   Encino, California A good traditional sausage stuffing
◆◆◆◆◆◆◆◆◆◆◆◆◆◆◆◆◆◆◆◆◆◆◆◆ from Mrs. Whiter's father-in-law.
Her husband likes to add fresh sliced mushrooms. An important element here
is letting the bread dry for three days before making the stuffing. If it's too late
for that, put the bread, broken into small pieces, on cookie sheets in a slow
(200° F.) oven until it feels dry.

8 tablespoons butter

3–4 onions, chopped

1 cup sliced mushrooms
(optional)

1 pound fresh sausage
meat

1½ loaves white bread,
left to dry 3 days (see
above)

1 tablespoon poultry
seasoning

Salt and freshly ground
black pepper to taste

¼ teaspoon dried sage, or
to taste

*Makes enough stuffing for
an 18-pound turkey.*

In a skillet, over medium heat, melt the butter and lightly
sauté the onions. Add the mushrooms, if using, and sauté
them also. Set aside.

In another skillet, over medium heat, fry the sausage meat
lightly and discard the fat. Break up the bread into small
pieces and put into a large bowl. Add the seasonings, to
taste. Pour the onion mixture over the bread. Add the
sausage and a dash of water. Work the stuffing in your hands
until it's thoroughly mixed.

OYSTER STUFFING

◆◆◆◆◆◆◆◆◆◆◆◆◆◆◆◆◆◆◆◆◆◆◆◆◆◆◆◆◆◆◆

Barbara Dehner   Pensacola, Florida This very fine stuffing recipe
◆◆◆◆◆◆◆◆◆◆◆◆◆◆◆◆◆◆◆◆◆◆◆◆◆◆◆◆ originated in Pennsylvania, where
Barbara Dehner's family used to fuss elaborately over its preparation. Everyone
would have to taste before the stuffing went into the bird to make sure it had
just the right amount of sage, or broth, or salt, or whatever. Afterward, there'd
be generous amounts of self-congratulation for knowing just what was needed.

Turkey giblets and neck

9 cups dry bread cubes

1 medium onion, diced

1 cup diced celery

*1 pint oysters, drained
and chopped, liquid
reserved*

*1 teaspoon celery seed, or
to taste*

*1 teaspoon dried sage, or
to taste*

*½ teaspoon salt, or to
taste*

*¼ teaspoon freshly ground
black pepper, or to taste*

**Makes enough stuffing for
an 18-pound turkey.**

Simmer the turkey pieces in 3 cups water for at least 1 hour.

Place the bread cubes in a large bowl. Add the onion, celery, and oysters. Season to taste with the celery seed, sage, and salt and pepper.

Remove the turkey pieces and add the drained oyster liquid to the broth. While it is still hot, drizzle the broth over the bread mixture and toss until moistened.

If the turkey is small, put any leftover stuffing in a buttered loaf pan and bake uncovered the last hour with the turkey.

CHESTNUT TART

◆◆◆

Laurey Andreas   West Collingswood, New Jersey An excellent sa-
◆◆◆◆◆◆◆◆◆◆◆◆◆◆◆◆◆◆◆◆◆◆◆◆◆◆◆◆◆◆◆◆◆◆◆ vory pie, per-
fect for Thanksgiving with turkey, goose, or roast beef. If you're looking for a
very unusual side dish, this is it.

*1 cup cooked and pureed
  chestnuts*

¾ cup ricotta cheese

½ cup heavy cream

2 eggs

2 tablespoons beef stock

*2 tablespoons unsalted
  butter, melted*

2 scallions, minced

1 teaspoon salt

½ teaspoon white pepper

*¼ teaspoon nutmeg,
  preferably freshly grated*

*1 tablespoon freshly grated
  Parmesan cheese*

*1 (10-inch) partially
  baked pie shell*

*Roasted chestnuts
  (optional)*

Serves 8 to 10.

Preheat oven to 375° F.

Combine the chestnut puree, ricotta, cream, eggs, beef stock, melted butter, scallions, salt, white pepper, nutmeg, and Parmesan. Mix well and pour into the partially baked pie shell.

Bake 25 minutes, or until set. Serve warm with roasted chestnuts, if you wish.

NEVER-FAIL YORKSHIRE PUDDING

◆◆◆◆◆◆◆◆◆◆◆◆◆◆◆◆◆◆◆◆◆◆◆◆◆◆◆◆◆◆

Fran Johnson   Regina, Saskatchewan A classic Yorkshire pudding.

◆◆◆◆◆◆◆◆◆◆◆◆◆◆◆◆◆◆◆◆◆◆◆◆◆◆ It's very important to put this together early in the day and refrigerate the batter until the beef is done and ready to rest before carving.

1 egg

¾ cup milk

¾ cup all-purpose flour, sifted

½ teaspoon salt

Roast beef drippings

Makes 6 individual servings or one pudding serving 6 to 8.

The pudding can be made in either the roasting pan or in individual muffin cups or a muffin tin.

Four hours before the roast beef goes into the oven, mix the pudding together—it can also be made the night before and left in the refrigerator. Beat the egg and add the milk, flour, and salt. Beat well, but it's all right if the batter remains a little lumpy.

When the roast is taken out of the oven, turn the oven to 375° F. Pour the drippings out of the roasting pan and measure out ¼ cup—try to get as much of the dark drippings as possible. Or if you're using muffin tins or cups, measure 1 teaspoon of drippings into each cup. Have the pans sizzling hot in the oven before you beat the batter again and pour it into the roasting pan. If you're using muffin cups or tins, fill them half full.

Bake the pudding 20 to 30 minutes, until it's well risen, crusty, and golden brown. Serve at once.

SPICED PEARS

◆◆◆◆◆◆◆◆◆◆◆◆◆◆◆◆◆◆◆◆◆◆◆◆◆◆◆◆◆

Evelyn Ortner Brooklyn, New York Irresistible, fresh-tasting spicy
◆◆◆◆◆◆◆◆◆◆◆◆◆◆◆◆◆◆◆◆◆◆◆◆◆◆◆ pears—perfect for winter pears
and a snap to make.

*4 pounds Anjou pears,
  peeled, cored, and cut
  into 1-inch chunks*

*¾ cup freshly squeezed
  lemon juice*

1 cup honey

½ teaspoon ground cloves

*2 teaspoons ground
  cinnamon*

½ cup currants

*2 (2-inch) pieces stick
  cinnamon*

Serves 10.

Mix all the ingredients except currants and cinnamon pieces in a medium saucepan. Simmer, uncovered, for 35 to 45 minutes, until sauce thickens. Pears will remain crunchy.

Add currants and simmer another 15 minutes, partially covered. Add cinnamon sticks and refrigerate until ready to serve. The pears will keep at least a week in the refrigerator.

MAMA SUGAR'S FRIED APPLES

◆◆◆◆◆◆◆◆◆◆◆◆◆◆◆◆◆◆◆◆◆◆◆◆◆

Rose Kreher Holyoke, Colorado There's a story behind this recipe.
◆◆◆◆◆◆◆◆◆◆◆◆◆◆◆◆◆◆◆◆◆◆◆◆◆ Rose Kreher says, "Mama Sugar,
my paternal grandmother, is the essence of the fine old Southern cook. Fried
apples are her specialty. I tried for years to duplicate them but they never
turned out like hers: individual slices of caramelized apple, hot and rich and
chewy.

"For what must have been the fiftieth time, I asked my grandmother, 'Now,
how do you make your fried apples?'

" 'Well,' she replied for the fiftieth time, 'you slice up some real tart apples,
brown 'em in butter, add some sugar and a little spice, cover 'em up, and cook
'em till they get real brown.'

"I went home, tried again, and finally came as close as I ever had. I just
hadn't been listening all those years. I hadn't browned the apples before adding
the sugar. So simple a step, but so crucial.

"I called Mama Sugar to tell her I was on my way to making real Southern
fried apples, but they still weren't exactly like hers, not quite so brown and
chewy.

"She answered, 'I was frying apples one day, and the dog got into the chicken
yard, so I took out after 'im and let those apples almost burn. They tasted so
good I made 'em that way ever since.' "

*6 medium tart cooking
  apples*

3 tablespoons butter

½ teaspoon ground mace

*½ cup sugar (or less, to
  taste)*

Serves 4.

Wash the apples but do not peel. Cut into ⅛-inch
sections and remove cores with the small end of a
melon baller.

Melt the butter in a large, heavy skillet over medium-high

heat. When the butter stops foaming, add the apple slices. Sauté until lightly browned, 10 to 15 minutes. Turn frequently but gently.

Reduce heat to medium. Sprinkle the mace and sugar evenly over the apples. Stir gently to mix. Cover and cook until syrup caramelizes and the apples are glazed, about 15 minutes, stirring occasionally.

Serve as a side dish with pork or ham, or for breakfast.

AMBER BAKED ONIONS

◆◆◆◆◆◆◆◆◆◆◆◆◆◆◆◆◆◆◆◆◆◆◆◆◆◆◆◆◆◆◆◆◆◆◆◆◆◆◆

Elizabeth Mulgrew   Millbourne, Pennsylvania This superb recipe
◆◆◆◆◆◆◆◆◆◆◆◆◆◆◆◆◆◆◆◆◆◆◆◆◆◆◆◆◆◆◆◆◆◆◆◆◆◆◆ was found among
Elizabeth Mulgrew's grandmother's papers. It's perfect for Thanksgiving or
Christmas with a roast.

*12 large onions, peeled
and cut in half
crosswise*

*2 tablespoons melted pan
drippings or bacon
drippings*

4 tablespoons tomato juice

2 teaspoons salt

4 tablespoons honey

¼ teaspoon paprika

Serves 12 to 14.

Preheat oven to 350° F. Have ready a large roasting pan,
well greased.

Place the onions in the baking pan. Combine the
drippings, tomato juice, salt, honey, and paprika. Mix well
and pour over onions. Cover pan with foil and bake 1 hour.

ST. DAVID'S DAY LEEKS

◆◆

Frances Fouche   Hastings-on-Hudson, New York These delecta-

◆◆ ble leeks are

basically stewed in butter, baked, then broiled with an Italian touch—Parmesan cheese. They go very well with roast beef, lamb, or duck, and they're just right for helping your Welsh friends celebrate St. David's Day.

1 dozen leeks, including most of the green

6 tablespoons butter, cut into pieces

1½ teaspoons salt

½ cup grated Parmesan cheese

⅓ cup fresh bread crumbs

2 tablespoons butter, melted, if needed (see instructions)

Serves 6.

Trim the leeks of any old leaves, then cut off the root and ends of leaves. Slice the leeks from root to tips, starting about an inch above the root. Turn the leeks on their sides and slice through again. Wash them well under running water, pulling the leaves apart to make sure all the grit is removed, or you'll have sand in your dish.

Arrange the leeks in a round or oval pot in which they can fit in 2 layers. Pour 4 cups water over the leeks; it should come just below the level of the top layer. Add the 6 tablespoons butter and the salt.

On top of the stove, bring the leeks to a boil; put the lid on the pot but leave a tiny breathing space and reduce heat to simmer. In 30 minutes or so the leeks should be tender. When they are, preheat oven to 325° F.

Arrange the cooked leeks in a gratin dish and pour the cooking juices over them. Put a piece of foil over them, loosely, and bake 20 to 30 minutes, until they begin to turn golden.

Just before serving, sprinkle the leeks with the Parmesan and bread crumbs and add any remaining pan juices. If there is no juice, add 2 tablespoons of melted butter. Run under the broiler just until the cheese is melted and turning golden brown.

PECAN-TOPPED CARROTS

◆◆◆◆◆◆◆◆◆◆◆◆◆◆◆◆◆◆◆◆◆◆◆◆◆◆◆◆◆◆◆◆

Marlene Luitwieler   Tulsa, Oklahoma A very attractive, tasty side
◆◆◆◆◆◆◆◆◆◆◆◆◆◆◆◆◆◆◆◆◆◆◆◆◆◆◆◆◆◆◆◆ dish that Marlene Luitwieler
evolved from a sweet potato recipe in an old *Sunset* magazine. Her family now
insists on having it for both Thanksgiving and Christmas dinner.

*2–3 pounds carrots,
    cooked and mashed, to
    yield 6 cups*

2 eggs, beaten

*¾ cup firmly packed
    brown sugar*

*8 tablespoons butter,
    melted*

¾ teaspoon baking powder

1 teaspoon salt

1 teaspoon cinnamon

*¾–1 cup freshly squeezed
    orange juice*

1 cup pecan halves

Serves 6 to 8.

Preheat oven to 375° F. Butter a 2-quart casserole and set aside.

Combine the carrots, eggs, ¼ cup of the brown sugar, 4 tablespoons of the butter, baking powder, salt, cinnamon, and enough orange juice to get a moist and fluffy consistency.

Spread evenly in the casserole. Either cover the casserole and refrigerate it until ready to bake or arrange the pecan halves over the top (in rows for a rectangular dish or concentric circles for a round one). Sprinkle with remaining brown sugar and remaining melted butter.

Bake uncovered for 20 minutes, or until heated through.

BAKED PARSNIPS WITH APPLES AND ORANGES

◆◆◆◆◆◆◆◆◆◆◆◆◆◆◆◆◆◆◆◆◆◆◆◆◆◆◆◆◆

Mandy Kutz   New York, New York A very simple but tasty dish, not
◆◆◆◆◆◆◆◆◆◆◆◆◆◆◆◆◆◆◆◆◆◆◆◆◆◆◆◆◆ too sweet, that particularly com-
plements poultry and game birds. The source is Marian Morash's *Victory Garden
Cookbook.*

1 pound parsnips

2 apples

1 orange

*3 tablespoons butter,
   melted*

2 tablespoons brown sugar

*3 tablespoons freshly
   squeezed orange juice*

Serves 4.

Preheat oven to 325° F. and butter a baking dish.

Peel the parsnips and cut into 3-inch pieces. Peel and
core the apples and cut each into 8 wedges. Slice the
unpeeled orange into ¼-inch slices, cutting the 4 or 5 largest
slices in half.

Combine the butter, sugar, and orange juice; add this mixture
to the parsnips and fruit, stirring well to coat. Put into the
buttered baking dish, cover, and bake 30 minutes, stirring
constantly. Uncover and bake 15 minutes longer to glaze.
Baste with juices and serve.

SWEET POTATOES WITH APPLES AND CHESTNUTS

◆◆◆◆◆◆◆◆◆◆◆◆◆◆◆◆◆◆◆◆◆◆◆◆◆◆

Judy Wolfe   Temple, New Hampshire This recipe, which first appeared in *Gourmet,* is an excellent holiday side dish, good with poultry, pork, beef, just about anything. The three main flavors here complement one another beautifully.

3 pounds sweet potatoes of the same size, well scrubbed

1½ cups chestnuts, with X cuts in rounded tops of shells

3 medium apples, preferably Golden Delicious

Juice of 1 lemon

8 tablespoons unsalted butter

½ cup brown sugar

½ cup honey

4 tablespoons dark rum

1 teaspoon cinnamon

Dash of mace

Serves 8.

Preheat oven to 350° F. Butter a large (9 × 13 × 2-inch) casserole, and set aside.

Put the sweet potatoes in an ungreased shallow pan along with the chestnuts. Bake for 25 to 30 minutes, until sweet potatoes and chestnuts are soft but not overcooked. The chestnuts may require more time.

Skin the sweet potatoes when they are cool enough to handle, and remove the eyes. Cut into ⅓-inch-thick slices and layer in the prepared casserole.

Skin and peel the cooled chestnuts and cut them in half crosswise. Layer the chestnut halves evenly on top of the sweet potatoes.

Peel and core the apples and slice into ⅓-inch-thick rings; cut the rings in half and drop them in the lemon juice to keep from darkening. Place apples evenly on top of chestnut layer. Increase oven temperature to 400° F.

In a small saucepan, melt the butter and add the brown sugar, honey, rum, cinnamon, and mace. Cook over medium heat until sugar is melted.

Pour butter-sugar mixture evenly over casserole layers. Bake for 30 to 40 minutes, basting frequently.

AUTHENTIC OLD-FASHIONED SWEET POTATO PUDDING

◆◆◆◆◆◆◆◆◆◆◆◆◆◆◆◆◆◆◆◆◆◆◆◆◆◆◆◆◆◆◆

Mrs. David Butler   Jackson, Mississippi As the title indicates, this
◆◆◆◆◆◆◆◆◆◆◆◆◆◆◆◆◆◆◆◆◆◆◆◆◆◆◆◆◆ dish is the real thing—classic Southern cooking in the grand tradition. The recipe comes from Mrs. Butler's Aunt Ash, Alice Fearn of Flora, Mississippi. It's over eighty years old and is always served with fresh roast pork in the fall or with turkey at Thanksgiving. It's frankly sweet and aromatic and has a delectable crunchy crust at the edges.

8 tablespoons butter

*4 cups grated raw sweet
  potato*

*1–1½ cups light brown
  sugar, or to taste*

2 cups milk

½ teaspoon baking soda

½ cup all-purpose flour

*1 teaspoon nutmeg,
  preferably freshly grated*

2 eggs, beaten

Serves 6 to 8.

Preheat oven to 350° F.

Melt the butter in an 8-inch baking dish. Mix all other ingredients together, eggs last, pour into the hot baking dish, and bake. When a crust forms at the edges, after 20 minutes or so, turn under, stir, and let a crust form again. Total baking time is 45 to 50 minutes.

GRANDMA SLOAN'S MACARONI PIE

◆◆◆◆◆◆◆◆◆◆◆◆◆◆◆◆◆◆◆◆◆◆◆◆◆

Diane Hrynczyszyn   Alvin, Texas This delicious macaroni and cheese
◆◆◆◆◆◆◆◆◆◆◆◆◆◆◆◆◆◆◆◆◆◆◆◆◆ dish is very easy to make and should
rest a little before serving, so it's perfect for a buffet table. This is another
grandmother dish—Grandmother Sloan was finally persuaded to measure the
ingredients, since she never uses recipes. The directions are a bit startling,
but do just as they say.

1 (10-ounce) package
   macaroni

1 pound medium-sharp
   Cheddar cheese, grated

3 eggs, beaten

2 cups milk

4 tablespoons butter

Salt and freshly ground
   black pepper to taste

1 teaspoon dry mustard
   (optional)

Dash of cayenne pepper
   (optional)

Grating of fresh nutmeg
   (optional)

Serves 8.

Preheat oven to 450° F.

Bring 1 quart water to boil and cook the macaroni to
the al dente stage, stirring occasionally to avoid sticking.
DO NOT DRAIN. Most of the water will be absorbed by the
pasta at this point.

Add all remaining ingredients, including the optional ones, if
using. Place mixture in a casserole and bake until the top
turns brown, about 30 to 45 minutes.

Let casserole sit a few minutes before serving; it will be
very hot.

OLD-FASHIONED CORN FRITTERS

Ruth Hill   Swiftwater, Pennsylvania   If you've never had corn fritters, you're in for a great treat. These are the real thing and should be made with young, sweet corn. Kernels from leftover corn on the cob are fine. These fritters are excellent for brunch, but they also make a good side dish, especially with pork or duck. Ruth Hill found this version in a column in the New York *Daily News*.

2 cups cooked corn kernels (about 3 ears' worth)

2 large eggs

2–4 tablespoons milk

½ cup all-purpose flour

1 teaspoon baking powder

1 teaspoon sugar

¾ teaspoon salt, or more to taste

Freshly ground black pepper to taste

Vegetable oil for frying

Serves 4 to 6.

Sift through the corn kernels with your fingers to make sure they are separate and set aside.

In a large bowl, beat the eggs lightly and beat in the milk.

Mix together the flour, baking powder, sugar, and ¾ teaspoon salt and gradually mix into liquid, stirring until you have a smooth batter.

Stir in the corn and add the pepper and, if you wish, more salt to taste. If the batter is too thick—it should fall slowly from the spoon—stir in a little more milk.

Fry in an inch of hot oil in a wide skillet over medium-high heat. Drop batter by heaping tablespoonfuls and cook until the fritters are crisp and golden on the bottom; then turn and cook the other side.

Drain on paper towels and serve hot.

AUNT ASH'S FRESH CORN PUDDING

Mrs. David Butler   Jackson, Mississippi   This old-fashioned recipe has been in Mrs. Butler's family since the turn of the century, when it was baked in a wood-burning stove. The family always serves it for the Fourth of July, usually with fried chicken.

6 ears fresh corn (not frozen)

4 eggs

2 cups light cream

1 teaspoon salt

¼ teaspoon freshly ground black pepper

1 tablespoon butter

Serves 6 to 8.

Preheat the oven to 350° F.

Scrape the corn from the ears—you should have about 2 cups of corn.

Beat the eggs; stir in the cream, salt, and pepper. Butter the bottom of a 1½-quart baking dish and pour the pudding into it. Place the dish in a roasting pan filled with enough water to come 2 inches up the side of the dish.

Bake 35 to 40 minutes; the corn will settle to the bottom of the dish.

CURRIED BRUSSELS SPROUTS IN CREAM

◆◆◆◆◆◆◆◆◆◆◆◆◆◆◆◆◆◆◆◆◆◆◆◆◆◆◆◆◆◆

Sibley Gillis Cockeysville, Maryland Creamy, nutty brussels sprouts
◆◆◆◆◆◆◆◆◆◆◆◆◆◆◆◆◆◆◆◆◆◆◆◆◆◆◆◆◆◆ enlivened with a touch of curry
powder. This unusual side dish is very good with pork, poultry, and roast beef.

*1½–2 pounds fresh
   brussels sprouts,
   washed and trimmed*

Salt to taste

½–1 cup heavy cream

*1 teaspoon curry powder,
   or to taste*

*Freshly ground black
   pepper to taste*

Serves 6.

Put the sprouts in a saucepan and cover with water. Bring to a boil and drain off the water. Return the sprouts to the pan and cover with hot water; add a dash of salt. Cook uncovered for 20 minutes. Drain and chop fine.

Put the sprouts back in the pan, cover with the cream, and sprinkle the curry powder on top. Season with pepper and mix well. Heat until nearly all the cream has been absorbed.

CHEESE GRITS

◆◆◆◆◆◆◆◆◆◆◆◆◆◆◆◆◆◆◆◆◆◆◆◆◆

Lee Harmer   Atlanta, Georgia   Lee Harmer has a Bostonian mother and
◆◆◆◆◆◆◆◆◆◆◆◆◆◆◆◆◆◆◆◆◆◆◆◆◆   a father from South Carolina, but neither
of them ever included cheese grits in the family kitchen repertoire. She
discovered them at church breakfasts in Georgia—as she says, they may be an
acquired taste, but these grits surely do acquire fast.

1 tablespoon salt

1 cup grits

*1 cup grated Cheddar
cheese*

4 tablespoons butter

Serves 6 to 8.

Put the salt into 4 cups water in a large saucepan, and bring to a boil. Add the grits and bring to a boil again, stirring. When all lumps have disappeared, turn the heat to low and cover, stirring occasionally to see if the grits are thick; it should take 15 to 20 minutes. When they are thick, add the cheese and butter, stirring until well blended and smooth.

NEVER-FAIL DUMPLINGS

◆◆◆

Mrs. Sherwin Palmer Cumberland, Wisconsin These dumplings are
◆◆◆ truly homey grand-
mother-style food, perfect for an intimate family dinner featuring stew or a
hearty homemade soup. This sort of meal serves as a respite from the elaborate
festive fare that tends to overwhelm us during the holidays. The recipe has
been handed down in the family for many years.

1⅓ cups all-purpose flour

*2 teaspoons baking
   powder*

1 teaspoon salt

1 egg

½ cup milk

*About 8 cups chicken or
   beef broth*

*Makes 2 dozen
   dumplings; serves 6.*

Sift the flour with the baking powder and salt. Beat the
egg and add the milk, then combine with the flour
mixture. Bring the broth to a boil, and drop the batter
by teaspoonfuls into boiling broth. Cover and steam for 20
minutes.

For a light lunch, serve the dumplings with the broth.

STUFFED VINE LEAVES

Brenda Heinrichs **Spruce Grove, Alberta** A pleasant, subtle filling for vine leaves that gives you one of those "soul food" reactions—you crave it every now and then.

⅔ cup olive oil

1 medium onion, chopped

½ cup medium-grain rice

2½ cups boiling water

½ cup pine nuts

½ cup golden raisins

½ teaspoon salt

Freshly ground black pepper to taste

Juice of 1 lemon

1 tablespoon snipped fresh dill

1 tablespoon minced fresh Italian parsley

1 teaspoon dried tarragon

1 (1-pound) jar vine leaves

Lemon wedges for garnish

Makes about 3 dozen; serves 12 to 16.

Heat ½ cup of the olive oil in a saucepan. Add the onion, and sauté gently until translucent. Add the rice and cook, stirring, 3 minutes. Add 1¼ cups boiling water, the pine nuts, raisins, salt, and pepper to taste. Simmer, covered, until the rice absorbs all the liquid, about 10 minutes. Add 1 tablespoon lemon juice and the herbs. Allow to cool.

Place the vine leaves in a bowl and let them soak in cold water a few minutes. Drain, soak again in cold water, then repeat the entire process. Gently separate the leaves and allow to drain on a tea towel.

Place a leaf, veined side up, on the work surface with the stem end closest to you. Place 1 or 2 heaping teaspoons (depending on the size of the leaf) of the filling near the stem end of the leaf. Fold the stem end up over the filling, then fold both sides toward the middle and roll up like a small cigar. Continue until the filling is used up.

Place a layer of unfilled leaves in the bottom of a heavy 2½- to 3-quart saucepan. Arrange the stuffed leaves tightly in layers, seam side down. Pour remaining oil, lemon juice, and boiling water over the leaves. Set a heatproof plate on top of the leaves to press them down and cover the saucepan. Bring to a boil, reduce heat, and simmer 45 minutes. Remove from the heat and cool.

Carefully remove the stuffed vine leaves and serve cold or at room temperature with lemon wedges. You can freeze them successfully in a covered container. Thaw for 24 hours in the refrigerator before using.

ZUCCHINI FRITTATA PANCAKES

◆◆◆◆◆◆◆◆◆◆◆◆◆◆◆◆◆◆◆◆◆◆◆

Terry Hill   Lafayette, California These savory pancakes can be served
◆◆◆◆◆◆◆◆◆◆◆◆◆◆◆◆◆◆◆◆◆◆ hot or cold—perfect, as Terry Hill
points out, for a picnic. Although they sound authentically Italian, they're her
own invention.

*4 unpeeled medium
    zucchini, grated*

½ cup chopped onion

2 cloves garlic, chopped

*½ cup chopped fresh
    parsley*

*2 tablespoons minced
    fresh rosemary or 2
    teaspoons dried
    rosemary*

*½ teaspoon dried
    marjoram*

½ cup olive oil

4 large eggs, lightly beaten

½ cup dry bread crumbs

*1 cup freshly grated
    Parmesan cheese*

Serves 4.

Set the zucchini aside in a colander to drain for an hour.
Sauté the onion, garlic, parsley, and herbs in 1 tablespoon of the olive oil. When the onion has softened—
about 5 minutes—remove from heat and allow to cool. Add
the eggs.

Put the zucchini, bread crumbs, and cheese in a medium
bowl. Add the onion mixture to the bowl. The mixture should
be thicker than pancake mixture. Don't overmix; a wooden
spoon is best for this procedure. Add more bread crumbs if
necessary.

Heat the remaining olive oil in a skillet, and when it's hot
add the pancakes, using about ½ cup of batter to a pancake.
Turn when brown on the first side and brown the other side,
about 5 minutes altogether. Drain on paper towels when
done.

TUTTA

◆◆◆

Deborah DeMarco Philadelphia, Pennsylvania A great buffet
◆◆ dish—it's particularly attractive baked and served in a ceramic dish. Or cut it in squares and
serve it on a platter; smaller squares would be good with cocktails.

*1½ cups long-grain white
rice*

3 cups chicken broth

*8 tablespoons butter, plus
2 tablespoons for the
pan*

1 medium onion, minced

1 bunch scallions, minced

*1 (10-ounce) package
frozen chopped spinach*

*Salt and freshly ground
black pepper to taste*

*1 large clove garlic,
minced*

*8 ounces good-quality
cream cheese*

4 eggs

*1 cup grated Parmesan
cheese*

½ cup dry bread crumbs

*Serves 8 as a side dish or
24 as an appetizer.*

Place the rice and the chicken broth in a saucepan and
bring to a boil. Immediately lower the heat to a simmer,
cover the saucepan, and cook 17 minutes, or until the
rice is just done. Transfer the rice to a large bowl.

Heat the 8 tablespoons butter in a skillet and sauté the onion
and scallions over medium heat until they turn golden. Add
them to the rice.

Cook the spinach according to the instructions on the package,
squeeze dry, and add to the bowl. Season with the salt and
pepper and add the garlic. Mix well and allow to cool to
lukewarm. Add the cream cheese and mix well. Add 3 of the
eggs and the Parmesan cheese.

Preheat oven to 350° F.

Butter an 11 × 14-inch baking pan with the 2 tablespoons
butter and shake the bread crumbs all over the bottom and
sides. Spread tutta mixture in the pan. Beat the remaining
egg, and pour over the top. Smooth the top evenly and draw
ridges across it with a fork.

Bake the tutta for 45 minutes. The top should be nicely
browned. Allow to cool for 30 minutes. Cut into squares to
serve.

ONION PIE

◆◆◆◆◆◆◆◆◆◆◆◆◆◆◆◆◆◆◆◆◆◆◆◆◆◆◆◆◆◆◆◆◆◆◆◆◆◆◆

Rose Drinkwater   North Billerica, Massachusetts This unusual pie
◆◆◆◆◆◆◆◆◆◆◆◆◆◆◆◆◆◆◆◆◆◆◆◆◆◆◆◆◆◆◆◆◆◆◆◆ is a regional specialty from Gaeta, Italy, where Rose Drinkwater's grandmother learned to make
it as a child. The onions are cooked very gently, which brings out their native
sweetness. This pie is a good addition to the buffet table, served hot or at
room temperature, and it also makes a good light luncheon dish with a salad
and a glass of wine.

3 tablespoons olive oil

*2 very large sweet yellow
onions, sliced thin*

1 egg

*½–¾ cup grated
Parmesan cheese*

*1 tablespoon chopped fresh
Italian parsley*

*4 fresh basil leaves, torn
in small pieces, or ½
teaspoon dried basil*

*Freshly ground black
pepper to taste*

Salt to taste

*1 recipe white bread
dough or 1 package
frozen bread dough or
1 package pizza dough*

Serves 6 to 8.

Preheat oven to 375° F. and have ready a 9-inch greased
pie pan. Put the oil and onions into a large skillet over
medium-low heat and cook the onions until they begin
to soften. Add ¼ cup water, cover, and simmer until the
onions are completely soft. With a slotted spoon remove
onions to a bowl, discarding most of the liquid.

Add the remaining ingredients, except the dough, and stir
until well blended. Taste for salt. Set mixture aside.

Halve the dough and place it on a well-floured board. Roll it
into a circle larger than the pie pan, about ⅛ inch thick (if
you're using pizza dough, it will be very thin). Gently lift the
bottom crust into the pie pan, pressing to fit. Add the onions.

Roll the rest of the dough to the same size and make several
decorative slashes for steam in the center of the crust. Fit
the top crust onto the pie and firmly seal the edges. Brush
a little olive oil on top.

Place the pie on the middle rack. Bake for about 30 minutes,
or until the pie is light brown and sounds hollow when tapped.
Remove to a wire rack and let cool about 15 minutes.

GRAM'S BAKED BEANS

◆◆◆◆◆◆◆◆◆◆◆◆◆◆◆◆◆◆◆◆◆◆◆◆◆◆◆◆◆◆◆

Emily Hollman   Windsor, Connecticut   Mrs. Hollman is a Connecticut
◆◆◆◆◆◆◆◆◆◆◆◆◆◆◆◆◆◆◆◆◆◆◆◆◆◆◆◆◆◆ Yankee who should know her
beans, and these are very good indeed. Her grandmother passed down the
recipe. These beans are sweet and mellow—if you like them more savory, use
less sugar, increase the mustard, and add a chopped onion when the beans go
into the oven.

2 cups dried pea beans,
   soaked overnight in
   water to cover

1 teaspoon baking soda

1 teaspoon salt

1 teaspoon–1 tablespoon
   dry mustard

¾ cup–2 cups dark brown
   sugar

¼ pound deeply scored
   salt pork

1 onion, chopped
   (optional)

Serves 12.

Rinse the beans and put them into a saucepan with water
to cover. Boil them 45 minutes, or until the skins peel.
Preheat oven to 300° F.

Put the beans into a bean pot or other ovenproof ceramic
pot with a cover, and add the rest of the ingredients. Water
should come to just under the top level of the beans. Bake
4 to 6 hours, until beans are tender.

Main Dishes

QUEBEC ROASTED TURKEY

◆◆◆◆◆◆◆◆◆◆◆◆◆◆◆◆◆◆◆◆◆◆◆◆◆◆◆◆◆

Emily Rankin   Mississauga, Ontario   When Mrs. Rankin was married
◆◆◆◆◆◆◆◆◆◆◆◆◆◆◆◆◆◆◆◆◆◆◆◆◆◆◆   thirty years ago, her husband
informed her that he didn't like bread dressing in poultry. She soon discovered
this very unusual recipe in a newspaper column by the famous Madame Benoît
and has used it ever since. Our testers raved about this turkey; they all thought
it was the best they'd ever eaten. There's no need to baste the bird since the
covering seals in all the juices.

1 (16-pound) turkey

7 tablespoons butter

3 onions, minced

8 cups cooked mashed
    potatoes, still warm
    (8 large potatoes)

1½ teaspoons savory or ¼
    teaspoon poultry spice

2 tablespoons salt

1 teaspoon freshly ground
    black pepper

2 tablespoons plus ½
    teaspoon dry mustard

8 tablespoons unsalted
    butter, softened to room
    temperature

3 tablespoons all-purpose
    flour

2 thick slices bacon

Serves 12.

Remove the turkey giblets and chop them into small pieces. Melt 3 tablespoons of the butter and sauté the giblets. Add the onions and sauté until translucent. Set aside.

In a large bowl, combine the mashed potatoes, 4 tablespoons butter, cut into small pieces, the savory, 1 tablespoon of the salt, ½ teaspoon of the pepper, and ½ teaspoon of the dry mustard. Add the sautéed giblets and onions. Mix well.

Preheat oven to 325° F.

Put the stuffing into the prepared turkey and place in a roasting pan breast side up. If you'd like to remove the stuffing easily and completely, line the cavity with cheesecloth before stuffing the turkey.

Meanwhile, prepare a covering mixture by creaming together the unsalted butter and remaining 2 tablespoons dry mustard, 1 tablespoon salt, ½ teaspoon pepper, and the flour. Spread the mixture evenly over the breast and legs of the turkey. Place a slice of bacon over each leg.

Roast the turkey for 18 to 20 minutes per pound; check to see that the leg joint moves easily for doneness.

STUFFED CROWN ROAST OF PORK

◆◆◆◆◆◆◆◆◆◆◆◆◆◆◆◆◆◆◆◆◆◆◆◆◆◆◆◆◆

Virginia Stalder   Nokesville, Virginia This delicious and gorgeous
◆◆◆◆◆◆◆◆◆◆◆◆◆◆◆◆◆◆◆◆◆◆◆◆◆◆◆◆ crown roast makes an impressive presentation. Virginia Stalder published the recipe several years ago in
Southern Living.

*1 crown pork roast (about
    5 pounds)*

Vegetable oil

*Salt and freshly ground
    black pepper to taste*

4 tablespoons butter

*3 scallions, sliced,
    including the green*

4 large mushrooms, sliced

2 tart apples, diced

3 cups herbed stuffing mix

*½ cup applesauce, or
    more if needed*

*3 tablespoons plus ½ cup
    apple brandy*

*1 (10-ounce) jar apricot
    preserves*

*Preserved kumquats for
    decoration (optional)*

Serves 6.

Remove the meat from the refrigerator about an hour before roasting. Brush with vegetable oil and rub salt and pepper into it. Place the roast on a triple thickness of aluminum foil the same diameter as the roast.

Preheat the oven the 325° F.

Heat the butter in a large skillet over medium heat until it bubbles. Add the scallions, and cook and stir until tender. Add the mushrooms, and cook and stir until mushrooms are just tender. Add the apples; cook and stir 1 minute. Stir in the stuffing, applesauce, and 3 tablespoons of the brandy (add more applesauce if stuffing seems dry). Pack in the prepared roast, mounding high, and cover the stuffing with a foil cap.

Roast 2½ hours. Remove foil cap from the stuffing. Heat the apricot preserves and ¼ cup of the brandy in a small saucepan over medium heat. Reserve ¼ cup of the mixture for serving. Brush the preserves-brandy mixture on the roast every 10 minutes, until a meat thermometer inserted in the roast comes to 170° F.; this should take about 30 minutes.

Remove roast from oven. Let stand 15 minutes. Cut the ends off the kumquats, if using, and scoop out centers with a melon baller. Garnish the tips of the ribs with the kumquats. Heat the remaining ¼ cup preserves mixture and float the last ¼ cup brandy on top. Ignite the brandy and pour mixture over the roast. Serve immediately.

TURKEY WITH CHINESE RICE STUFFING

◆◆◆◆◆◆◆◆◆◆◆◆◆◆◆◆◆◆◆◆◆◆◆◆◆◆◆

Sandra Wong   Cochrane, Alberta   For those die-hard Chinese food fans
◆◆◆◆◆◆◆◆◆◆◆◆◆◆◆◆◆◆◆◆◆◆◆◆◆◆◆ who can't bear to spend even
Thanksgiving without the joys of Chinese flavors or for those who long for
something exotic with their turkey, this dish will be a godsend. The recipe has
been in Sandra Wong's family for three generations.

2 cups long-grain rice

1 cup glutinous short-grain rice

5–6 dried Chinese black mushrooms

3 dry Chinese sausages

2 tablespoons peanut oil

1 medium onion, finely chopped

2 stalks celery, finely chopped

Turkey giblets, chopped

¼ cup dried Chinese shrimp, chopped

¼ cup soy sauce

1 teaspoon salt

½ teaspoon freshly ground black pepper

1 teaspoon sugar

1½ tablespoons sesame oil

3 tablespoons Chinese barbecue sauce (Hoisin sauce)

In a large saucepan, combine the 2 rices and cover with
cold water to ¾ inch above the rice mixture. Bring to a
boil over high heat, cover, and simmer over low heat
about 8 minutes, or until water level is below rice.

Meanwhile, soak the mushrooms in 1 cup hot water for 15
minutes. Drain, reserving mushroom liquid for basting turkey.
Discard stems and chop mushroom caps. Set aside.

Add the sausages to the rice and continue to simmer, covered,
for another 8 minutes, or until sausages are tender and rice
is cooked.

Remove sausages from cooked rice. Set aside the rice and
chop the sausages.

In a large sauté pan, heat the peanut oil and add the onion
and celery. Then add the giblets, sausages, shrimp, and
mushrooms. Sauté over medium heat until the onion is
translucent.

Remove from heat and add soy sauce, salt, pepper, sugar,
sesame oil, and Hoisin sauce. Add this mixture to the cooked
rice and combine well until thoroughly mixed.

Preheat oven to 350° F. Stuff the turkey with the rice, truss,
and place in a roasting pan. Roast at 20 minutes per pound.
Baste with reserved mushroom liquid.

1 (16-pound) turkey

Makes about 8 cups stuffing, enough for a 16-pound turkey.

Note: For a more flavorful turkey, baste with the following sauce: ¾ cup reserved mushroom liquid, 2 tablespoons soy sauce, 1½ tablespoons peanut oil, 1½ tablespoons sesame oil, and 1 teaspoon sugar.

FRUITED STUFFED GOOSE

◆◆◆◆◆◆◆◆◆◆◆◆◆◆◆◆◆◆◆◆◆◆◆◆◆◆◆◆◆◆◆◆

Virginia Stalder   Nokesville, Virginia   An easily prepared goose rec-
◆◆◆◆◆◆◆◆◆◆◆◆◆◆◆◆◆◆◆◆◆◆◆◆◆◆◆◆◆◆ ipe with a succulent fruit stuffing. Virginia Stalder says this is her favorite Thanksgiving recipe, found in a
rural Minnesota newspaper years ago.

6 slices bacon

½ cup chopped scallion

*½ cup chopped green
 pepper*

*1 (8-ounce package)
 herbed stuffing mix*

1 cup chopped peaches

*½ cup seeded and chopped
 dates*

1 egg, slightly beaten

1 (8-pound) goose

*Salt and freshly ground
 black pepper to taste*

*Makes 6 cups dressing;
 serves 6 to 8.*

In a skillet, cook the bacon until crisp. Remove, drain on
paper towels, and crumble; set aside. Add the scallion and
green pepper to the drippings and sauté over medium heat
until tender.

Combine the stuffing, bacon, vegetables, 1¼ cups water,
peaches, dates, and egg.

Preheat oven to 325° F.

Wash the goose inside and out. Season the cavity with salt
and pepper. Pack the stuffing lightly into the cavity. Place
on rack in roasting pan. Roast for 3 hours, or until done.

BARBECUED CORNED BEEF

◆◆◆◆◆◆◆◆◆◆◆◆◆◆◆◆◆◆◆◆◆◆◆◆◆◆

Donia Tyner Ponte Vedra, Florida An unusual way to serve corned
◆◆◆◆◆◆◆◆◆◆◆◆◆◆◆◆◆◆◆◆◆◆◆◆◆ beef, this very easy recipe is just
right for a large crowd.

1 (3–5-pound) front-cut
  corned beef brisket

3 tablespoons Dijon
  mustard

½ cup brown sugar

4 shakes Tabasco sauce

2 tablespoons white
  vinegar

¼ teaspoon garlic juice

Serves 12 to 20.

In a large kettle, cover the brisket with water and simmer until tender, about 4 hours. Meanwhile, mix together the rest of the ingredients and set aside.

When the brisket is done, drain, dry thoroughly, brush on both sides with the sauce, and put on a hot grill, about 5 inches from the flame. Baste frequently. The meat can also be broiled in the oven. Cooking time is 5 minutes to a side, under a preheated broiler.

The meat will probably catch fire and blacken, but that's fine. To serve, slice thin, against the grain.

DOT'S ROAST LAMB WITH DILLSEED

◆◆◆◆◆◆◆◆◆◆◆◆◆◆◆◆◆◆◆◆◆◆◆◆◆◆◆◆◆◆◆◆

June Paul   Burnaby, British Columbia   This is one of the more un-
◆◆◆◆◆◆◆◆◆◆◆◆◆◆◆◆◆◆◆◆◆◆◆◆◆◆◆◆◆◆◆◆◆ usual recipes we received—
it seems to date from the days of stouthearted ovens with great insulation. In
any case, it's perhaps 5 minutes' worth of preparation altogether, and you're
rewarded with a very succulent, rustic-style roast—the aroma alone will drive
you wild. Because ovens differ and the size of legs of lamb can vary from 5 to
10 pounds, rely on a meat thermometer for accurate roasting. A good Bordeaux
goes beautifully with lamb, and you'll want a hearty red for the roasting.

6 medium onions, sliced

3 tablespoons dillseed

*1 leg of lamb, skin and
fat removed*

*1 quart buttermilk or
yogurt*

*1 (10½-ounce) can beef
broth plus equal
amount of dry red
wine, mixed*

Three days before serving, lay half of the onions in a
roasting pan and sprinkle with half of the dillseed. Lay
the lamb on the bed of onions, pour the buttermilk over
it, and finish with the rest of the onions and dillseed. Cover
the pan with foil and refrigerate.

Twice a day, turn the lamb over and spoon the buttermilk
and some onion over the top.

On serving day, drain the meat, reserving the onions, and
bring to room temperature. Preheat the oven to 500° F.

Put the onions back on the bottom of the roasting pan and
the lamb on top of them. Add the broth and wine. Put the
roast into the oven for 20 to 40 minutes, depending on its
size—you want it nicely browned—then turn off the oven
and leave the lamb in it for 3 hours. Don't open the door.

Preheat the oven to 350° F. before serving the roast. Warm
the lamb about 20 minutes, or as needed to reach the right
temperature. Check the temperature of the meat on a meat
thermometer. For a good pink roast, it should register 140–
145° F.; a truly rare roast will be 130° F.

You'll have the wonderfully tasty onions to serve alongside
the juicy lamb; the dillseed simply melts into the sauce.

LOIS HUNT'S FRIED CHICKEN

◆◆◆◆◆◆◆◆◆◆◆◆◆◆◆◆◆◆◆◆◆◆◆◆◆◆◆◆

Mary Lepp Yankton, South Dakota A particularly tasty, lightly crisp
◆◆◆◆◆◆◆◆◆◆◆◆◆◆◆◆◆◆◆◆◆◆◆◆◆◆◆◆ fried chicken with a wonderful
down-home flavor. One of the secrets here is the heavy use of salt and pepper.
The interior meat remains moist and succulent. Perfect for a picnic, but then
it's hard to imagine when fried chicken wouldn't be perfect. This recipe comes
from the *Des Moines Register*.

*3 pounds frying chicken,
  cut into serving pieces*

*Oil for frying, preferably
  peanut or corn oil*

2 cups all-purpose flour

2 tablespoons salt

*2 tablespoons freshly
  ground black pepper*

1 tablespoon paprika

Dash of garlic salt

Serves 4.

Remove fat from chicken and wash it thoroughly. Soak in cold salted water for 10 to 15 minutes. In a roasting pan or Dutch oven, pour oil to a depth of 2 inches. Be sure the pan is very deep or the oil will bubble up dangerously and may even run over the sides. Heat oil over low heat while preparing the chicken.

In a large brown paper bag, mix the flour, salt, pepper, paprika, and garlic salt. Put 3 or 4 pieces of chicken in the bag and shake to cover chicken well. Increase heat under oil to medium-high and when a cube of bread sizzles in the oil, add the chicken. Turn the chicken frequently. Fry until golden brown, about 15 minutes for white meat and up to 25 minutes for dark meat. Drain on paper towels.

Note: Chicken prepared this way would also be delicious cocktail food. Get the butcher to bone a whole chicken and cut it in chunks about the size of a finger. Cook in a heavy iron skillet, using 8 tablespoons of melted butter to replace the oil. In this case, you'll be sautéing rather than frying, so the heat should be lower—medium-low is the right temperature.

STEAMED HARD-SHELL CRABS

◆◆◆◆◆◆◆◆◆◆◆◆◆◆◆◆◆◆◆◆◆◆◆◆◆◆◆◆◆◆◆◆◆◆◆◆◆

Conway Davenport Baltimore, Maryland In Maryland, where the
◆◆◆◆◆◆◆◆◆◆◆◆◆◆◆◆◆◆◆◆◆◆◆◆◆◆◆◆◆◆◆◆◆◆◆ crabs are wonderful, they
are the traditional centerpiece for Memorial Day, the Fourth of July, and Labor
Day. Here's an authentic method for preparing them. Start off with live crabs,
fresh from the water if possible. If they seem too feisty, subdue them on ice
or in the refrigerator for an hour.

Serve the crabs with ice-cold beer or iced tea. Some Marylanders insist on
having fresh baked bread and butter with their crabs, which is also traditional.

*12 ounces beer or mixture
of 1 cup water, 1 cup
vinegar*

*Fresh live hard-shell
crabs, 1 or 2 per
person*

Salt

*Freshly ground black
pepper*

Dry mustard

Crushed red pepper flakes

Kosher salt

You'll need a clam steamer for this project or a similar
pot in 2 sections, so that the crabs can be separated
by a rack from the steaming brew.

In the lower section of the steamer, pour the beer (flat is all
right) or water and vinegar.

Put the top section of the steamer and add 1 layer of crabs—
the Davenports' own steamer will hold 4 dozen crabs, so
judge accordingly, depending on the quantity you're steaming.
Cover this layer and each successive layer with a dash of
each of the other ingredients, in the order listed. Continue
adding crabs and spices until the pot is full or you've run out
of crabs. Cover the steamer.

Steam over high heat for 45 minutes.

ARCTIC SALMON COOKED IN A DISHWASHER

◆◆◆◆◆◆◆◆◆◆◆◆◆◆◆◆◆◆◆◆◆◆◆◆◆◆◆◆◆◆◆

Sage German   Old Chelsea, Quebec   The cooking utensil here is indeed
◆◆◆◆◆◆◆◆◆◆◆◆◆◆◆◆◆◆◆◆◆◆◆◆◆◆◆◆◆◆ the dishwasher, and the method
seems to have been developed by Eskimo women—this tidbit was passed along
during Montreal's Expo 67, when the Eskimo were in town to demonstrate
their crafts. Intrigued by the image of hundreds of igloos with electric dishwashers
cooking fish, Mrs. German had to try it. Now she never cooks fish any other
way, and since there's a shortage of well water in her area, she does the dishes
at the same time. Best of all, it really works; the texture is perfect and all the
juices stay in the fish.

*1 (3–4-pound) whole char
or salmon*

1 bunch fresh dill

*Seasonings of your choice
(optional)*

Serves 4 to 6.

It's important that the dishwasher have a drying cycle;
otherwise the recipe won't work.

Place the fish on 2 sheets of heavy-duty aluminum foil,
add the bunch of dill and any other favorite seasonings, and
wrap the foil well around the fish.

Put the wrapped fish on the top rack in the dishwasher and
run through one complete wash and dry cycle. Unwrap the
fish, remove the skin, and serve hot or cold.

TRIPLE MEAT MARINADE

◆◆◆◆◆◆◆◆◆◆◆◆◆◆◆◆◆◆◆◆◆◆◆◆◆◆◆◆◆◆◆◆◆

Kathleen Gordon   Kalamazoo, Michigan   A good choice for a holiday
◆◆◆◆◆◆◆◆◆◆◆◆◆◆◆◆◆◆◆◆◆◆◆◆◆◆◆◆◆◆◆◆ buffet. This hearty dish can
be quickly put together, made ahead of time, and glamorized with cut vegetables.

4 cups high-quality rare
    roast beef, thinly sliced

1 cup smoked ham, thinly
    sliced

1 cup roast turkey, thinly
    sliced

1 cup minced scallion,
    including some green

1 cup minced celery,
    including leaves

4 (3-inch) sour dill
    pickles, minced

6 hard-cooked egg yolks

1 tablespoon Dijon mustard

1 cup extra virgin olive oil

1 clove garlic

1 teaspoon salt

3/4 teaspoon freshly ground
    black pepper

1/4 teaspoon lemon pepper
    or freshly squeezed
    lemon juice

1/3 cup tarragon white
    wine vinegar

2 dashes hot pepper sauce

Serves 16.

Cut all the meats into squares and place them, mixed together well, in a bowl with the scallion, celery, and pickles. Put the rest of the ingredients in a blender and blend until smooth. Pour the dressing over the meats, mix well, and refrigerate for at least 12 hours before serving.

NEW ORLEANS RED BEANS AND RICE

◆◆◆◆◆◆◆◆◆◆◆◆◆◆◆◆◆◆◆◆◆◆◆◆◆◆◆◆

Pat Chopin   Metairie, Louisiana This recipe was developed by Pat
◆◆◆◆◆◆◆◆◆◆◆◆◆◆◆◆◆◆◆◆◆◆◆◆◆◆ Chopin herself—but it has the classic
taste of great soul food. You can make it all ahead of time, even a day or so
ahead, and it reheats beautifully. Serve it over hot rice. This dish would be
especially good luck on New Year's Day, according to Southern folklore.

*1 pound dried red beans
    or kidney beans*

*6 slices bacon or 2
    tablespoons bacon
    drippings*

⅓ cup all-purpose flour

1 large onion, chopped

4 cloves garlic, chopped

¼ teaspoon dried thyme

¼ teaspoon Tabasco sauce

*1 tablespoon
    Worcestershire sauce*

3 bay leaves

*12 ounces Polish sausage,
    cut into ½-inch pieces*

Salt to taste

Serves 10.

Soak the beans overnight in water to cover, then drain.
In a large Dutch oven, fry the bacon until crisp and
remove. Alternatively, melt the bacon drippings. To
the drippings add the flour and stir constantly over medium
heat until golden brown.

Add the onion and garlic and sauté until tender. Gradually
add 5½ cups water and all remaining ingredients. Simmer
for 3 hours, or until the beans are very tender and the liquid
has thickened.

TALMADGE COUNTRY CURED HAM

Louise Dodd   Wrightsville, Georgia In Georgia, no matter what the holiday, the one essential is country ham. This recipe, which comes originally from Betty Talmadge of Lovejoy, Georgia, is the one to beat.

1 country cured ham
6 onions
3 cups light brown sugar
2 cups white vinegar
2 bay leaves
24 whole cloves, plus
    more for decoration
2 teaspoons dry mustard
Serves 20.

Wash the ham thoroughly, soak it overnight, and drain. Place in a roasting pan with 2 cups of water; add the onions, 2 cups of the brown sugar, the vinegar, bay leaves, and 24 cloves.

Cover the roasting pan and bring it to a simmer on top of the stove. Continue to simmer—do not boil—20 minutes to the pound. The ham is done when the small bone at the hock end can be twisted out.

Preheat oven to 450° F.

Let the ham cool in the liquid. Then remove the skin and cut off excess fat, score, and insert whole cloves in a decorative pattern. Mix the remaining 1 cup brown sugar with the mustard to make a glaze; press it onto the ham. Bake 20 minutes to glaze.

To serve, slice thinner than you would a commercial ham.

CHRISTMAS BEEF

◆◆◆◆◆◆◆◆◆◆◆◆◆◆◆◆◆◆◆◆◆◆◆◆◆◆◆◆

Emily Rankin   Mississauga, Ontario   A very distinctive recipe that's
◆◆◆◆◆◆◆◆◆◆◆◆◆◆◆◆◆◆◆◆◆◆◆◆◆◆◆ been in Emily Rankin's family for
many years. This beef was always made only for Christmas. Now that we have
refrigerators it can be made any time of the year and will keep for weeks. It's
an excellent choice for buffets and should be served sliced thin so that the
sweet cured beef flavor can be savored.

1 tablespoon saltpeter
(potassium nitrate at
the drugstore)

3 ounces ground allspice

1 teaspoon ground mace

1 teaspoon ground cloves

1 cup salt

1 cup light brown sugar

1 (12-pound) top round of
roast beef

Serves 40.

Combine all the dry ingredients and mix well. Rub mixture throughly into the beef, using your hands, and place in a covered crock in a cool but unrefrigerated place.

Turn meat every day for 3 weeks and baste with the liquid that has leached out of the meat. Tie meat securely in 2 or 3 layers of cheesecloth, securing the ends and wrapping twice around the middle.

Place in a large kettle and cover with water. Bring to a boil and simmer partially covered for 6 hours. Remove meat from water and cool.

Wrap meat in plastic wrap and refrigerate after each use. It will keep for several weeks.

ALEUT FISH PIE

◆◆◆◆◆◆◆◆◆◆◆◆◆◆◆◆◆◆◆◆◆◆◆◆◆◆◆◆◆◆

Sharon Lestenkof   Seattle, Washington   Certainly this recipe is among
◆◆◆◆◆◆◆◆◆◆◆◆◆◆◆◆◆◆◆◆◆◆◆◆◆◆   the more unusual ones: it
comes from the Pribilof Islands, Alaska, the seal rookeries of the Bering Sea.
Sharon Lestenkof is married to an Aleut whose mother makes this traditional
dish. It's easy to assemble and can be made well ahead of time and varied to
suit the availability of fish—salmon works well in this pie, but so does shredded
corned beef, with a layer of cabbage leaves on top. A bit Irish, but actually the
Aleuts of Kodiak are fond of this variation.

*Double recipe of piecrust
  or 2 packages frozen
  piecrust*

3 cups pearl rice

1 bay leaf

*2–3 pounds halibut or
  salmon fillets*

*Salt and freshly ground
  black pepper to taste*

1 medium onion, diced

Milk

Serves 8 to 10.

Divide piecrust dough in two, and roll out half to fit a
9 × 13-inch baking dish, covering the sides as well as
the bottom of the dish. Set aside other half.

Cook the rice with bay leaf until done, then remove bay leaf
(which will stain the rice if left in) and cool the rice. Preheat
oven to 350° F.

Cut the fish fillets in half through the middle if they are not
already thinly sliced. Put half the rice over the bottom crust
of the pie and sprinkle with salt and pepper to taste. Lay on
the fish fillets, which should cover the surface with a little
crowding. Salt and pepper the fish and add half the onion.

Add the rest of the rice, more salt and pepper, and the rest
of the onion. Put on the top crust, seal around the edges,
and brush with milk. Cut a few vent holes in the pastry and
bake for 1 hour. The fish will be moist and perfectly cooked.

Cool the pie for about 10 minutes and slice into squares. The
traditional accompaniments are butter and seafood sauce.

The pie can be prepared several hours ahead of time—
refrigerate it uncooked, wrapped in plastic wrap. Cook about
10 minutes longer.

CRAWFISH STEW

◆◆◆◆◆◆◆◆◆◆◆◆◆◆◆◆◆◆◆◆◆◆◆◆◆◆◆◆◆◆◆◆◆◆◆

Jane Muirhead   Shreveport, Louisiana   This recipe is the real thing,
◆◆◆◆◆◆◆◆◆◆◆◆◆◆◆◆◆◆◆◆◆◆◆◆◆◆◆◆◆◆ from Louisiana. If your fish
store isn't shipping in lots of crawfish, make it with shrimp. The real secret of
this dish is the roux, which should be made attentively. This stew is good
served over rice.

½ cup all-purpose flour

½ cup bacon drippings or
oil

1 large onion, chopped

½ cup chopped green
pepper

2 cloves garlic, minced

3 ribs celery, chopped

1½ cups chicken broth

1 teaspoon salt

1 teaspoon freshly ground
black pepper

¼ teaspoon Tabasco
sauce, or to taste

1 pound crawfish tails,
cleaned

½ cup chopped fresh
parsley

½ cup chopped scallion,
including the green

Serves 4 to 6.

In a heavy pot, make the roux with the flour and bacon
drippings. Set the pot over a medium flame and stir the
flour and bacon drippings mixture constantly until it be-
comes very dark brown but not burned. Be patient—this will
take about 15 minutes.

After the roux is dark brown, add the onion, green pepper,
garlic, and celery. Cook over low heat, covered, about 5
minutes. Add the chicken broth, salt, pepper, and Tabasco.
Cover and let simmer for 1 hour. Add the crawfish tails and
cook for about 5 minutes. Just before serving, add the parsley
and scallion.

OAKWOOD FEED STORE CHILI

◆◆◆◆◆◆◆◆◆◆◆◆◆◆◆◆◆◆◆◆◆◆◆

Del Smith Burke, Virginia This very meaty, peppery chili is far from
◆◆◆◆◆◆◆◆◆◆◆◆◆◆◆◆◆◆◆◆◆◆ the usual offering. Del Smith has been working on the recipe for four years now, and it's already been a prizewinner in
regional chili cook-offs. The Oakwood Feed Store can be found in a small town
in western Oklahoma where Mr. Smith's eighty-three-year-old father still lives.
They must have mouths of steel there: this is very spicy chili indeed, and
unless you really love your chili flammable, you'll want to cut down on the
Tabasco and jalapeños.

*1½ pounds bacon,
chopped*

*3 pounds lean beef chuck
roast, cut into small
cubes*

*2 pounds coarsely ground
pork roast*

*8 large cloves garlic,
pressed*

*3 large onions, coarsely
chopped*

*5 tablespoons freshly
ground dried Mexican
chile peppers (cascabels
and chiles de arbol)*

*2 tablespoons freshly
ground ancho chilies*

*2 tablespoons fresh, high-
quality, commercial
chili powder*

*1½ tablespoons
Hungarian paprika*

*4 tablespoons freshly
ground cumin seeds*

In a heavy cast-iron skillet, fry the bacon over medium
heat until very crisp. Remove bacon and reserve. In the
same skillet, using 2 tablespoons of the bacon fat (reserve
the rest), brown the meat along with the garlic.

In a large kettle (at least 8-quart-size) place the remainder
of the bacon fat and sauté the onions until soft. Add the
browned meats along with the crisp bacon. Immediately add
the rest of the ingredients.

Simmer uncovered over low heat about 2 hours, checking
occasionally to stir so the chili doesn't scorch. If possible,
leave the chili refrigerated overnight to cure; the flavor will
be much better. The chili will keep for several days; it also
freezes well.

1 tablespoon freshly
  ground black pepper

2 tablespoons MSG
  (optional)

1 tablespoon Tabasco
  sauce

2 tablespoons
  Worcestershire sauce

1 small (4-ounce) can
  chopped green chilies

6 large, fresh jalapeño
  peppers, chopped

2 cups beef stock

Serves 10 to 12.

PAT'S CHILI ROAST

◆◆◆◆◆◆◆◆◆◆◆◆◆◆◆◆◆◆◆◆◆◆◆◆◆◆

Pat Burt   Camarillo, California   One of the easiest recipes imaginable,
◆◆◆◆◆◆◆◆◆◆◆◆◆◆◆◆◆◆◆◆◆◆◆◆◆◆ this is not haute Mexican cuisine, but
it's very tasty and great to have on hand for impromptu parties—the shredded
beef can be tucked into tacos, burritos, chimichangas, or tostadas.

1 (3–4-pound) pot roast
*1 (7-ounce) can green
    chile salsa*

Serves 20.

Place the pot roast in a slow cooker and cover with the salsa. Cook on high a minimum of 6 hours, until the meat is very tender.

When ready to serve, shred the meat with 2 forks, removing fat and gristle.

Breads

PUMPKIN BREAD

◆◆◆◆◆◆◆◆◆◆◆◆◆◆◆◆◆◆◆◆◆◆◆

Barb Williams   Listowel, Ontario A very moist, beautifully golden loaf
◆◆◆◆◆◆◆◆◆◆◆◆◆◆◆◆◆◆◆◆◆◆ that's on the sweet side. We liked it
especially with whipped cream cheese.

3 cups sugar

1 cup vegetable oil

4 eggs, beaten

2 cups pumpkin puree

3½ cups all-purpose flour

2 teaspoons baking soda

2 teaspoons salt

1 teaspoon baking powder

*1 teaspoon nutmeg,
    preferably freshly grated*

1 teaspoon ground allspice

1 teaspoon cinnamon

½ teaspoon ground cloves

Makes 2 loaves.

Preheat oven to 350° F. Butter and flour 2 (9 × 5-inch)
loaf pans and set aside.

Mix the sugar and oil. Add the eggs and pumpkin and
mix well. Sift together the dry ingredients. Add alternately
to the batter with ⅔ cup water. Pour into the prepared pans.

Bake for 1½ hours, or until a tester inserted in the center
comes out clean. Let cool in pans for 10 minutes, then turn
out and let cool completely before slicing.

BLACK WALNUT PUMPKIN BREAD

◆◆◆◆◆◆◆◆◆◆◆◆◆◆◆◆◆◆◆◆◆◆◆◆◆◆◆◆◆◆◆◆

Dorothy Michel   Spokane, Washington   A very tasty, easy-to-prepare
◆◆◆◆◆◆◆◆◆◆◆◆◆◆◆◆◆◆◆◆◆◆◆◆◆◆◆◆◆◆   pumpkin bread, with the unusual addition of black walnuts. The bread freezes well, should it happen to be
around that long.

3 cups sugar

*3½ cups sifted all-purpose
    flour*

1½ teaspoons salt

½ teaspoon baking powder

2 teaspoons baking soda

1 teaspoon ground cloves

1 teaspoon cinnamon

*1 teaspoon nutmeg,
    preferably freshly grated*

4 eggs

1 cup vegetable oil

*2 cups pumpkin puree,
    preferably fresh*

*1 cup black walnuts,
    chopped*

Makes 2 loaves.

Preheat oven to 350° F. and grease 2 (9½ × 5½-inch) loaf pans.

In a large mixing bowl, combine the sugar, flour, salt, baking power, baking soda, and spices. Add the eggs, oil, 1 cup of cold water, and pumpkin. Mix well and blend until smooth. Stir in the nuts. Bake for 1 to 1½ hours, until sides of bread begin to come away from the pan and a toothpick inserted in the middle comes out clean. Let bread cool before removing from pan.

WHOLE GRAIN PUMPKIN MUFFINS

◆◆◆◆◆◆◆◆◆◆◆◆◆◆◆◆◆◆◆◆◆◆◆◆◆◆◆◆◆◆◆◆◆

Deborah Tuosto   Watsonville, California These nutritious moist, light
◆◆◆◆◆◆◆◆◆◆◆◆◆◆◆◆◆◆◆◆◆◆◆◆◆◆◆ muffins are not too sweet.
Serve them warm with brunch or as an accompaniment to soups and salads.
They're particularly delicious with thick apricot preserves.

¾ cup all-purpose flour

½ cup whole wheat flour

2 tablespoons sugar

½ cup toasted wheat germ

2½ teaspoons baking
   powder

½ teaspoon salt

½ teaspoon cinnamon

½ teaspoon nutmeg,
   preferably freshly grated

2 egg whites

¾ cup skim milk

½ cup pumpkin puree

¼ cup vegetable oil

1 teaspoon vanilla extract

½ cup raisins (optional)

½ cup toasted sunflower
   seeds (optional)

Makes 12 muffins.

Preheat oven to 400° F. Butter a muffin pan and set aside.

Stir together the flours, sugar, wheat germ, baking powder, salt, and spices.

Mix together the egg whites, milk, pumpkin, oil, and vanilla and blend well. Pour into the flour mixture and mix until just blended. Blend in the raisins and sunflower seeds, if using.

Spoon the batter into the muffin pan. Bake 20 to 25 minutes, or until muffins spring back to the touch. Cool in pan for 2 minutes and serve warm.

Note: Adding the optional seeds and raisins produces a hearty breakfast muffin.

SPICY PUMPKIN BREAD

◆◆◆◆◆◆◆◆◆◆◆◆◆◆◆◆◆◆◆◆◆◆◆◆◆◆◆◆◆◆◆

Brenda Flasowski   Dallas, Texas A particularly flavorful, spicy, full-
◆◆◆◆◆◆◆◆◆◆◆◆◆◆◆◆◆◆◆◆◆◆◆◆◆ bodied bread, good even without the
nuts. This is one of the very few recipes we tried that tasted fine made with
commercially prepared pumpkin.

1 cup shortening

1 can pumpkin pie filling

3 eggs

2½ cups sugar

3½ cups all-purpose flour

1 teaspoon cinnamon

1 teaspoon nutmeg,
   preferably freshly grated

1 teaspoon ground allspice

1 teaspoon ground cloves

1 teaspoon baking soda

½ teaspoon baking powder

1 cup toasted, chopped
   pecans (optional)

Makes 2 loaves.

Preheat oven to 325° F. Butter and flour 2 (9 × 5-inch) loaf pans. Beat together the shortening, pumpkin, and eggs. Gradually beat in sugar.

Stir together the dry ingredients, except the nuts. Add gradually to the pumpkin mixture. Stir in the nuts, if using. Bake for 1 hour, cool 10 minutes, then remove from pans. This bread freezes well.

FINNISH SOUR RYE BREAD

◆◆◆◆◆◆◆◆◆◆◆◆◆◆◆◆◆◆◆◆◆◆◆◆◆◆

Marguerite Re Elmhurst, Illinois This is a truly unusual, delicious
◆◆◆◆◆◆◆◆◆◆◆◆◆◆◆◆◆◆◆◆◆◆◆◆◆ bread—you just have to remember
to make the starter 4 days ahead of baking. It's very good sliced thin and
served with buffet meats and cheeses. But be sure to display one of the whole
loaves alongside the slices; this is gorgeous earthy-looking bread, with its rough
shape and its fork-tine design under the glaze.

3½ cups rye flour

*3 cups warm liquid (flat
    beer, buttermilk, potato
    water, etc.)*

A few grains yeast

1 envelope active dry yeast

2 tablespoons salt

1 egg

Makes 2 loaves.

Four days ahead: Combine 1 cup of the rye flour, 1 cup
of the warm liquid, and the grains of yeast. Cover with
wax paper and set aside in a warm place. Stir once or
twice a day.

On baking day: Turn the soured starter into a large bowl.
Add the remaining 2 cups warm liquid and stir until smooth.

Dissolve the envelope of yeast and salt in ¼ cup lukewarm
water and stir it into the soured mix. Gradually beat in the
remaining 2½ cups flour until mixture is the consistency of
biscuit dough—it will be a little sticky. Knead until smooth.

Divide the dough into 2 parts, shape into balls, and place in
2 greased bowls. Turn dough to grease all sides. Cover with
a tea towel and let rise 1½ hours. Punch down the dough.

Shape each ball into a round loaf. Place the loaves on a
greased baking sheet and let rise 40 minutes.

Preheat oven to 400° F. Prick the loaves all over with a fork.
Bake 35 minutes. Mix the egg and 1 tablespoon water to
make a glaze and brush the loaves with the glaze. Bake 10
minutes more. Cool on a wire rack.

DAIRY HOLLOW HOUSE GINGERBREAD MUFFINS

◆◆

Crescent Dragonwagon   Eureka Springs, Arkansas These light,
◆◆ airy, but moist
muffins with streusel topping are perfect for breakfast or afternoon coffee.
They're a specialty of Dairy Hollow House, a restored country inn in the
Ozarks, where breakfast is a favorite meal.

1½ cups unbleached all-
  purpose flour

¾ cup sugar

2 teaspoons ground ginger

1 teaspoon cinnamon

8 tablespoons butter

¾ cup chopped walnuts

1 egg

3 tablespoons blackstrap
  molasses

1 teaspoon baking soda

½ teaspoon salt

1 cup buttermilk

½ cup raisins

Makes 12 muffins.

Preheat oven to 375° F. Have ready a well-greased muffin pan. Combine the flour, sugar, ginger, and cinnamon; stir thoroughly. Cut in the butter until the mixture resembles cornmeal. Set aside a quarter of this mixture for topping, adding to it the chopped walnuts.

To the remaining flour-butter mixture add the egg and molasses. Dissolve the baking soda and salt in the buttermilk, and stir this into the batter. When thoroughly blended, stir in the raisins.

Spoon the batter into the prepared muffin pan, filling each cup two-thirds full. Sprinkle with the reserved topping.

Bake for about 15 minutes, or until a tester inserted in the center of a muffin comes out clean. Turn out of the pan and serve warm or let cool on a rack.

BROWN BREAD

◆◆◆◆◆◆◆◆◆◆◆◆◆◆◆◆◆◆◆◆◆◆◆◆◆◆◆

Seretta Corl   Milan, Pennsylvania A quick and easy, particularly tasty
◆◆◆◆◆◆◆◆◆◆◆◆◆◆◆◆◆◆◆◆◆◆◆◆◆◆ bread that Mrs. Corl's grandchil-
dren beg for when they know she's coming to visit.

2 cups graham flour

1 cup all-purpose flour

¾ cup sugar

1 teaspoon salt

2 teaspoons baking soda

1¾ cups sour milk or
   buttermilk

1 tablespoon butter or
   shortening, melted

½ cup molasses
   (unsulfured)

1 egg, beaten

Makes 2 loaves.

Preheat oven to 350° F. Grease 2 (9 × 5-inch) loaf pans and set aside.

Thoroughly mix all the dry ingredients with a spoon or whisk. Add the milk, butter, molasses, and egg and stir until well mixed.

Pour into prepared pans and let sit 20 minutes. Bake 45 minutes, or until toothpick inserted in center comes out clean. Let cool in pans 10 minutes, then turn the breads out of the pans and cool on a rack.

CRACKED WHEAT ROLLS

◆◆◆◆◆◆◆◆◆◆◆◆◆◆◆◆◆◆◆◆◆◆◆◆◆◆◆◆◆◆◆◆◆◆

Darnell Moser Wenatchee, Washington These whole-grain whole-
◆◆◆◆◆◆◆◆◆◆◆◆◆◆◆◆◆◆◆◆◆◆◆◆◆◆◆◆◆ some rolls are also really
delicious—good enough to accompany elegant meals at the holiday table, but
also homey and nutritious.

⅔ cup cracked wheat

2 cups raw oats

½ cup whole wheat flour

⅓ cup unprocessed bran

4 teaspoons salt

*2 envelopes active dry
yeast*

1½ cups milk

2 tablespoons oil

3 tablespoons honey

1 tablespoon molasses

*About 3 cups all-purpose
flour*

Cornmeal

1 egg white

Makes 2 dozen rolls.

Stir the cracked wheat and 2 cups boiling water together and set aside. Meanwhile, whirl the oats in a blender until powdery. Mix together all the dry ingredients, except the flour. Heat the milk, oil, honey, and molasses until warm and blended. Beat the warm liquids into the flour. Drain the cracked wheat and add it to the mixture.

Add enough all-purpose flour to make the dough clean the bowl. Knead until smooth and firm. Place in an oiled bowl to rise. Cover with a tea towel and let rise until doubled in bulk. Punch down and let rise again.

Shape into 2½-inch balls, tuck ends under, and place on a cookie sheet sprinkled with cornmeal. Let rise 20 minutes. Preheat oven to 375° F.

Bake for 15 minutes. Meanwhile, prepare an egg wash by mixing the egg white and 1 tablespoon water thoroughly. Brush the rolls with the egg wash and bake 20 minutes more.

Let the rolls cool on a rack.

TEX'S BREAD

◆◆◆◆◆◆◆◆◆◆◆◆◆◆◆◆◆◆◆◆◆◆◆◆◆◆◆◆◆◆◆◆◆◆◆◆◆

Monika McCollum   Goldsboro, North Carolina These very tasty
◆◆◆◆◆◆◆◆◆◆◆◆◆◆◆◆◆◆◆◆◆◆◆◆◆◆◆◆◆◆◆◆◆ sweetish rolls are
extremely easy to make and would be welcome at just about any meal.

1 cup vegetable shortening

¾ cup sugar

3 eggs

*2 envelopes active dry
  yeast*

1½ teaspoons salt

6 cups all-purpose flour

Makes 3 dozen rolls.

Cream the shortening and sugar and pour 1 cup boiling
water over them. Let cool. Beat the eggs separately
and add them. Dissolve the yeast in 1 cup lukewarm
water and add to the mixture.

Add the salt and about 2 cups of the flour. Mix well. Add
the remaining flour a little at a time until a firm dough is
formed. Place in an oiled bowl, cover with a tea towel, and
let rise until doubled in bulk.

Preheat oven to 350° F. Grease a muffin pan.

Roll the dough into small balls to fit inside muffin pan cups—
or make 3 little balls for each cup of the muffin pan. Bake
20 to 30 minutes, until golden. Cool the rolls on a rack.

ENSAIMADA FILIPINA

◆◆◆◆◆◆◆◆◆◆◆◆◆◆◆◆◆◆◆◆◆◆◆◆◆◆◆◆◆◆

Elena Ugarte Seattle, Washington This unusual bread is a cross between the Spanish *ensaimada* and the French brioche. The recipe wasn't easy to come by; although Elena Ugarte had several versions, somehow the secrets were always left out. When she moved to America, her neighbor's daughter had the solution.

1½ tablespoons plus ¾ cup sugar

1½ envelopes active dry yeast

½ cup potato flour

5 cups all-purpose flour, sifted

1 cup butter, at room temperature

½ teaspoon salt

8 egg yolks

½ cup grated aged Gruyère cheese

Makes 2 dozen rolls.

Dissolve 1½ tablespoons of the sugar in ¾ cup warm water. Add the yeast and potato flour. Let stand until the yeast is softened. Add 1 cup of the all-purpose flour gradually, blending well. Cover with a damp cloth and set aside in a warm place for 30 to 60 minutes.

Cream the butter and the remaining ¾ cup sugar thoroughly. Add the salt and egg yolks, one at a time, beating well after each addition. Add the remaining 4 cups flour gradually, blending well. Combine the flour mixture with the yeast mixture and mix thoroughly.

Put the dough in a greased bowl, turn to grease all sides of the dough, and cover with a slightly damp tea towel. Whack the bowl on the counter top about 100 times. Set aside in a warm place to rise until doubled, about 2 hours.

To make the rolls: Divide dough in 24 parts. Roll each part out very thin, rub over with soft butter, and sprinkle lightly with Gruyère. Roll up jelly roll style, coil, and place in a greased brioche pan. Let rise again for 2 to 3 hours.

Preheat oven to 400° F. Bake rolls for 40 minutes. Paint the rolls with melted butter when they come out of the oven, and sprinkle with sugar. Cool on a rack.

ORANGE BREAD

◆◆◆◆◆◆◆◆◆◆◆◆◆◆◆◆◆◆◆◆◆◆◆◆◆◆◆◆◆

Shirley Baker   La Grange, Georgia In the course of raising five chil-
◆◆◆◆◆◆◆◆◆◆◆◆◆◆◆◆◆◆◆◆◆◆◆◆◆◆◆◆ dren, Shirley Baker often found it
necessary to make meals out of leftovers, creating something new each time
and never quite managing to repeat it. The children learned to save their orange
peels for this invention, which is deeply flavored with oranges, moist, not too
sweet, and nicely textured. Best of all, it's very easy to make.

1 cup orange peel, grated

*½ cup plus 6 tablespoons
   sugar*

4 tablespoons butter

1 egg, well beaten

*1¾ cups all-purpose flour,
   sifted*

1 teaspoon baking powder

1 teaspoon salt

1 cup milk

Makes 2 loaves.

Preheat oven to 350° F. Grease 2 (9 × 5-inch) loaf pans
and set aside. Cover the orange peel with 1 cup of cold
water and boil 5 minutes. Repeat this step twice more,
draining the peel well after each boiling and adding fresh
water.

Add ½ cup of the sugar and cook slowly until all moisture
has evaporated. Cream the butter, the remaining 6 tablespoons sugar, and the egg. Sift the flour, baking powder,
and salt, and add to the creamed butter and sugar mixture.
Stir in the milk. Add the orange peel.

Pour the batter into the pans and bake 1 hour. Let the bread
cool in the pans.

APRICOT BREAD

◆◆◆◆◆◆◆◆◆◆◆◆◆◆◆◆◆◆◆◆◆◆◆◆◆◆◆◆◆◆

Peggy S. Whiter   Encino, California   This very tasty apricot bread came
◆◆◆◆◆◆◆◆◆◆◆◆◆◆◆◆◆◆◆◆◆◆◆◆◆◆◆ from Mrs. Whiter's grandmother
Julia, born in Vermont in 1876. Mrs. Whiter thinks the warm, sunny quality of
the apricots must have had a special appeal in the cold Vermont winter. But
it's hard to think of a season in which this satisfying bread wouldn't be a very
welcome sight.

1 cup dried apricots

1 cup sugar

*2 tablespoons shortening,
    softened*

1 egg

*½ cup freshly squeezed
    orange juice*

2 cups all-purpose flour

*2 tablespoons baking
    powder*

¼ teaspoon baking soda

1 teaspoon salt

*½ cup chopped nuts
    (walnuts or pecans)*

Serves 10.

Cover the apricots with warm water and leave to soak
30 minutes. Drain and cut into small (about ¼-inch)
pieces.

Grease a 9 × 5-inch loaf pan, line with wax paper, and grease
the paper, too. Mix the sugar, shortening, and egg thoroughly.
Stir in ¼ cup water and the orange juice.

Sift together the flour, baking powder, baking soda, and salt,
and stir. Blend in the liquid ingredients, nuts, and apricots.
Pour the batter into the pan and let stand for 20 minutes
before baking.

Preheat the oven to 350° F.

Bake until a toothpick tester comes out clean, 55 to 75
minutes. Remove paper immediately and let bread cool on a
rack.

LEMON TEA BREAD WITH BLACK WALNUTS

◆◆◆◆◆◆◆◆◆◆◆◆◆◆◆◆◆◆◆◆◆◆◆◆◆◆◆◆◆◆◆◆◆

Barbara Belew   Charlotte, North Carolina This unusual recipe was
◆◆◆◆◆◆◆◆◆◆◆◆◆◆◆◆◆◆◆◆◆◆◆◆◆◆◆◆◆◆◆ a great favorite with our
testers. Although Barbara Belew now lives in North Carolina, the recipe comes
from her hometown, Ann Arbor, Michigan, where it appeared in *Culinary Clues
II,* the Women's City Club's cookbook. The surprise additions of thyme and
black walnuts give this bread a unique and delicious flavor. Baked in mini-loaves,
it makes a perfect holiday gift. This bread freezes beautifully.

6 tablespoons butter,
   softened to room
   temperature

1⅓ cups sugar

2 eggs

Grated zest of 1 lemon

½ cup all-purpose flour

1 teaspoon baking powder

1 teaspoon salt

½ cup milk

1 teaspoon dried thyme

½ cup chopped black
   English walnuts

Juice of 1 lemon

Serves 10.

Preheat oven to 325° F. Grease a 9 × 5-inch loaf pan or
2 mini-loaf pans.

Cream the butter, 1 cup of the sugar, the eggs, and
lemon zest. Sift the flour, baking powder, and salt, add to
the mixture, and blend well. Add the milk, thyme, and
walnuts; mix thoroughly.

Pour into the pan and bake 1 hour.

Combine the lemon juice and the remaining ⅓ cup sugar for
a glaze and pour over the bread while still hot. Cool in the
pan 15 to 20 minutes.

THREE-GRAIN PEANUT BREAD

Eileen E. Perlman   Granada, California Children and everyone else will love this very tasty bread with its deep peanut flavor. We think it's especially good served warm for breakfast.

1 cup all-purpose flour

½ cup quick-cooking oats

½ cup yellow cornmeal

½ cup dried powdered milk

½ cup sugar

3 teaspoons baking powder

1 teaspoon salt

⅔ cup peanut butter

1 egg

1½ cups fresh milk

Serves 10.

Preheat oven to 325° F. Grease and flour a 9 × 5-inch loaf pan and set aside. In a mixing bowl, combine the flour, oats, cornmeal, dried milk powder, sugar, baking powder, and salt. Cut in the peanut butter. Blend and pour in the egg and fresh milk.

Mix well and turn into prepared pan; spread evenly. Bake for 70 minutes, or until a toothpick inserted in the center comes out clean. Cool 10 minutes and remove from pan.

AUNT SUSIE'S PASKE (EASTER BREAD)

Linda Peters   Morden, Manitoba   These gorgeous airy loaves of yeasty bread seem like Easter itself. You may feel as though you've wandered into Maurice Sendak's Night Kitchen while you're making this bread—it rises and rises, 6 hours altogether, and sprawls all over as you try to corral it for the kneading. Don't worry; that's normal. To gild the lily, spread the bread with your favorite butter icing.

2 envelopes active dry yeast

1 tablespoon plus 2 cups sugar

2 cups milk

8–10 eggs, separated, at room temperature

7–10 cups all-purpose flour

1 cup butter

1 teaspoon vanilla extract

2 teaspoons salt

Makes 4 loaves; serves 24.

Soak the yeast with the tablespoon of sugar in 1 cup warm water. Bring the milk to a boil and set aside to cool. Beat the egg whites until soft peaks form. Set aside the yolks, covered.

When the milk is cool, mix it with the yeast and egg whites. Add enough flour—about 4 cups—to make a smooth paste. Set paste aside to rise 1 hour.

Shortly before the paste is ready, melt the butter and mix it with 1 cup of the sugar and the vanilla. Mix the reserved yolks with the remaining cup of sugar and the salt. Finally, mix the butter mixture and yolk mixture into the paste.

Add enough flour to make a soft dough and begin kneading. This will be difficult; use a pastry scraper to scoop the dough up when it starts to stick. Knead for about 10 minutes. Set the dough ball aside to rise in a buttered bowl; turn once to grease all the sides, and cover with a tea towel. Let rise 1½ hours. Punch down again and let rise for 1½ hours. At this point the dough can be made into 4 round loaves, a number of large buns, or rings in tube pans. You can expect the dough to rise double again, so be sure the pan you use is large enough and well buttered.

Let rise again for 2 hours. Preheat oven to 250° F. Bake for 1 hour or until golden.

MOLASSES BREAD

◆◆◆◆◆◆◆◆◆◆◆◆◆◆◆◆◆◆◆◆◆◆◆◆◆◆◆◆◆◆◆

Sheila Marjoribanks   Toronto, Ontario   A simple but excellent bread
◆◆◆◆◆◆◆◆◆◆◆◆◆◆◆◆◆◆◆◆◆◆◆◆◆◆◆◆◆◆◆   from a very old recipe handed
down by the early settlers in Pickering Township, Ontario. It's particularly nice
for tea, but also good for brunch or with fresh fruit for dinner.

1 egg

1 cup milk

½ cup sugar

3 cups all-purpose flour

1 cup molasses

1 cup walnuts, chopped

1 cup raisins

1 teaspoon baking soda

Makes 2 loaves.

Preheat oven to 350° F. and butter 2 (9 × 5-inch) loaf
pans; set aside. Beat the egg; add the milk, sugar, and
1½ cups of the flour. Pour in the molasses and mix
well.

Add the walnuts and raisins. Add the remaining 1½ cups
flour and the baking soda dissolved in a little hot water. Mix
thoroughly, pour into the buttered pans, and bake 1 hour.
Cool in pans 15 minutes.

SWEDISH RYE BREAD

◆◆◆◆◆◆◆◆◆◆◆◆◆◆◆◆◆◆◆◆◆◆◆◆◆◆◆

Jody LaFrance   Wyandotte, Michigan This earthy, delicious rye bread
◆◆◆◆◆◆◆◆◆◆◆◆◆◆◆◆◆◆◆◆◆◆◆◆◆ has been made in Jody La-
France's family for generations; it came along when her great-grandparents
emigrated from Sweden.

½ cup brown sugar

1 teaspoon salt

1 teaspoon caraway seed

1 teaspoon anise

1 tablespoon butter

1 cake compressed yeast
   or 1 envelope active dry
   yeast

3½ cups all-purpose flour,
   sifted

2 cups rye flour (stir it in
   the bag; do not sift)

Makes 2 loaves.

Grease 2 (9 × 5-inch) pans and set aside. In a saucepan,
combine 2 cups water, the sugar, salt, caraway seed,
anise, and butter, and cook 3 minutes, over medium
heat, or until butter and sugar are melted. Cool to lukewarm
and soften yeast in this mixture.

Add the all-purpose flour and mix to a soft dough. Let rise
1½ hours. Add the rye flour to make a stiff dough. Knead
lightly. Place in a greased bowl, turn once to grease the
surface of the dough, cover with a damp tea towel and let
rise until doubled in bulk—about 2 hours.

Knead the dough again and divide into 2 portions. Cover with
a tea towel and let rest 10 to 15 minutes.

Mold the dough into 2 loaves; place in greased bread pans
and let rise until doubled in bulk.

Preheat oven to 375° F. Bake 35 to 40 minutes and brush
tops of finished loaves with melted butter. Remove bread
from pans and cool on a rack.

GRAM'S BLUE RIBBON DATE NUT BREAD

◆◆◆◆◆◆◆◆◆◆◆◆◆◆◆◆◆◆◆◆◆◆◆◆◆◆◆◆◆◆

Mary Williams   Imlay City, Michigan A particularly tasty, perfectly
◆◆◆◆◆◆◆◆◆◆◆◆◆◆◆◆◆◆◆◆◆◆◆◆◆◆◆◆◆ textured bread that won Mary
Williams and her sister blue ribbons at the local agricultural fair. The source is
their grandmother, Annie Fitzgibbon.

2 teaspoons baking soda
1½ cups chopped dates
8 tablespoons butter
2 cups sugar
2 eggs, beaten
4 cups all-purpose flour
1 teaspoon salt
2 teaspoons vanilla extract
1 cup chopped walnuts

Makes 2 loaves.

Preheat oven to 350° F. Butter and flour 2 (9x5-inch) loaf pans and set aside.

Sprinkle the baking soda over the dates and pour 2 cups boiling water over this mixture. Allow to sit until lukewarm.

Cream together the butter and sugar. Add the beaten eggs and mix well. Alternating, add the flour, date mixture, and salt. Do not overmix. Add the vanilla and then the walnuts. Divide equally and pour into the pans. Bake for 1¼ hours, or until a toothpick inserted in the center of the bread comes out clean. Let cool in pans 15 minutes.

JALAPEÑO CORN BREAD

Carla Patterson   Arlington, Texas   The Pattersons always eat this spicy corn bread with black-eyed peas (for good luck) on New Year's Day. For the best flavor, serve this bread the moment it's ready.

8 tablespoons butter

1 cup cornmeal

½ cup all-purpose flour

½ teaspoon baking soda

1 teaspoon salt

1 cup canned cream-style corn

2 or more jalapeño peppers, to taste, minced (seeds removed; see Note)

¼ pound Cheddar cheese, shredded

2 eggs

1 cup buttermilk

Serves 8.

Preheat oven to 450° F.

Melt the butter in an 8-inch skillet and set aside. In a large bowl, combine all the dry ingredients, stir, and add remaining ingredients. Turn into the skillet and bake 25 to 30 minutes, or until the bread springs back to the touch. Let stand 5 minutes, then serve immediately.

Note: Peppers are very hot; don't touch your eyes or mouth while you're working with them.

SQUASH ROLLS

◆◆◆◆◆◆◆◆◆◆◆◆◆◆◆◆◆◆◆◆◆◆◆◆◆◆◆◆◆◆◆◆◆◆◆◆

Fleurette Clough   East Freetown, New York A grandmother's rec-
◆◆◆◆◆◆◆◆◆◆◆◆◆◆◆◆◆◆◆◆◆◆◆◆◆◆◆◆◆◆◆◆◆◆◆ ipe for delicious sweet
rolls. For dinner, you might want to cut the sugar to ½ cup; for breakfast, the
sweetness is perfect as written. We used butternut squash, but any winter
squash, or pumpkin, is fine. The dough can also be made into small loaves of
bread.

1 envelope active dry yeast

*2 cups cooked, mashed
winter squash*

1 cup sugar

1 tablespoon salt

*8 tablespoons butter or
vegetable shortening*

*6½–7½ cups all-purpose
flour*

Makes 3 dozen rolls.

Dissolve the yeast in 1 cup lukewarm water. Stir in the
squash, sugar, salt, and butter or shortening. Add flour
a cup at a time, mixing well after each addition.

Place the dough in a greased bowl, turn to grease the dough
on all sides, cover with a tea towel, and set aside to rise
until doubled in bulk. Punch down the dough, form into small
balls, and place on a baking sheet. Let rise again until doubled
in bulk. Preheat oven to 350° F.

Bake 30 to 45 minutes, or until browned and hollow-sounding
when tapped. Remove rolls from pan and let cool on rack.

OATMEAL BUNS

◆◆◆◆◆◆◆◆◆◆◆◆◆◆◆◆◆◆◆◆◆◆◆◆◆◆◆◆◆◆◆◆

Linda Christian Carlson   De Soto, Texas These rolls are constantly
◆◆◆◆◆◆◆◆◆◆◆◆◆◆◆◆◆◆◆◆◆◆◆◆◆◆◆◆◆ requested at potluck Texas
barbecues, where they're used as hamburger buns. They're faintly sweet and
make unusual but delicious dinner rolls. Mrs. Carlson likes to substitute a cup
of whole wheat flour for one of the cups of white flour—an excellent idea, for
taste as well as nutrition.

1 cup rolled oats

2 tablespoons butter, melted

2 tablespoons lard

1 envelope active dry yeast

½ tablespoon granulated sugar

¾ cup brown sugar

1½ teaspoons salt

5 cups all-purpose flour, plus 1 cup for kneading

Chopped walnuts or pecans (optional)

Makes 2 dozen rolls.

Pour 2 cups boiling water over the rolled oats. Add the melted butter and lard. Let stand until lukewarm.

Dissolve the yeast in ½ cup water and add the granulated sugar. Add this mixture to the oatmeal. Mix in the brown sugar, salt, and 5 cups of the flour. Mix well.

Knead, using the additional cup of flour. The dough should remain sticky. Cover and let rise until doubled in bulk. With well-greased hands, shape the dough into buns, pinching the edges to the back to form a smooth top.

Place on cookie sheets, cover with a tea towel, and let rise again until doubled in bulk.

Preheat oven to 375° F.

Bake about 25 minutes, or until tops are nicely browned. Cool on a rack.

BLUEBERRY MUFFINS

◆◆◆◆◆◆◆◆◆◆◆◆◆◆◆◆◆◆◆◆◆◆◆◆◆◆◆◆◆◆◆◆

Marie Edna Reynolds Gardiner, Maine These are sweet, cakelike
◆◆◆◆◆◆◆◆◆◆◆◆◆◆◆◆◆◆◆◆◆◆◆◆◆◆◆◆◆◆◆◆ blueberry muffins—from
Maine, of course, where they've already won a prize. Because we were testing
in December, we had to use frozen blueberries, but the muffins were still
excellent. For an interesting variation add a dash of nutmeg to the batter and
mix a little cinnamon into the sugar topping.

8 tablespoons butter

1 cup sugar, plus 2
    teaspoons for tops of
    muffins

2 eggs

2 cups all-purpose flour

2 teaspoons baking
    powder

½ teaspoon salt

½ cup milk

1 teaspoon vanilla extract

2½ cups blueberries,
    preferably fresh

Makes 12 muffins.

Preheat oven to 375° F. and grease a muffin pan well—
around the top, too—with butter.

With mixer on low speed, cream the butter and 1 cup
of the sugar until fluffy. Add the eggs 1 at a time, mixing
until blended.

Sift the dry ingredients and add alternately to the batter with
the milk and vanilla. Mash ½ cup of the blueberries and stir
in by hand, mixing well. Add the remaining 2 cups blueberries,
still whole, and pile batter high in muffin cups. Sprinkle the
tops with the remaining 2 teaspoons sugar. Bake 25 to 30
minutes. Let cool in pan at least 30 minutes, tilting the pan
on its side while cooling so the bottoms of the muffins don't
get soggy.

Desserts

PEACH SHORTCAKE

◆◆◆◆◆◆◆◆◆◆◆◆◆◆◆◆◆◆◆◆◆◆◆◆

Betty Montfoort Newton, Kansas This light, lovely dessert is like no
◆◆◆◆◆◆◆◆◆◆◆◆◆◆◆◆◆◆◆◆◆◆◆◆ other shortcake, and it's also easy
to prepare. Don't try it if peaches aren't in season, though—it's the fresh ripe
peach flavor that's so fine here. We liked it even more with a little brandy and
cinnamon added.

2 cups all-purpose flour
(half whole wheat, if
you like)

½ teaspoon salt

2 teaspoons baking
powder

9 tablespoons butter

½ cup milk

8 peaches, the same size

1½ cups sugar

¼ cup brandy (optional)

½ teaspoon cinnamon
(optional)

Serves 8.

Butter a baking dish large enough to hold the peaches
comfortably. Preheat oven to 375° F.

Combine the flour, salt, and baking powder. Cut in 8
tablespoons of the butter, then add the milk, a little at a
time. Form the dough into a ball. Roll the dough out, no
more than ½ inch thick. Cut in long strips wide enough to
wrap around the peaches, leaving the top and bottom open.
Peel the peaches but leave the pits in place. Put each peach
on a strip of dough and wrap it, in a rolling motion. Place
the wrapped peaches in the buttered dish.

In a saucepan, combine the sugar, 2 cups of water, and the
remaining 1 tablespoon butter along with the brandy and
cinnamon, if using. Let the syrup come to a boil and boil for
3 minutes. Pour the syrup over the peaches and bake 20 to
35 minutes, depending on the size of the peaches.

FRESH PEACH ICE CREAM

◆◆◆◆◆◆◆◆◆◆◆◆◆◆◆◆◆◆◆◆◆◆◆◆◆◆◆

Carla Patterson   Arlington, Texas Carla Patterson makes this glorious
◆◆◆◆◆◆◆◆◆◆◆◆◆◆◆◆◆◆◆◆◆◆◆◆◆ old-fashioned ice cream every Fourth
of July, using peaches ripened on her own trees. You may need to make this
in batches if your ice cream freezer is small. Purists will want to substitute 1½
cups heavy cream for the Cool Whip.

4 eggs

2¼ cups sugar

¼ teaspoon salt

1 teaspoon vanilla extract

*½ teaspoon almond
    extract*

*4 cups peaches, pureed in
    blender*

1 quart half-and-half

*1 (12-ounce container)
    Cool Whip*

*Milk to fill freezer can (if
    using)*

Serves 12 or more.

Have ready a home ice cream maker. Beat the eggs
until thick and lemon-colored. Add the sugar, salt,
vanilla, and almond extract. Add the peaches, half-and-
half, and Cool Whip. If using a hand-crank freezer of the old-
fashioned variety, pour the mixture into the freezer can and
add enough milk to bring it to the proper level. With other
kinds of freezers, omit the extra milk and follow instructions
for your ice cream maker.

THE EASIEST PIECRUST

◆◆◆◆◆◆◆◆◆◆◆◆◆◆◆◆◆◆◆◆◆◆◆◆◆◆◆◆◆

Donna Russell   Louisville, Kentucky This recipe seems too good to
◆◆◆◆◆◆◆◆◆◆◆◆◆◆◆◆◆◆◆◆◆◆◆◆◆◆◆ be true: a nearly instant made-
from-scratch piecrust that's very flaky and browns easily. We were amazed.
For the many cooks who simply can't deal with pastry, this is the answer—for
the bottom crust, at least. This bright idea isn't a new one; Donna Russell's
great-grandmother is the source.

2 cups sifted all-purpose
   flour
Pinch of salt
⅔ cup vegetable oil

Makes 1 pie shell.

In a small bowl, mix one third of the flour with ¼ cup water
and the salt. Stir to make a paste. In a medium bowl,
combine the remaining flour with the vegetable oil and
beat well. Combine the 2 mixtures and blend thoroughly. Pat
into pie pan. Bake as your recipe directs.

OLD-FASHIONED CHESS PIE

◆◆◆◆◆◆◆◆◆◆◆◆◆◆◆◆◆◆◆◆◆◆◆◆◆◆◆

Virginia Prosise **Miami, Florida** Virginia Prosise's mother-in-law found
◆◆◆◆◆◆◆◆◆◆◆◆◆◆◆◆◆◆◆◆◆◆◆◆◆ this recipe in a cookbook containing
recipes from country people in Blackstone, Virginia. The women who submitted
it were from Danville and said it had been in their family over one hundred
years. We loved this pie, which forms a crisp topping as it bakes. And it's
extremely easy to make.

2 eggs
1 cup sugar
4 tablespoons butter,
   melted
¼ teaspoon vanilla extract
1 (9-inch) unbaked pie
   shell

Serves 8.

Preheat oven to 350° F. In a large mixing bowl, beat the
eggs until light. Add the sugar and continue beating
until well blended and light. Add the melted butter and
vanilla. Beat again to mix well.

Pour the mixture into the pie shell and bake 35 to 40 minutes,
or until a knife inserted into the center of the pie comes out
clean.

BUTTERMILK PIE

◆◆◆◆◆◆◆◆◆◆◆◆◆◆◆◆◆◆◆◆◆◆◆◆◆◆◆◆◆◆◆

Debbie Cox Oklahoma City, Oklahoma This pie is nearly an instant
◆◆◆◆◆◆◆◆◆◆◆◆◆◆◆◆◆◆◆◆◆◆◆◆◆◆◆◆ creation, and as long as you
have some buttermilk in the refrigerator, it can be made without running to the
store for ingredients. But best of all, it's an excellent pie with a thin crispy top
that adds to its terrific flavor.

8 tablespoons butter,
    softened to room
    temperature

2 cups sugar

3 tablespoons all-purpose
    flour

3 eggs, beaten

1 cup buttermilk

1 teaspoon vanilla extract

1 (9-inch) unbaked pie
    shell

Serves 8.

Preheat oven to 350° F. Cream the butter and sugar
together. Add the flour and eggs. Beat well.

Stir in the buttermilk and vanilla. Pour the mixture into
the pie shell and bake 45 to 50 minutes. Place on a wire rack
to cool completely.

TATER PIE

◆◆◆◆◆◆◆◆◆◆◆◆◆◆◆◆◆◆◆◆◆◆◆◆◆◆◆

Phyllis Gore   Middleburg, Florida This sweet potato pie is just incre-
◆◆◆◆◆◆◆◆◆◆◆◆◆◆◆◆◆◆◆◆◆◆◆◆ dibly good—it has not only an outstanding flavor but a wonderful aroma while baking and a beautiful dark glossy
appearance at the table. It's the creation of Phyllis Gore's daddy, who can't
quite remember how he came to put it together—but he's already won a prize
with it.

½ cup dark brown sugar

1 teaspoon cinnamon

½ teaspoon ground
   allspice

½ teaspoon nutmeg,
   preferably freshly grated

½ teaspoon salt

1½ cups cooked, mashed
   sweet potatoes*

2 eggs, slightly beaten

¼ cup evaporated milk

2 tablespoons butter,
   melted

½ cup Jim Beam bourbon

1 (9-inch) unbaked pie
   shell

1 cup heavy cream,
   whipped

4 ounces crystallized
   ginger, slivered

Serves 6 to 8.

Combine the sugar, spices, and salt and stir into the
sweet potatoes. Combine the eggs, milk, ¼ cup water,
the butter, and bourbon and mix well. Stir into the
potato mixture until thoroughly blended.

Preheat oven to 400° F.

Pour the pie filling into the pie shell and bake for 40 minutes,
or until a knife inserted in the center comes out clean. Chill
for at least 4 hours. Top with whipped cream and sprinkle
with slivered ginger.

* For this amount of mashed sweet potatoes, start with 3–4 large whole ones.
  Bake the potatoes well in advance, even the night before, at 400° F. for
  about an hour, until they are mushy. Cool them completely before trying to
  peel them. The skins will pull away in the cooling process and make peeling
  much easier.

CHOCOLATE RASPBERRY SEDUCTION

◆◆◆◆◆◆◆◆◆◆◆◆◆◆◆◆◆◆◆◆◆◆◆◆◆◆◆◆◆◆◆◆◆

Cathy Power   Medfield, Massachusetts The very idea of raspberries
◆◆◆◆◆◆◆◆◆◆◆◆◆◆◆◆◆◆◆◆◆◆◆◆◆◆◆◆◆ and chocolate seems wickedly
seductive, and this recipe lives up to its name. It's very moist and very rich,
so slice it in small pieces.

CAKE

4 (1-ounce) squares
   unsweetened chocolate

8 tablespoons butter

3 large eggs

1½ teaspoons vanilla
   extract

1⅓ cups sugar

1 cup all-purpose flour

⅔ cup chopped walnuts

½ cup seedless raspberry
   jam

FROSTING

1½ (1-ounce) squares
   unsweetened chocolate

3 tablespoons butter

4 tablespoons seedless
   raspberry jam

⅔ cup confectioner's
   sugar

Serves 12.

Grease 2 (9-inch-square) pans with butter, line with foil, then butter the foil. Set aside. Preheat oven to 350° F.

Melt the chocolate with the butter in a heavy saucepan over low heat. Stir well to combine and let cool. Beat the eggs with the vanilla and sugar until smooth and thick. Blend in the chocolate mixture. Stir in the flour and nuts just until blended.

Pour half the batter into each pan and bake for approximately 12 minutes—check after 10 minutes to make sure this brownie base is staying fudgy and not getting dry.

Cool completely, then carefully lift out of pan with the foil. Cut each square in half, making 4 layers. Layer one on top of the other, spreading each generously with the raspberry jam. Frost the top and sides with the frosting below.

In a medium-size heavy saucepan, melt the chocolate with the butter over low heat and then let cool. Beat in the jam and sugar until the mixture is thick and smooth.

MELON BALLS IN RUM-LIME SAUCE

◆◆◆◆◆◆◆◆◆◆◆◆◆◆◆◆◆◆◆◆◆◆◆◆◆◆◆◆

Albie Johnson   Lebanon, Tennessee   Here is that elusive dessert we're
◆◆◆◆◆◆◆◆◆◆◆◆◆◆◆◆◆◆◆◆◆◆◆◆◆◆   always looking for: light, refreshing, and superb. It's a great ending for a heavy meal, and virtually seasonless.

½ cup sugar

*½ cup freshly squeezed
lime juice (the juice of
about 4 limes)*

½ cup light rum

*1 tablespoon grated lime
zest (only the green)*

*1 quart melon balls (any
combination of
cantaloupe, honeydew,
Persian, watermelon,
etc.), chilled*

*Mint leaves or sprigs for a
garnish*

Serves 6 to 8.

In a small saucepan, combine the sugar and ¼ cup water and bring to a boil to dissolve the sugar. Allow to cool. Add the lime juice, rum, and grated zest. Chill.

Add the chilled melon balls to the rum-lime sauce at least 30 minutes before serving. Garnish each serving with a mint leaf, or strew mint sprigs over the melon balls in a serving dish.

JUDHAB AL-KHUBZ

◆◆◆◆◆◆◆◆◆◆◆◆◆◆◆◆◆◆◆◆◆◆◆◆◆◆◆◆◆◆◆◆◆◆

John Nuttall   Vancouver, British Columbia   Although we received a
◆◆◆◆◆◆◆◆◆◆◆◆◆◆◆◆◆◆◆◆◆◆◆◆◆◆◆◆◆◆ number of very unusual
recipes, surely this one is unique. As Mr. Nuttall says, it is straight out of the
Arabian Nights. It comes from a cookbook written in Baghdad in 1226, discovered
by an Iraqi scholar in 1934 and published in a journal of Islamic culture. The
original cook was one Muhammad ibn al-Karim al-Katib al-Baghdadi.

Although its curiosity value is obviously very high, and that may be reason
enough to serve it, it's also strangely delicious—unlike anything else. A perfect
dessert after curries, Middle Eastern dishes, or large salads. It's very rich, so
count on small portions.

*White bread, cut in cubes
  (we used pita bread)*

Heavy cream

Butter

Honey

Sliced almonds

**Makes 1 serving to each
  ½ cup bread.**

Exact quantities are difficult to prescribe here, since they
depend on the bread. Start off with 1 cup heavy cream,
2 tablespoons butter, 2 tablespoons honey, and a handful
of sliced almonds, and add more as needed.

Place the bread in a bowl and pour on it just enough cream
to moisten it—for 3 large pitas breads, start with about ½
cup of cream. Toss to make sure all the bread is moistened.

Preheat the broiler.

In a skillet, heat the butter till it foams and fry the bread
until it is golden brown. Use a fairly high heat but watch
carefully to avoid burning. The bread should be crisp on the
outside but still moist inside.

Transfer the bread to an ovenproof serving platter, drizzle
the honey over it, and top with the sliced nuts. Place under
the broiler just long enough to brown the nuts.

Serve hot. The dish can be made ahead and reheated.

BRIL'S V.I.P. PECAN PIE

◆◆◆◆◆◆◆◆◆◆◆◆◆◆◆◆◆◆◆◆◆◆◆◆◆◆◆◆◆◆

Clare Urion   Dover, Massachusetts This recipe comes from Clare
◆◆◆◆◆◆◆◆◆◆◆◆◆◆◆◆◆◆◆◆◆◆◆◆◆◆◆◆ Urion's mother, who was famous
for it. The secret is to use only light corn syrup, which yields a moist, delicious,
delicate flavor—old-fashioned but elegant. It freezes well and should be served
warm, preferably with a big scoop of the best vanilla ice cream.

1 cup light corn syrup

*2 tablespoons unsalted
    butter, melted*

⅛ teaspoon salt

3 eggs, slightly beaten

1 cup sugar

1 teaspoon vanilla extract

1 cup pecans

*1 (9-inch) unbaked deep-
    dish pie shell*

Serves 8.

Preheat oven to 400° F. Mix all ingredients except the
pie shell, adding pecans last. Pour into the pie shell.

Bake for 15 minutes at 400° F., then lower oven
temperature to 350° F. and bake 45 minutes more.

ALASKAN BLUEBERRY BUCKLE

◆◆◆◆◆◆◆◆◆◆◆◆◆◆◆◆◆◆◆◆◆◆◆◆

Beverly Reid   Petersburg, Alaska   A particularly good blueberry dessert—the best we found, and there
◆◆◆◆◆◆◆◆◆◆◆◆◆◆◆◆◆◆◆◆◆◆◆◆
were a lot of entries. Blueberries peep through the crispy topping, making it a very attractive dessert as well. Serve with whipped cream or vanilla ice cream on the side.

¼ cup shortening

1 cup sugar

1 egg

1⅓ cups all-purpose flour

1½ teaspoons baking powder

½ teaspoon salt

⅓ cup milk

2 cups blueberries (fresh or frozen)

½ teaspoon cinnamon

4 tablespoons butter, softened to room temperature

Serves 6 to 8.

In a large mixing bowl, combine the shortening, ½ cup of the sugar, the egg, 1 cup of the flour, the baking powder, salt, and milk. Mix well. Pour into a greased 9x13-inch pan. Sprinkle the blueberries over the batter.

Preheat oven to 350° F. In a small bowl, combine the remaining ½ cup sugar and ⅓ cup flour, the cinnamon, and butter. Mix to make a crumbly mixture. Sprinkle over the top of the blueberries.

Bake for 45 minutes. Serve warm.

BETSY'S PEACH COBBLER

◆◆◆◆◆◆◆◆◆◆◆◆◆◆◆◆◆◆◆◆◆◆◆◆◆◆◆◆◆◆◆◆◆◆

Betsy Crampe   Charlotte, North Carolina An easy, attractive des-
◆◆◆◆◆◆◆◆◆◆◆◆◆◆◆◆◆◆◆◆◆◆◆◆◆◆◆◆◆◆◆◆◆ sert that's particularly good
with home-canned peaches. Of course, it can also be made with fresh peaches,
in which case you should slice them and leave them to rest for an hour or so
with a little sugar, to taste, before proceeding with the recipe.

Serve with vanilla ice cream or whipped cream.

4 tablespoons butter

½ cup sugar

½ cup milk

¾ cup all-purpose flour

*1½ teaspoons baking
     powder*

⅛ teaspoon salt

*2 cups canned sliced
     peaches, drained*

Serves 6 to 8.

Preheat oven to 350° F. Put the butter in an 8-inch loaf pan, and set the pan in the oven to melt the butter.

In a medium bowl, combine the sugar, milk, flour, baking powder, and salt. Mix well. Pour over the melted butter. DO NOT STIR. Distribute the peaches evenly over the top.

Bake for 1 hour. Batter should rise during baking.

CHOCOLATE MARIE CAKE

◆◆◆◆◆◆◆◆◆◆◆◆◆◆◆◆◆◆◆◆◆◆◆◆◆

Carole Fuller   Bowie, Texas   An absolutely delectable cake that has been
◆◆◆◆◆◆◆◆◆◆◆◆◆◆◆◆◆◆◆◆◆◆◆ in Carole Fuller's family for over sixty
years. It's very easy to put together, and it doesn't need an icing.

¾ cup butter, softened to
    room temperature

2 cups sugar

2 eggs

2½ cups all-purpose flour,
    sifted

4 tablespoons cocoa

¼ teaspoon salt

1½ cups buttermilk

1 teaspoon vanilla extract

1 teaspoon baking soda

1 cup chopped pecans

Serves 10.

Preheat oven to 400° F. Butter a bundt pan and set aside.

In a large mixing bowl, cream together the butter, sugar, and eggs. Sift together the flour, cocoa, and salt.

Mix together the buttermilk, vanilla, and baking soda. To the butter-sugar mixture add the flour mixture alternately with the buttermilk mixture, starting and ending with the flour. Add the pecans and stir to mix.

Pour into the prepared bundt pan and bake for 1 hour, or until a tester inserted into the center of the cake comes out clean.

BUTTERMILK WALNUT CAKE

◆◆◆◆◆◆◆◆◆◆◆◆◆◆◆◆◆◆◆◆◆◆◆◆◆◆◆◆◆◆◆◆◆◆◆◆◆

Janis Zarkowsky   Milledgeville, Georgia A lovely cake with good
◆◆◆◆◆◆◆◆◆◆◆◆◆◆◆◆◆◆◆◆◆◆◆◆◆◆◆◆◆◆◆◆◆ flavor and texture; it has
been in this Georgia family for generations. They always serve it for Christmas
dinner, but we think it would also be wonderful for Christmas breakfast, served
hot with butter.

This cake is well complemented by ice cream or whipped cream.

CAKE

*3 cups all-purpose flour,
   sifted*

2 cups sugar

½ teaspoon baking powder

½ teaspoon baking soda

½ teaspoon salt

*1 cup butter, melted and
   slightly cooled*

4 large eggs

1 cup buttermilk

2 teaspoons vanilla extract

¾ cup chopped walnuts

¾ cup ground walnuts

GLAZE

*1 cup confectioner's
   sugar, sifted*

1 teaspoon vanilla extract

*1 tablespoon freshly
   squeezed orange juice*

*1 tablespoon freshly
   squeezed lemon juice*

Preheat oven to 300° F. Grease and flour a 9-inch
springform pan. Mix together the flour, sugar, baking
powder, baking soda, and salt. Add the remaining
ingredients and beat well.

Pour into the pan and bake 1 hour, or until a knife comes
out clean when inserted in the center of the cake—it may
take as much as 1½ hours. Meanwhile, prepare glaze, *which
must be applied the moment the cake is removed from oven.*

Combine all ingredients and mix well. Pour over the hot
cake. Return cake to oven for 2 seconds only.

Serve warm, or let cool, as you like. Wrap well to freeze.

CHOCOLATE SHEET CAKE

◆◆◆◆◆◆◆◆◆◆◆◆◆◆◆◆◆◆◆◆◆◆◆◆◆◆◆◆◆◆◆◆

Cynthia Hines Lower Sackville, Nova Scotia A really delicious
◆◆◆◆◆◆◆◆◆◆◆◆◆◆◆◆◆◆◆◆◆◆◆◆◆◆◆◆◆◆ chocolate cake. Cynthia Hines got the recipe from her mother-in-law when she was first dating the man who became her husband. This cake makes 50 big pieces, enough for all the guests to have more than they should. We especially liked it topped with chocolate shavings.

CAKE

8 tablespoons butter

½ cup vegetable oil

4 tablespoons cocoa

2 cups sugar

2 cups all-purpose flour

½ teaspoon salt

½ teaspoon vanilla extract

2 large eggs

1 teaspoon baking soda

½ cup sour milk or
buttermilk

ICING

4 tablespoons butter,
softened to room
temperature

2 cups confectioner's
sugar, sifted

1 large egg

½ teaspoon vanilla extract

Chocolate shavings
(optional)

Serves 50.

Preheat oven to 400° F. Grease the bottom of a 15 × 11 × 1-inch pan with butter and set aside. In a medium saucepan, combine the butter, oil, 1 cup cold water, and the cocoa. Bring to a full rolling boil and remove from the heat.

In a large bowl, mix together the sugar, flour, salt, vanilla, and eggs. Mix well. Add the baking soda to the sour milk and add to the batter. Add the chocolate mixture and mix well.

Pour the batter into the pan. Bake for 25 minutes, or until cake springs back when lightly touched. Remove to a cake rack to cool completely before frosting.

In a mixing bowl, cream together the butter and sugar. Add the egg and beat until creamy. Add the vanilla and mix well. Spread over the cooled cake.

Decorate with chocolate shavings, if desired.

STRAWBERRY FOOL

◆◆◆◆◆◆◆◆◆◆◆◆◆◆◆◆◆◆◆◆◆◆◆◆◆◆◆◆◆◆◆◆

Adrienne Jackson   Milwaukee, Wisconsin This is a nearly instant
◆◆◆◆◆◆◆◆◆◆◆◆◆◆◆◆◆◆◆◆◆◆◆◆◆◆◆ dessert, a sort of straw-
berry shortcake without the cake. Make this only with perfectly ripe strawberries
in season.

2 cups heavy cream

¼ cup sugar

*1 quart strawberries,
    quartered*

Serves 4.

Whip the cream, add the sugar, and fold in the strawberries. Stir before serving.

HYER'S DRUGSTORE POUND CAKE

◆◆◆◆◆◆◆◆◆◆◆◆◆◆◆◆◆◆◆◆◆◆◆◆◆◆◆◆◆◆◆◆

Mary Ann Shivers   Easley, South Carolina This old and very good
◆◆◆◆◆◆◆◆◆◆◆◆◆◆◆◆◆◆◆◆◆◆◆◆◆◆◆◆◆◆ recipe is from a real
drugstore in North Augusta, South Carolina. We especially liked it spread with
butter and toasted, for tea or afternoon coffee. And of course you can use all
butter.

8 tablespoons butter
½ cup shortening
8 tablespoons margarine
3 cups sugar
5 large eggs
3 cups all-purpose flour
1 cup milk
2 teaspoons vanilla extract
1 teaspoon baking powder
Makes 24 slices.

Grease a bundt pan with butter and set aside. *Do not preheat the oven.*

In a large mixing bowl, cream together the fats and the sugar. Add the eggs 1 at a time, beating well after each addition. Add the flour alternately with the milk, starting and ending with the flour. Add the vanilla and mix until well blended. At the very last minute, add the baking powder and mix.

Pour the batter into the prepared pan. Turn oven to 350° F.—the cake is supposed to go into a cold oven. Bake for 70 minutes, or until a tester inserted into the center comes out clean.

GRANDMA KHOURY'S RAISIN CAKE

◆◆◆◆◆◆◆◆◆◆◆◆◆◆◆◆◆◆◆◆◆◆◆◆◆◆◆◆◆◆◆◆◆◆

Annamarie Childers   Hawthorne, California A very moist, old-fash-
◆◆◆◆◆◆◆◆◆◆◆◆◆◆◆◆◆◆◆◆◆◆◆◆◆◆◆◆◆◆◆ ioned cake that would
be good served with applesauce. This is another of those excellent "grandmother"
cakes, always made for Christmas, with the recipe handed down carefully to
the next generation.

2 cups raisins

1¼ teaspoons baking soda

1 cup shortening

1¼ cups sugar

⅛ teaspoon salt

½ teaspoon cinnamon

½ teaspoon nutmeg,
preferably freshly grated

½ teaspoon ground ginger

½ teaspoon ground
allspice

2½ cups all-purpose flour

1 teaspoon vanilla extract

Makes 24 slices.

Preheat oven to 275° F. Butter a 9x13x2-inch pan and set aside.

In a medium saucepan, combine the raisins and 2 cups water. Boil until the water is almost gone. Remove from the heat and pour the raisins into a large mixing bowl. Add 1 cup cold water. Add the baking soda and mix well. Add the shortening, sugar, salt, and spices. Mix well. Add the flour and beat well. Add the vanilla and mix in.

Pour into the prepared pan. Bake for 1 hour, or until a tester inserted into the center of the cake comes out clean.

TWO-HUNDRED-DOLLAR CARROT CAKE

◆◆◆◆◆◆◆◆◆◆◆◆◆◆◆◆◆◆◆◆◆◆◆◆◆◆◆

Mairi Stevenson   Toronto, Ontario Mairi Stevenson got this recipe
◆◆◆◆◆◆◆◆◆◆◆◆◆◆◆◆◆◆◆◆◆◆◆◆◆◆◆ thirdhand from a woman who re-
portedly paid a chef in California $200 for it. She got her money's worth, we
think; this cake is truly delicious—rich, nutty, spicy, delectable.

CAKE

1 cup vegetable oil

1 cup sugar

*3 eggs, at room
    temperature*

1⅓ cups all-purpose flour

*1½ teaspoons baking
    powder*

1½ teaspoons baking soda

1½ teaspoons cinnamon

2 cups finely grated carrot

*1 cup chopped and lightly
    toasted walnuts*

ICING

4 tablespoons butter

*1 (8-ounce) package
    cream cheese*

2 teaspoons vanilla extract

*2 cups confectioner's
    sugar, sifted*

*Grated carrots or walnut
    halves for decoration
    (optional)*

Serves 10 to 12.

Preheat oven to 350° F. Butter and flour a 10-inch bundt pan and set aside.

Mix together the oil and sugar. Beat in the eggs 1 at a time, blending well after each addition.

Sift together the flour and spices. Add slowly to the egg mixture and blend well; if using a mixer, keep on low speed.

Stir in the carrots and nuts. Pour into the prepared pan and bake 1 hour. The cake will begin to pull away from the edges of the pan when done.

Cool 10 to 15 minutes before removing from pan. Cool completely before icing.

Whip the butter and cream cheese together until smooth, then slowly beat in the vanilla and confectioner's sugar until the icing is fluffy.

Split the cake into 3 layers and ice, leaving sides of cake unfrosted. Decorate with grated fresh carrots or walnut halves, if desired.

GINGER PUMPKIN BUNDT CAKE

◆◆◆◆◆◆◆◆◆◆◆◆◆◆◆◆◆◆◆◆◆◆◆◆◆◆◆◆◆◆

Georgette Hilliard Kaleva, Michigan A dense, moist, shiny cake with
◆◆◆◆◆◆◆◆◆◆◆◆◆◆◆◆◆◆◆◆◆◆◆◆◆◆ a "quick bread" texture and an
excellent flavor. For decoration, we suggest cutting petals of crystallized ginger.

CAKE

6 eggs

*1 (16-ounce) can pumpkin
    puree*

1½ cups honey

⅔ cup butter, melted

½ cup plain yogurt

1 cup wheat germ

3 cups all-purpose flour

2 teaspoons baking soda

½ teaspoon salt

2 teaspoons ground ginger

1 teaspoon cinnamon

*1 teaspoon nutmeg,
    preferably freshly grated*

½ teaspoon ground cloves

GLAZE

1 cup sugar

½ teaspoon baking soda

½ cup plain yogurt

1 tablespoon light corn syrup

8 tablespoons butter

1 teaspoon vanilla extract

Makes 1 (10-inch) cake.

Preheat oven to 350° F. Butter and flour a 10-inch tube pan or bundt pan and set aside.

Beat the eggs in a large bowl. Stir in the pumpkin, honey, butter, yogurt, and wheat germ.

Sift the flour and remaining cake ingredients together, then stir into the pumpkin mixture.

Pour into the prepared pan and bake 50 to 60 minutes. The cake will begin to pull away from the sides of the pan when done. Cool in the pan on a rack 10 minutes, then invert onto the rack.

Combine all the glaze ingredients except the vanilla in a saucepan and bring to a boil. Reduce heat and simmer 2 minutes, stirring constantly. Remove from the heat and stir in the vanilla.

Place the cooled cake on its rack over a tray or a piece of foil. Spoon the glaze over it while the glaze is still hot. Scoop up the drips and continue to apply the glaze until absorbed.

GINGER SPICE CAKE

Eleanor Forbes   Islington, Ontario This terrific ginger cake is from a very old recipe—Mrs. Forbes's husband's grandmother brought it from her family, and it's become a favorite. In the great tradition of Scottish baking, this is a dense, moist, succulent cake with an expecially delicious praline buttercream frosting.

1 cup dark brown sugar

8 tablespoons butter

2 eggs, beaten

1 cup all-purpose flour

1 teaspoon cinnamon

½ teaspoon ground cloves

1 teaspoon baking soda

½ cup sour cream

½ cup crystallized ginger, chopped

½ cup walnuts or pecans, chopped

ICING

1 heaping cup light brown sugar

¼ cup heavy cream

2 tablespoons butter

1 tablespoon corn syrup

Serves 12.

Preheat oven to 325° F. Butter and flour a 9-inch-square pan and set aside.

Cream the brown sugar and butter together well and add the eggs.

Sift the flour, spices, and baking soda together, and add them to the mixture alternately with the sour cream. Mix in the ginger and nuts.

Bake for 35 to 45 minutes, or until the cake begins to pull away from the sides of the pan and the top springs back to the touch. Cool in the pan.

Put all ingredients in a heavy saucepan and bring to a boil. Cook over medium heat for 2 minutes. Cool briefly, then beat with a wooden spoon until the icing is thick enough to spread on cake. This happens very quickly; if the icing gets too hard to spread, never mind—it makes delicious candy and this cake is rich enough without icing!

Alternatively, use a candy thermometer and cook the icing until it's just over 250° F., then pour it into a mixing bowl and beat until you reach the right consistency.

LAZY DAISY CAKE

Linda Schwerin **Aurora, Colorado** This excellent cake comes from Linda Schwerin's Scandinavian mother—it's great with fudge frosting, and it makes a splendid strawberry shortcake base. Best of all, it's extremely easy to make.

2 large eggs

1 cup sugar

1 teaspoon vanilla extract

1 cup all-purpose flour, sifted

½ teaspoon salt

½ teaspoon baking powder

½ cup milk

1 tablespoon butter

Preheat oven to 350° F. Grease an 8-inch-square baking pan and set aside.

In a large mixing bowl, beat the eggs; gradually add the sugar and vanilla. Sift together the flour, salt, and baking powder. Add to the egg-sugar mixture; beat well.

Heat the milk and butter in a saucepan to a boil. Add all at once to the previous mixture. Beat well. (The batter will be thin.)

Pour into the prepared pan. Bake for 30 minutes, or until golden.

Remove from the oven and, while hot, spread icing over the cake. Place under broiler until bubbly and lightly browned. Cool in the pan on a rack.

ICING

3 tablespoons butter, melted

5 tablespoons dark brown sugar

2 tablespoons cream

½ cup shredded coconut

Serves 8 to 10.

Combine all ingredients and mix well.

MOMMA G'S APPLESAUCE CAKE

◆◆◆◆◆◆◆◆◆◆◆◆◆◆◆◆◆◆◆◆◆◆◆◆◆◆◆◆◆◆◆◆◆◆

Tracy Gilmore   Ann Arbor, Michigan The recipe for this excellent
◆◆◆◆◆◆◆◆◆◆◆◆◆◆◆◆◆◆◆◆◆◆◆◆◆◆ cake was handed down from
Tracy Gilmore's great-grandmother, but not in the usual way. Ms. Gilmore
never met her great-grandmother, and the recipe was found tucked in her
savings account passbook, saved for the next generation. Some cooks may find
the cream cheese icing a bit too rich and sweet; if so, try using a simple glaze
(see page 139).

2 cups all-purpose flour

2 teaspoons baking soda

1 teaspoon baking powder

2 teaspoons cinnamon

1 teaspoon ground cloves

*1 teaspoon nutmeg,
preferably freshly grated*

1 cup raisins

*1 cup chopped nuts
(walnuts or pecans)*

1 cup sugar

*8 tablespoons butter,
softened to room
temperature*

1 large egg

1 teaspoon vanilla extract

2 cups applesauce

Serves 24.

Preheat oven to 350° F. Grease and flour a 9 × 13-inch pan and set aside.

Sift together the flour, baking soda, baking powder, cinnamon, cloves, and nutmeg. Remove ½ cup of the flour mixture and combine with the raisins and nuts to coat well.

Cream together the sugar and butter. Add the egg and vanilla and beat until well blended. Add the dry ingredients alternately with the applesauce, beating until well blended. Stir in the flour-coated raisins and nuts.

Pour into the prepared pan and bake for 25 to 30 minutes, or until a toothpick inserted into the center of the cake comes out clean. Put on a rack to cool. When completely cooled, spread cream cheese icing over top.

CREAM CHEESE ICING

2 (3-ounce) packages
  cream cheese, softened
  to room temperature

2 tablespoons butter,
  softened to room
  temperature

2 teaspoons vanilla extract

4 cups sifted confectioner's
  sugar

1 tablespoon milk
  (optional)

In a mixing bowl, combine the cream cheese, butter, and vanilla. Beat until blended. Gradually add the sugar, beating until fluffy. If necessary, add a tablespoon of milk to reach spreading consistency.

BANANA COCONUT CAKE

◆◆◆◆◆◆◆◆◆◆◆◆◆◆◆◆◆◆◆◆◆◆◆◆◆◆◆◆◆◆◆◆

Shirley Koehler   Long Beach, California A very attractive cake that's
◆◆◆◆◆◆◆◆◆◆◆◆◆◆◆◆◆◆◆◆◆◆◆◆◆◆◆◆◆ also delectable. The coco-
nut browns as the layers bake.

CAKE

¾ cup shortening

1½ cups sugar

2 large eggs

1 cup mashed banana

2 cups cake flour

1 teaspoon baking powder

¼ teaspoon salt

1 teaspoon baking soda

½ cup buttermilk

½ cup chopped pecans

1 cup shredded coconut

CREAMY NUT FILLING

½ cup sugar

2 tablespoons all-purpose
  flour

½ cup heavy cream

2 tablespoons butter,
  softened to room
  temperature

½ cup chopped pecans

½ teaspoon vanilla extract

WHITE SNOW FROSTING

1 egg white, at room
  temperature

4 tablespoons butter

Preheat oven to 375° F. Grease and flour 2 (9-inch) round cake pans.

In a large mixing bowl, blend the shortening and sugar. Add the eggs and beat for 2 minutes on medium speed. Add the banana and beat for another 2 minutes.

Sift the dry cake ingredients together. Add to the banana mixture alternately with the buttermilk, beginning and ending with the flour. Beat well for 2 minutes. Stir in the chopped pecans.

Pour into the prepared cake pans. Sprinkle ½ cup of the shredded coconut on top of the batter in each pan. Bake for 25 to 30 minutes.

Place a piece of wax paper over each layer when you remove it from the pan. Turn onto another rack so that the coconut will be on top. Cool completely.

Put the first 4 filling ingredients into a heavy saucepan and cook over medium heat until thickened, stirring constantly to prevent scorching. Remove from the heat and stir in the nuts and vanilla. Cool.

Place the first cake layer with the coconut side down and spread with the cooled filling. Place the second layer on top with the coconut side up.

Beat the egg white until stiff. Add the butter, shortening, coconut extract, and sugar. Beat all ingredients until light and fluffy.

¼ *cup shortening*

½ *teaspoon coconut extract*

2 *cups confectioner's sugar*

Serves 10.

Frost around the cake sides and about 1 inch around the top edge of the cake, leaving the browned coconut on the top exposed in the center.

CHERRY NUT CAKE

♦♦♦♦♦♦♦♦♦♦♦♦♦♦♦♦♦♦♦♦♦♦♦

George Wertke   Plano, Illinois A truly delectable cake that Mr. Wertke
♦♦♦♦♦♦♦♦♦♦♦♦♦♦♦♦♦♦♦♦♦♦♦ always makes on or around George
Washington's Birthday. He thinks it dates from the 1940s. In any case, it's
utterly delicious. We think the layers alone would be great served with vanilla
ice cream.

CAKE

8 tablespoons butter

2 cups sugar

*4 large eggs, separated, at
   room temperature*

*2 teaspoons baking
   powder*

2 cups all-purpose flour

1 cup milk

*1 cup chopped walnuts or
   pecans*

*1 cup drained, chopped
   maraschino cherries,
   juice reserved*

CHERRY FROSTING

*5 tablespoons butter, at
   room temperature*

*4 cups confectioner's
   sugar*

*6 tablespoons reserved
   cherry juice*

Serves 10.

Preheat oven to 350° F. Grease and flour 3 (9-inch) round cake pans and set aside.

In a large mixing bowl, cream together the butter and sugar. Add the egg yolks 1 at a time, beating well after each addition.

Sift together the baking powder and flour and add to the butter-sugar mixture alternately with the milk. Stir in the nuts and cherries.

Beat the egg whites until stiff and then fold into the batter. Pour into the prepared pans and bake for 20 to 25 minutes, until the center springs back to the touch. Cool completely and frost with Cherry Frosting.

Combine all ingredients in mixing bowl and beat until well blended and smooth. Spread between layers and on top and sides of cake.

STELLA'S LEMON CAKE

◆◆◆◆◆◆◆◆◆◆◆◆◆◆◆◆◆◆◆◆◆◆◆◆◆◆◆◆◆◆◆

Fay Buckley   Plymouth, Massachusetts This delectable cake comes
◆◆◆◆◆◆◆◆◆◆◆◆◆◆◆◆◆◆◆◆◆◆◆◆◆◆◆◆◆◆◆ from an old Swedish recipe.
It's even better baked a day ahead; the flavor deepens overnight.

5 tablespoons butter,
   melted

1⅓ cups sugar

2 eggs

1½ cups all-purpose flour

1 teaspoon baking powder

1 teaspoon salt

½ cup milk

2 teaspoons grated lemon
   zest (only the yellow)

½ cup chopped walnuts or
   almonds (optional)

3 tablespoons freshly
   squeezed lemon juice

Serves 10.

Preheat oven to 350° F. Butter and flour a 9 × 5-inch loaf pan and set aside.

In a large mixing bowl, mix together the butter, 1 cup of the sugar, and eggs. Sift together the flour, baking powder, and salt. Add to the butter-sugar mixture alternately with the milk. Stir in the lemon zest and the nuts, if using.

Pour the batter into the prepared pan and bake for 40 to 45 minutes. While the cake is baking, mix together in a non-metallic saucepan the lemon juice and remaining ⅓ cup sugar and heat gently to dissolve the sugar. Let stand at room temperature. As soon as the cake is taken from the oven, spoon glaze over the top. Cool in the pan 20 minutes.

STIBBLES SCOTTISH SHORTBREAD

◆◆◆◆◆◆◆◆◆◆◆◆◆◆◆◆◆◆◆◆◆◆◆◆◆

Norma Stealy   Lake Wales, Florida This recipe comes from Dundee,
◆◆◆◆◆◆◆◆◆◆◆◆◆◆◆◆◆◆◆◆◆◆◆◆◆ Scotland, where Norma Stealy's
family, the Stibbles, had a confectionery store. This is one of the rare shortbreads
made with brown sugar; it's only vaguely sweet, wonderfully rich, and hard to
leave alone. It also looks splendid, with its rustic fork tine marks—which can
be done in a design if you like. It can be made in just a few minutes.

*1 cup butter, minus 1
    tablespoon*

*½ cup lightly packed light
    brown sugar*

2 cups all-purpose flour

Serves about 20.

Preheat oven to 325° F. Butter an 8-inch pie pan and set
aside.

Knead all the ingredients together with your hands—
it's not cricket to use utensils—until you have a soft, shiny
ball of dough. Pat it into the pan. Prick the dough all over
with a fork. Using the tines of the fork, press down around
the edges of the dough.

Bake for 55 minutes, or until lightly browned. Cool in the
pan 20 minutes. Break into pieces with fork tines to serve;
the Stibbles would be horrified to see someone cutting
shortbread with a knife.

JEWISH APPLE CAKE

◆◆◆◆◆◆◆◆◆◆◆◆◆◆◆◆◆◆◆◆◆◆◆◆◆◆◆◆◆◆◆◆◆

Susan Menetrey   Fort Sam Houston, Texas Mrs. Menetrey's Jewish

◆◆◆◆◆◆◆◆◆◆◆◆◆◆◆◆◆◆◆◆◆◆◆◆◆◆◆◆◆◆◆ apple cake, which appeared in the *Sweet Energy Cookbook,* is a heavy, moist cake with a wonderful chewy crust on top. It smells terrific while it's baking, and it's not quite like any other cake. Serve it with vanilla ice cream.

6 Granny Smith apples,
   thinly sliced

2 heaping teaspoons
   cinnamon

5–6 tablespoons
   granulated sugar, or to
   taste

3 cups all-purpose flour

2¼ cups sugar, half
   granulated and half
   dark brown

3 teaspoons baking
   powder

½ teaspoon salt

4 eggs

1 cup vegetable oil

2½ teaspoons vanilla
   extract

⅓ cup freshly squeezed
   orange juice

Serves 12.

Oil and flour a tube pan—not a fluted one—or angel food cake pan. Set aside. Preheat oven to 350° F.

In a medium bowl, mix the apples, cinnamon, and sugar.

In a large bowl, mix the rest of the ingredients together and beat with a wooden spoon until the mixture is smooth.

Scoop half the batter into the prepared pan and cover with half the apple mixture. Scoop a second layer of batter over apples and top with remaining apple mixture.

Bake for about 1¾ hours. The crust should be crunchy. Cool in the pan for 15 minutes and remove to a wire rack to finish cooling.

INDIAN CORN PUDDING

◆◆◆◆◆◆◆◆◆◆◆◆◆◆◆◆◆◆◆◆◆◆◆◆◆◆◆◆◆◆◆◆◆◆◆

Linda Ratcliff   Darrington, Washington   An interesting version of the
◆◆◆◆◆◆◆◆◆◆◆◆◆◆◆◆◆◆◆◆◆◆◆◆◆◆◆◆◆◆◆◆   classic Indian pudding—in this
case, milk is slowly absorbed and evaporated into the cornmeal, leaving a
naturally caramelized subtle taste that's unusual and very good. You have to
give it a stir every 30 minutes for four hours, so plan to stay around the house
for a while.

1 cup cornmeal

¼ cup sugar

½ cup dark molasses

2 eggs

¼ teaspoon salt

¼ teaspoon baking soda

6 cups hot milk

8 tablespoons butter

½ teaspoon cinnamon

*½ teaspoon nutmeg,
    preferably freshly grated*

Serves 8.

Preheat oven to 400° F. Mix the first 6 ingredients together in a bean pot or a 3-quart baking dish with a cover. Stir until lumps are out.

Add 3 cups of the hot milk and the butter. Cover the pot and put it in the oven until the pudding boils. After it boils, add the remaining milk. Set the oven to 275° F. and bake for 4 hours, stirring every 30 minutes. Add the spices during the last 30 minutes of baking.

SARAH'S PERSIMMON PUDDING

◆◆

Charyl Borgwald-Lawrence   Danville, Illinois   In the Midwest, per-
◆◆ simmons ripen and fall
to the ground in November, after the heavy frosts. Then they are gathered
and, in the Borgwald-Lawrence family, turned into this lovely pudding, which
is their traditional Thanksgiving dessert. It is good topped with hard sauce or
whipped cream with a little ground mace added.

2 cups persimmon pulp

3 eggs

1¼ cups sugar

1½ cups all-purpose flour

1 teaspoon baking powder

1 teaspoon baking soda

½ teaspoon salt

*8 tablespoons butter,
  melted*

2½ cups milk

2 teaspoons cinnamon

*½–1 cup pecans or
  walnuts, chopped
  (optional)*

Serves 6 to 8.

Preheat oven to 350° F. Butter a 2-quart casserole dish and set aside. In a large mixing bowl, combine all ingredients and beat well until all lumps have disappeared.

Pour the pudding into the prepared dish and bake for 1 hour, or until firm. Serve warm. (The pudding can be reheated in a moderate oven.)

LIME CHEESECAKE

◆◆◆◆◆◆◆◆◆◆◆◆◆◆◆◆◆◆◆◆◆◆◆◆

Bill Hinrich   Pensacola, Florida This zesty cheesecake tastes very
◆◆◆◆◆◆◆◆◆◆◆◆◆◆◆◆◆◆◆◆◆◆ similar to Key lime pie. It's especially
pretty decorated with very thin half slices of lime with a little lime zest strewn
over it. As cheesecakes go, it's a cinch—you don't bake it.

1½ cups graham cracker
crumbs

5 tablespoons butter,
melted

1 (8-ounce) package
cream cheese, softened
to room temperature

14 ounces sweetened
condensed milk

1 teaspoon grated lime
zest (only the green)

¾ cup freshly squeezed
lime juice (the juice of
about 6 limes)

1 envelope unflavored
gelatin

1 cup heavy cream,
whipped

Serves 10.

Combine the crumbs and butter. Mix well. Press into an
8½-inch springform pan, building up the sides. Chill.

In a mixing bowl, combine the cream cheese and
condensed milk. Beat until smooth. Add the grated lime zest
and lime juice. Blend well.

In a small saucepan, soften the gelatin in ¼ cup water. Warm
over low heat to dissolve. Gradually stir into the cream
cheese mixture. Fold the whipped cream into the cream
cheese mixture. Pour into the crust.

Chill to set.

PUMPKIN CHEESECAKE

◆◆◆◆◆◆◆◆◆◆◆◆◆◆◆◆◆◆◆◆◆◆◆◆◆◆◆

Linda Sloan   Beaumont, Alberta A mildly flavored mellow cheesecake
◆◆◆◆◆◆◆◆◆◆◆◆◆◆◆◆◆◆◆◆◆◆◆◆◆◆ with a zippy gingersnap crust. This
may be the ultimate Thanksgiving dessert.

20 gingersnaps

*4 tablespoons butter,
melted*

*5 eggs, separated, at room
temperature*

*2 (8-ounce) packages
cream cheese, softened
to room temperature*

1 cup granulated sugar

2 teaspoons cinnamon

*1 teaspoon nutmeg,
preferably freshly grated*

1 teaspoon ground ginger

Large pinch of salt

*2 cups pumpkin puree (see
page 197)*

¼ cup light brown sugar

1 cup sour cream

*¼ cup walnuts or pecans,
chopped*

Serves 8 to 12.

Preheat oven to 350° F.

Crush the gingersnaps into crumbs and combine with
the melted butter; press the mixture into the sides and
bottom of a 9-inch springform pan.

Bake the crust 10 to 15 minutes, until it colors.

Beat the egg yolks at high speed until they are thick and
lemon-colored. Add the cream cheese and beat until smooth.

Gradually beat in the granulated sugar mixed with the spices
and salt. Add the pumpkin and blend well.

Beat the egg whites until stiff but not dry. Fold into the
pumpkin mixture. Pour the mixture into the crust and bake
about 1½ hours, until a knife comes out clean when inserted
in the center of the cake.

Increase oven temperature to 450° F.

Combine the brown sugar and sour cream. Spread over the
cheesecake. Sprinkle the nuts on top and bake another 5
minutes.

Cool the cheesecake and refrigerate it in the pan until ready
to serve.

ORANGE CHEESECAKE

◆◆◆◆◆◆◆◆◆◆◆◆◆◆◆◆◆◆◆◆◆◆◆◆

Liz Sirois Edmonton, Alberta Several of our test cooks felt this was
◆◆◆◆◆◆◆◆◆◆◆◆◆◆◆◆◆◆◆◆◆◆ the best cheesecake they'd *ever* tasted.
It's a superb cheesecake with a delicious orange sauce and a chocolate glaze.
As Liz Sirois points out, it's very rich, so it goes a long way. It also takes more
than the usual time to prepare, but it's definitely worth the extra fuss. The
cheesecake is also excellent served on its own, but we loved the sauce-and-
glaze combination.

CRUST

*1 cup sifted all-purpose
flour*

¼ cup sugar

*1 tablespoon grated
orange zest*

8 tablespoons butter

1 egg yolk

½ teaspoon vanilla extract

Preheat oven to 400° F.

Combine the flour, sugar, and orange zest. Cut the
butter in with a pastry blender until the mixture is the
consistency of coarse meal. Add the egg yolk and vanilla;
blend well.

Place half of the dough on the bottom of a 9-inch springform
pan; pat down evenly to cover the bottom. Bake for 5
minutes, or until golden brown. Remove from the oven and
cool. Pat the remaining dough evenly around the sides to ½
inch from the top, and set aside.

Leave oven at 400° F.

FILLING

*5 (8-ounce) packages
cream cheese, softened
to room temperature*

1¾ cups sugar

*3 tablespoons all-purpose
flour*

*1 tablespoon grated
orange zest*

¼ teaspoon salt

In a large mixing bowl, combine the cream cheese, sugar,
flour, orange zest, salt, and vanilla. Beat with an electric
mixer at low speed until smooth. Add eggs and yolks 1 at a
time; beat well after each addition. Stir in the orange juice.

Pour the filling into the prepared pan, place on a cookie
sheet, and bake 8 to 10 minutes, or until crust is lightly
browned. Reduce heat to 225° F. and bake 80 minutes

¼ teaspoon vanilla extract

5 eggs plus 2 egg yolks

¼ cup frozen orange juice concentrate, thawed

further. When the cake is done, a knife inserted in the center should come out clean. Cool to room temperature and then refrigerate.

ORANGE SAUCE

1 (11-ounce) can mandarin orange sections, undrained

¼ cup frozen orange juice concentrate, thawed

¼ cup water or orange liqueur

2 tablespoons cornstarch dissolved in 1 tablespoon water, or more cornstarch mixture as needed

Heat the oranges and other liquids to a slow boil. Thicken the sauce with the cornstarch; if it's not quite thick enough, add a little more.

CHOCOLATE GLAZE

½ pound dark chocolate, melted

2 tablespoons orange liqueur (optional)

Orange slices (optional, for a garnish)

Chocolate curls (optional, for a garnish)

Melt the chocolate in a double boiler over low heat and add liqueur, if desired. Cool.

To serve: Cut thin slices of cheesecake and serve them on their sides, topped with a little orange sauce and chocolate glaze dribbled over that. Decorate with orange slices or chocolate curls, if desired.

COCONUT CHEESECAKE

◆◆◆◆◆◆◆◆◆◆◆◆◆◆◆◆◆◆◆◆◆◆◆◆◆◆◆◆

Megan Balterman   Cincinnati, Ohio An unusual cheesecake with a
◆◆◆◆◆◆◆◆◆◆◆◆◆◆◆◆◆◆◆◆◆◆◆◆◆◆◆◆ good coconut texture—a perfect
summer cheesecake, especially suited to follow an Indian or Mexican meal.

1½ cups graham cracker crumbs

1 cup sugar

Juice and grated zest of 1 lime, plus 1 teaspoon lime juice

5 tablespoons butter, softened to room temperature

3 (8-ounce) packages cream cheese, softened to room temperature

3 eggs

2 cups toasted shredded coconut

Pinch of salt

2 tablespoons dark rum

¾ cup cream of coconut

Shredded coconut or lime slices for a garnish

Serves 10.

To prepare the crust: Combine the crumbs, ½ cup sugar, the juice and zest of the lime, and the butter. Pat into the sides and bottom of a 9-inch springform pan.

Preheat oven to 350° F.

In a food processor or mixer, combine the cream cheese and remaining ½ cup sugar and beat until smooth. Add the eggs, 1 at a time.

Add the coconut, 1 teaspoon lime juice, salt, rum, and cream of coconut, mixing only just until they are combined.

Bake for 40 to 55 minutes, or until lightly browned. Cool and decorate with coconut or lime slices. Refrigerate overnight.

RICH CHOCOLATE CHEESECAKE

◆◆◆◆◆◆◆◆◆◆◆◆◆◆◆◆◆◆◆◆◆◆◆◆◆◆◆◆◆

Kathy Musto Chicago, Illinois This recipe comes originally from Charleston, South Carolina, and once appeared in *Southern Living* magazine. It's an extremely rich, smooth cheesecake with a deep chocolate taste—just about irresistible.

1½ cups chocolate wafer
  crumbs

¼ teaspoon nutmeg,
  preferably freshly grated

8 tablespoons butter,
  melted

2 (8-ounce) packages
  cream cheese, softened
  to room temperature

¾ cup sugar

3 eggs

1 cup sour cream

6 (1-ounce) squares
  semisweet chocolate,
  melted

1 tablespoon plus ¾
  teaspoon cocoa

1½ teaspoons vanilla extract

½ cup heavy cream, whipped

Additional whipped cream
  (optional, for a garnish)

Chocolate curls (optional,
  for a garnish)

Almonds (optional, for a
  garnish)

Serves 10 to 12.

Preheat oven to 300° F. Combine the crumbs, nutmeg, and butter, mixing well, and press into the bottom of a 9-inch springform pan; chill.

Beat the cream cheese with a mixer until light and fluffy. Gradually add the sugar, mixing well. Add the eggs, 1 at a time, beating well after each addition. Stir in the sour cream, melted chocolate, cocoa, and vanilla; mix well.

Gently fold in the whipped cream, then spoon the batter into the prepared pan. Bake for 1 hour. Turn oven off and allow cheesecake to cool in oven 30 minutes. Open oven door, and allow cheesecake to cool in oven an additional 30 minutes. Refrigerate for 8 hours, still in the pan.

To serve, remove sides of pan and garnish with additional whipped cream, chocolate curls, and almonds, if desired.

AUNT MARY'S NEW YORK CHEESECAKE

◆◆

Christine Jean Appleyard   Mountain Top, Pennsylvania

◆◆

Christine Appleyard had a real Aunt Mary who would send her recipes collected here and there; then they would try the best ones when Aunt Mary came to visit in the summer. This recipe seemed to say, "I'm good, try me." We felt the same way, and sure enough, it's very good, and relatively light.

9 squares graham crackers, in crumbs

1 pound ricotta cheese

2 (8-ounce) packages cream cheese, softened to room temperature

1½ cups sugar

4 extra-large eggs

Juice of 1 lemon plus 1 tablespoon lemon juice

1 teaspoon vanilla extract

3 tablespoons all-purpose flour

2 cups sour cream

1 cup butter, melted

Serves 10 to 12.

Preheat oven to 350° F. Pour the crumbs into a well-greased 9½-inch springform pan and set aside.

Combine the rest of the ingredients in order, 1 at a time. Use an electric mixer to mix well.

Pour the filling into the crumb-lined pan and bake for 1 hour. Turn the oven off and let stand in the oven for 2 more hours. Serve at room temperature.

CIRNAYA PASKA (RUSSIAN EASTER CHEESE)

Betty-Anne Malashenko   Montreal, Quebec For the Russian Ortho-
dox, Easter is a more
festive celebration than Christmas. It wouldn't be Easter without this glorious
Easter Cheese, served unmolded onto a plate decorated with nuts and candied
and dried fruits. Betty-Anne Malashenko got the recipe from her mother-in-
law; it's a much less rich paska than most, though it's not exactly light.

*3 pounds cottage cheese
(without curds)*

*1 cup butter, softened to
room temperature*

1 cup sugar

4 egg yolks

1 teaspoon vanilla extract

*½ cup dried fruit (raisins,
apricots) or candied
fruit*

*Nuts and candied and
dried fruits for
decoration*

Serves 12.

To drain the whey off the cheese, the best solution is to
use a clean, scrubbed 6-inch flowerpot that's completely
dry. Or you can make do with a large soufflé dish and
a tea towel. Have one of these systems ready.

Cream the butter into the sugar, and the egg yolks, and mix
well. Mix in the vanilla, cheese, and fruits.

Flowerpot method: Dampen 2 thicknesses of cheesecloth and
line the flowerpot with it. Add the cheese mixture and fold
the edges of the cheesecloth over the top. Cover with foil.
Weigh down with a heavy food can placed on a small plate.
Set the flowerpot on a rack over a shallow pan and place the
whole assembly in the refrigerator to drain for 24 hours.

Soufflé dish method: Put the tea towel in the soufflé dish and
pour in the cheese mixture. Fold the tea towel over the
mixture and weigh down with a heavy food can placed on a
plate. Refrigerate for 24 hours to drain.

Unmold the cheese onto a serving plate and decorate. Serve
in very small slices.

GRANDMA'S CREAM CAKE

◆◆◆◆◆◆◆◆◆◆◆◆◆◆◆◆◆◆◆◆◆◆◆◆◆◆◆◆◆◆

Rosanne Pantaleo   Miami, Florida   A beautifully textured delicate cake,
◆◆◆◆◆◆◆◆◆◆◆◆◆◆◆◆◆◆◆◆◆◆◆◆◆◆◆ rich with cream. This makes a
perfect base for strawberry shortcake or any other fruit, and it's very easy to
make.

6 large eggs

2 cups sugar

4 cups cake flour

*4 teaspoons baking
    powder*

2 cups heavy cream

2 teaspoons vanilla extract

Serves 10.

Preheat oven to 350° F. Grease a 10-inch tube pan and set aside.

In a large bowl, beat together the eggs and sugar. Mix in the flour and baking powder. Add the cream and vanilla and beat until well mixed.

Pour into greased pan and bake 50 to 55 minutes, or until a toothpick inserted in the center of the cake comes out clean.

Cookies

PECAN BALLS

◆◆◆◆◆◆◆◆◆◆◆◆◆◆◆◆◆◆◆◆◆◆◆◆◆◆◆◆◆◆

Mrs. George Davis   Arlington, Georgia These superb cookies are of
◆◆◆◆◆◆◆◆◆◆◆◆◆◆◆◆◆◆◆◆◆◆◆◆◆◆◆◆◆ the melt-in-your-mouth sort,
and they have the additional virtue of bits of pecan all through them. They're
easy and fun to make, too—you do it all with your hands. A little box of these
cookies would make a lovely holiday gift.

*2 cups all-purpose flour,
    sifted*

*1 cup butter, softened to
    room temperature*

*4 tablespoons granulated
    sugar*

2 teaspoons vanilla extract

1½ cups pecans, chopped

¼ teaspoon salt

*Confectioner's sugar (as
    needed)*

Makes about 2 dozen.

Preheat oven to 275° F. Work the flour and butter with your hands until it's smooth and shiny, then add the rest of the ingredients except the confectioner's sugar and work in well. Shape the dough into little balls and place on a cookie sheet lined with aluminum foil.

Bake for 20 minutes, then raise heat to 325° F. and bake for 10 minutes further. Roll the cookies in confectioner's sugar as soon as they're out of the oven, using a couple of spoons to avoid burning your fingers. Let them cool on a plate.

NORWEGIAN COOKIES

◆◆◆◆◆◆◆◆◆◆◆◆◆◆◆◆◆◆◆◆◆◆◆◆◆◆◆◆◆◆◆

Mary Henry   Scotts Valley, California These crisp, delicate cookies
◆◆◆◆◆◆◆◆◆◆◆◆◆◆◆◆◆◆◆◆◆◆◆◆◆◆◆ were always made for Christmas when Mary Henry was growing up, and sometimes for Easter as well.
The secret is to roll the dough very thin. This dough makes perfect cut cookies
that keep beautifully in tins.

8 tablespoons butter

1 cup sugar

1 egg, well beaten

3 tablespoons brandy or
　sherry

2 cups all-purpose flour,
　sifted

2 teaspoons baking
　powder

¼ teaspoon salt

Makes 4 dozen.

Cream the butter and sugar. Beat in the egg and brandy.
Stir the flour, baking powder, and salt into the mixture.
Form into a ball and chill for several hours.

Preheat oven to 350° F.

Roll out dough as thin as possible and cut the cookies. Bake
6 to 8 minutes, until there's just a hint of brown at the edges.

SPECULAAS

◆◆◆◆◆◆◆◆◆◆◆◆◆◆◆◆◆◆◆◆◆◆◆◆◆◆◆◆◆◆◆◆◆◆◆

Mrs. William Hilton   Kingston, New York Kingston was an early

◆◆◆◆◆◆◆◆◆◆◆◆◆◆◆◆◆◆◆◆◆◆◆◆◆◆◆◆◆◆ Dutch settlement in New York, and Mrs. Hilton researched this recipe in a cookbook published in honor of its recent Tercentennial. For the Dutch, St. Nicholas' Eve and Day (December 5 and 6) was the important festival, and they used foods for decoration rather than greens. There were always three oranges, a marzipan heart decorated with a pink sugar turtle dove, ginger, glazed fruit, and traditional cookies. The favorite was speculaas, often shaped in the initials of the children of the family. These are particularly interesting cookies because of the white pepper.

2 cups all-purpose flour

¼ teaspoon baking soda

1 teaspoon salt

1 teaspoon cinnamon

*1 teaspoon nutmeg,
    preferably freshly grated*

½ teaspoon ground mace

¼ teaspoon ground cloves

¼ teaspoon white pepper

*1½ teaspoons grated
    lemon zest*

⅔ cup dark brown sugar

¾ cup butter

3 tablespoons milk

*1 egg white thinned with 1
    tablespoon water*

¼ cup ground almonds

Makes 2 dozen.

Mix the dry ingredients and lemon zest with the brown sugar. Cut in the butter.

Stir in the milk to make a heavy dough. Wrap the dough in plastic wrap and store in refrigerator for several hours or overnight.

Roll out the dough on a lightly floured surface. Cut into rectangles, brush with the egg white mixture, and sprinkle with the ground almonds.

Preheat oven to 375° F.

Bake on a cookie sheet 6 to 8 minutes, or until lightly browned. Remove the cookies to a rack to cool.

HRUSTULE

◆◆◆◆◆◆◆◆◆◆◆◆◆◆◆◆◆◆◆◆◆◆◆◆◆◆◆

Kate Orsini   San Rafael, California This unusual cookie recipe comes
◆◆◆◆◆◆◆◆◆◆◆◆◆◆◆◆◆◆◆◆◆◆◆◆◆ from the island of Korčula in Yu-
goslavia—it's Kate Orsini's mother's recipe. The cookies are light, dry, and
crisp, not too sweet, with a hint of lemon.

6 eggs

¾ cup granulated sugar

*2½ tablespoons unsalted
   butter, melted and
   cooled*

3 teaspoons vanilla extract

2 teaspoons lemon extract

½ cup whiskey

*5–5½ cups all-purpose
   flour, sifted 3 times*

*1½ teaspoons baking
   powder*

1½ teaspoons salt

*Vegetable oil for deep
   frying*

Confectioner's sugar

Makes about 9 dozen.

Beat the eggs until thick and lemon-colored. Add the
sugar gradually, beating after each addition.

Add the melted and cooled butter, vanilla, lemon extract,
and whiskey. Mix well.

Add 1 cup of the sifted flour, the baking powder, and salt.
Mix well. Continue to add flour gradually until a fine, soft
dough is formed.

Turn the dough out onto a floured surface and knead in
additional flour until you have a smooth, firm ball. Divide the
dough into quarters and roll out each quarter on a floured
surface to ⅛ inch thick. With a pastry cutter, cut out 1½ × 4-
inch strips.

In a heavy pot, heat 2½ inches of oil to 350°–375° F. Layer
a tray with paper towels on which to drain the cookies.

Drop the strips in the hot oil. They will sink to the bottom,
then bubble up to the surface and inflate. Turn them over
and let brown on the other side. When light golden in color,
remove them with a slotted spoon and drain. Do not let them
get dark.

When the cookies are cool, sprinkle them with sifted confectioner's sugar.

BUTTER PECAN ICEBOX COOKIES

◆◆◆◆◆◆◆◆◆◆◆◆◆◆◆◆◆◆◆◆◆◆◆◆◆◆

Rose Jones   Brookdale, Manitoba An old recipe from Rose Jones's
◆◆◆◆◆◆◆◆◆◆◆◆◆◆◆◆◆◆◆◆◆◆◆◆◆ grandmother. These cookies are
very tasty and very easy to make, and you can even freeze the dough and bake
only as many as you want.

1 cup butter
1 cup light brown sugar
1 egg
¼ teaspoon salt
1 teaspoon vanilla extract
1 teaspoon cream of tartar
2 cups all-purpose flour
1 cup pecans

Makes 8 dozen.

Mix all ingredients in the order given. Form the dough into 2 rolls. Wrap in plastic wrap, and refrigerate until firm.

Preheat oven to 350° F.

Slice the dough into ¼-inch rounds. Place the cookies on greased baking sheets and bake 8 to 10 minutes. Cool on a rack.

COUSIN LEAL'S SOFT MOLASSES COOKIES

◆◆◆◆◆◆◆◆◆◆◆◆◆◆◆◆◆◆◆◆◆◆◆◆◆◆◆

Marion Lutz   Priest River, Idaho Marion Lutz used to make these
◆◆◆◆◆◆◆◆◆◆◆◆◆◆◆◆◆◆◆◆◆◆◆◆◆ cookies when she was a little girl—
c∩en somehow the Brer Rabbit molasses cookbook got itself lost and no one
se had the recipe. When she had her own children she began to hanker for
5 t₊se cookies and finally wrote to the Brer Rabbit people, who said they'd
s
t∠er heard of the recipe. Then years later her mother served some molasses
1 cupies one day, and Marion said, "Isn't this a Cousin Leal?" Her mother had
2 tabl̃ the book, all chewed up by mice, but the recipes were intact.
½ cup nk goodness; these are not only very easy but very good, worth writing
1 egg, be͡r.

Enough p͜
  (2½-inc̃tening
Makes 12. *plus more*
          cookies
       es
       ͜aking soda
       ground ginger
       cinnamon
       round cloves
       ͜tmeg,
       freshly grated
       alt
       ͜pose flour
       ilk

          dozen.

Mix the shortening, 1 cup sugar, the molasses, baking soda, ginger, cinnamon, cloves, nutmeg, and salt together. Add the flour and buttermilk.

The dough should be very stiff. Wrap it in plastic wrap and chill it for an hour or two before rolling out to ¼ inch thick.

Preheat oven to 375° F.

Cut out the cookies with a glass or cookie cutter, sprinkle sugar on top, and bake about 8 minutes, or until golden. Remove cookies from pan and cool on a rack.

MELTING MOMENTS

◆◆◆◆◆◆◆◆◆◆◆◆◆◆◆◆◆◆◆◆◆◆◆◆◆◆◆◆◆◆◆◆

Lorraine Klassen   Denver, Colorado Melting Moments are one of
◆◆◆◆◆◆◆◆◆◆◆◆◆◆◆◆◆◆◆◆◆◆◆◆◆◆◆◆◆◆◆ those legendary cookies that ex-
patriate British people are forever waxing nostalgic over—and indeed, we
received quite a few recipes for Melting Moments. This one is especially good,
and it's also fast and easy. The recipe makes many tiny cookies, moments if
you will, and so your guests can eat a few handfuls before they start feeling
guilty.

*1 cup butter, softened to
   room temperature*

*3 tablespoons
   confectioner's sugar,
   plus more for rolling
   cookies*

2 cups all-purpose flour

**Makes about 6 dozen tiny
   cookies.**

Cream together the butter and 3 tablespoons sugar. Add the flour, working it in by hand.

Preheat oven to 350° F.

Measuring by ½ teaspoonfuls, roll little balls of dough in the palm of your hand and place them on an ungreased cookie sheet. Bake for 10 to 15 minutes, until the cookies color slightly.

Pour some confectioner's sugar into a paper bag and add the hot cookies, shaking the bag well so that all sides of the cookies are covered.

PHIL'S FAVORITE MOLASSES COOKIES

◆◆◆◆◆◆◆◆◆◆◆◆◆◆◆◆◆◆◆◆◆◆◆◆◆◆◆◆◆◆◆

Martha Sgriccia   Studio City, California   Really good molasses cook-
◆◆◆◆◆◆◆◆◆◆◆◆◆◆◆◆◆◆◆◆◆◆◆◆◆◆◆◆ ies—these are crispy,
crinkly, chewy, and moist, with just the right molasses flavor. Martha Sgriccia
has been making them since she was a little girl.

*1½ cups sugar, plus more
for dipping cookies*

*1 cup butter, softened to
room temperature*

2 eggs, beaten

1 cup dark molasses

4 cups all-purpose flour

4 teaspoons baking soda

2 teaspoons cinnamon

1 teaspoon ground ginger

1 teaspoon salt

Makes 3 dozen.

Cream the 1½ cups sugar and butter well. Add the eggs and molasses, and mix well.

Sift all the dry ingredients together and add to the molasses mixture. At this point you can chill the dough several hours or overnight so it will be easier to work with. Then roll the dough into balls the size of walnuts, dip in sugar, and place on a greased cookie sheet.

Or, if you prefer not to chill it, drop the batter from a teaspoon onto the greased cookie sheet and sprinkle with sugar.

Preheat oven to 375° F.

Bake for 10 minutes. Remove the cookies from the pan and cool on a rack.

SOFT SUGAR COOKIES

◆◆◆◆◆◆◆◆◆◆◆◆◆◆◆◆◆◆◆◆◆◆◆◆

Frances Davis La Vale, Maryland This is a very old recipe in Mrs.
◆◆◆◆◆◆◆◆◆◆◆◆◆◆◆◆◆◆◆◆◆◆◆ Davis's family—at least one hundred
years old. The cookies have an unusual consistency and an excellent flavor.

2 cups sugar, plus more
   for dusting cookies

1½ cups vegetable
   shortening

4 eggs

1 teaspoon vanilla extract

4½ cups all-purpose flour

1 teaspoon baking powder

1 cup buttermilk mixed
   with 1 teaspoon baking
   soda

Makes about 3 dozen.

Cream together the 2 cups sugar, shortening, and eggs. Add the vanilla.

Mix the flour and baking powder together. Beginning with the flour mixture, add the flour and buttermilk alternately to the sugar mixture, ending with the flour mixture.

Preheat oven to 350° F.

Lightly flour a cookie sheet and drop batter from a soup spoon onto it. Dust the cookies lightly with sugar. Bake for 10 to 12 minutes, until lightly browned. Remove from pan and cool on a rack.

SHORTBREAD COOKIES

◆◆◆◆◆◆◆◆◆◆◆◆◆◆◆◆◆◆◆◆◆◆◆◆◆

Dianne Pawlik   High Level, Alberta This not-too-sweet shortbread
◆◆◆◆◆◆◆◆◆◆◆◆◆◆◆◆◆◆◆◆◆◆◆◆◆ makes lovely fragile cookies. The
recipe comes from Mrs. Pawlik's mother and is one of the easiest to make
we've encountered.

1 cup butter

1 cup all-purpose flour

½ cup cornstarch

*½ cup confectioner's
sugar*

*5–6 drops food coloring
(optional, for
decoration)*

*2 tablespoons granulated
sugar (optional, for
decoration)*

Makes 12 large cookies.

Beat the butter until light and fluffy. Measure the flour by stirring with a spoon, then very lightly lifting it into the measuring cup by spoonfuls. Shake the cornstarch into its measuring cup and spoon the confectioner's sugar in the same way as the flour. Sift these dry ingredients together into the butter and mix with a wooden spoon.

Preheat oven to 300° F.

Flour your hands and make small ¾-inch balls of dough. Place these on an ungreased cookie sheet and press with the tines of a fork.

Add decorations if desired:

Shake the food coloring—red or green or 2 batches, 1 color each—over the sugar in a small bowl. Work into all sugar grains, using a fork or spoon. Shake bits of the sugar onto the cookies before baking.

Bake for 20 to 25 minutes, until lightly colored. Remove from pan and cool on a rack.

KERRI'S ALMOND COOKIES

◆◆◆◆◆◆◆◆◆◆◆◆◆◆◆◆◆◆◆◆◆◆◆◆

M. Hintsa   Edmonton, Alberta These really delicious almond cookies
◆◆◆◆◆◆◆◆◆◆◆◆◆◆◆◆◆◆◆◆◆◆ are old-fashioned—the sort that friends
begin to hint for once the Christmas season is in sight.

1 cup butter
½ cup granulated sugar
½ cup light brown sugar
1 egg
1 teaspoon almond extract
2 cups all-purpose flour
¾ cup ground almonds
1 teaspoon baking soda

Makes 4 dozen.

Preheat the oven to 350° F. Butter a cookie sheet and set aside.

Cream the butter and sugars together. Add the egg and beat well. Add the almond extract and beat well.

Combine the flour, ground almonds, and baking soda. Add in 3 additions to the butter mixture, beating well after each addition.

Mold teaspoonfuls of the dough into balls and drop onto the prepared cookie sheet. Make indentations in each with your thumb. Bake until the edges of the cookies are barely light brown, about 8 to 10 minutes. Remove from the pan and cool on a rack.

CHEESECAKE COOKIES

◆◆◆◆◆◆◆◆◆◆◆◆◆◆◆◆◆◆◆◆◆◆◆◆◆◆◆◆◆

Sharon West DaRe   Lansing, Ohio These cheesecake squares are very
◆◆◆◆◆◆◆◆◆◆◆◆◆◆◆◆◆◆◆◆◆◆◆◆◆◆◆ good, and even better the second
day, if you can wait that long. They also freeze successfully.

1 cup all-purpose flour

5 tablespoons butter,
   softened to room
   temperature

⅓ cup firmly packed light
   brown sugar

½ cup chopped nuts
   (walnuts, pecans, or
   almonds)

1 (8-ounce) package
   cream cheese

¼ cup granulated sugar

1 egg

2 tablespoons milk

2 tablespoons freshly
   squeezed lemon juice

½ teaspoon vanilla extract

Makes 16 squares.

Preheat oven to 350° F.

Combine the flour, butter, and brown sugar. Blend until particles are fine. Stir in the nuts. Reserve 1 cup of the mixture for topping.

Press the remaining mixture into an ungreased 8-inch-square cake pan. Bake for 12 to 15 minutes, until lightly brown.

In the same mixing bowl, combine the remaining ingredients. Blend well, and spread on the crust. Sprinkle with the reserved crumbs. Bake for 25 to 30 minutes. Cool and cut into squares.

APRICOT BUTTER BARS

◆◆◆◆◆◆◆◆◆◆◆◆◆◆◆◆◆◆◆◆◆◆◆◆

Madelyn Miller   Dallas, Texas

◆◆◆◆◆◆◆◆◆◆◆◆◆◆◆◆◆◆◆◆◆◆◆◆

These sweet, nutty bars are moist and cakelike in texture, with the tang of apricots. Very good.

1 cup dried apricots

8 tablespoons unsalted butter, softened to room temperature

1¼ cups firmly packed light brown sugar

1⅓ cups all-purpose flour, sifted

½ teaspoon baking powder

¼ teaspoon salt

2 eggs

½ teaspoon vanilla extract

½ cup walnuts coarsely chopped

Makes 2 dozen.

Preheat oven to 350° F. Butter a 9-inch-square cake pan.

Rinse the apricots; place them in a saucepan and cover with cold water. Bring to a boil and simmer for 10 minutes. Drain; cool and chop into ¼-inch pieces.

Cut the butter into ¼ cup of the brown sugar and 1 cup of the flour until a crumbly mixture is formed. Press the mixture into the bottom of the pan, and bake 25 minutes, or until golden.

Meanwhile, sift remaining ⅓ cup flour with baking powder and salt. Beat the eggs until well blended. Beat in the remaining 1 cup brown sugar and then the flour mixture until well blended.

Add the vanilla, chopped nuts, and apricots. Evenly spread the apricot-nut mixture over the baked layer and continue to bake 30 minutes. Cool in the pan and cut into squares or bars.

MOLASSES SUGAR COOKIES

◆◆◆◆◆◆◆◆◆◆◆◆◆◆◆◆◆◆◆◆◆◆◆◆◆◆◆◆◆◆◆◆

Marguerite Buderus   Kingwood, Texas   An excellent cookie of a much
◆◆◆◆◆◆◆◆◆◆◆◆◆◆◆◆◆◆◆◆◆◆◆◆◆◆◆◆◆◆◆ adored sort—these have a
soft center with a crunchy exterior, and they're a lot easier than pie to make.

¾ *cup butter or
  shortening*

*1 cup sugar, plus more
  for rolling cookies*

¼ *cup molasses*

1 egg

*1 cup all-purpose flour,
  sifted*

2 teaspoons baking soda

1 teaspoon cinnamon

½ *teaspoon ground cloves*

½ *teaspoon ground ginger*

½ *teaspoon salt*

Makes 2 dozen.

Grease 2 cookie sheets and set aside.
Cream the butter or shortening and the 1 cup sugar.
Add the molasses and egg, and beat well.

Sift together the flour, baking soda, cinnamon, cloves, ginger, and salt. Add to the shortening-sugar mixture.

Mix all ingredients together well. Chill for at least 1 hour.

Preheat oven to 375° F.

Form the dough into 1-inch balls, roll in sugar, and place on the prepared cookie sheets, 2 inches apart.

Bake for 8 to 10 minutes. Remove from pan and cool on a rack.

PECAN TARTS

◆◆◆◆◆◆◆◆◆◆◆◆◆◆◆◆◆◆◆◆◆◆◆◆◆◆◆◆◆◆◆◆◆◆◆◆◆◆

Katherine Brower   Colonial Heights, Virginia   These absolutely de-
◆◆◆◆◆◆◆◆◆◆◆◆◆◆◆◆◆◆◆◆◆◆◆◆◆◆◆◆◆◆◆◆◆◆ licious tarts make
very attractive mini-treats, but they won't be around long even though this
recipe makes about 72 of them.

*1 cup butter, softened to
    room temperature*

*1 (8-ounce) package
    cream cheese, softened
    to room temperature*

2 cups all-purpose flour

*4 tablespoons butter,
    melted*

*1 (1-pound) package light
    brown sugar*

*3 large eggs, beaten until
    frothy*

*72 pecan halves (about 1
    pound)*

*Makes about 72 mini-
    tarts.*

In a large mixing bowl, combine the butter and cream
cheese. Blend well. Add the flour and stir until mixture
holds together. Cover and refrigerate for at least 30
minutes.

Form pastry into small balls about 1 inch in diameter. Press
into mini-muffin pans.

In a mixing bowl, combine the melted butter, brown sugar,
and beaten eggs. Mix with a fork until well blended.

Preheat oven to 350° F.

Spoon the filling into the pastry-lined pans, filling each hole
about half full. Top each mini-tart with a pecan half.

Bake for 20 to 25 minutes, or until filling is set and pastry
is light brown. Remove from pans and cool on cake racks.

KIFFLINS

◆◆◆◆◆◆◆◆◆◆◆◆◆◆◆◆◆◆◆◆◆◆◆◆◆

Katie Maxwell   Houston, Texas This delicious recipe, which originated
◆◆◆◆◆◆◆◆◆◆◆◆◆◆◆◆◆◆◆◆◆◆◆◆◆ in Germany, has been handed down in
Katie Maxwell's family for many generations. It had always been kept a family
secret until she got it—but she feels it's too good not to share.

2 cups butter

1 cup granulated sugar

2 cups pecans, grated (not
chopped) in food
processor

1 tablespoon vanilla
extract

4 cups all-purpose flour

Confectioner's sugar

1 vanilla bean, pounded
with a mortar and
pestle

**Makes 5 dozen small
crescents.**

Preheat oven to 300° F.

Cream the butter and sugar. Add the pecans and vanilla
extract. Add the flour until you can shape the cookies
into crescents, being careful not to add too much flour. Form
the dough into small crescents, about 2 inches long.

Place the crescents on a cookie sheet covered with aluminum
foil. Bake 10 to 12 minutes, but watch carefully, as the
cookies burn easily.

Cool on a rack, then roll the crescents in a mixture of the
confectioner's sugar and pounded vanilla bean. The cookies
keep very well in tins.

OLD ENGLISH ALMOND TARTS

◆◆◆◆◆◆◆◆◆◆◆◆◆◆◆◆◆◆◆◆◆◆◆◆◆◆◆◆

Joyce Sykes   Tulsa, Oklahoma   These excellent tarts go very well with
◆◆◆◆◆◆◆◆◆◆◆◆◆◆◆◆◆◆◆◆◆◆◆◆   tea or coffee. The recipe is from an
English flour manufacturer's cookbook.

1 teaspoon salt

2½ cups all-purpose flour

1 cup butter

*5 tablespoons ice water
     mixed with 2 teaspoons
     white vinegar*

¼ cup sugar

¼ cup ground almonds

1 egg, beaten

Raspberry jam

Makes 12 to 14.

Preheat oven to 425° F.

In a bowl, mix the salt with the flour. Cut the butter into the flour, sprinkle ice water mixture over, and mix, handling as little as possible.

Mix together the sugar, almonds, and part of the egg, just enough to make a soft paste.

Roll the pastry dough thin and cut into 3-inch circles with a fluted tart cutter or with any round tart cutter. Place the pastry rounds in tart tins or muffin pans.

Put ⅓ teaspoon jam in each pastry and add 1 teaspoon of the almond mixture. Cut thin strips of pastry and lattice across the tops of the tarts.

Bake the tarts for 15 to 20 minutes. Allow to cool in pans before serving.

ICEBOX COOKIES

◆◆◆◆◆◆◆◆◆◆◆◆◆◆◆◆◆◆◆◆◆◆◆◆◆

Nini Guidotti   Soledad, California   Nini Guidotti has been making these
◆◆◆◆◆◆◆◆◆◆◆◆◆◆◆◆◆◆◆◆◆◆◆◆◆   cookies since 1944, when she learned
how to bake them in her high school home ec. class. They're crisp and tasty,
and the recipe makes more than 100 cookies.

1½ cups butter

1 cup granulated sugar

1 cup dark brown sugar

3 eggs, slightly beaten

4½ cups all-purpose flour

2 teaspoons baking soda

1 teaspoon salt

1 teaspoon cinnamon

1 teaspoon ground cloves

*1 cup finely chopped
   walnuts*

Makes about 120 to 150.

Cream the butter and sugars well and add the eggs. Mix well. Add the flour, baking soda, salt, spices, and nuts. Mix well and form into rolls 1½ to 1¾ inches in diameter. Set the dough in the refrigerator for 24 hours, wrapped well in wax paper.

Preheat oven to 350° F. Grease 2 cookie sheets.

Slice the cookie dough ⅛ inch thick and place on the sheets. Bake for about 12 minutes, or until crisp. Remove from the pans and cool on a rack.

CHOCOLATE HALF-MOONS

◆◆◆◆◆◆◆◆◆◆◆◆◆◆◆◆◆◆◆◆◆◆◆◆◆

Anna Perina Riviera, Arizona These very unusual cookies have an
◆◆◆◆◆◆◆◆◆◆◆◆◆◆◆◆◆◆◆◆◆◆ unusual history. Anna Perina's mother
came from Czechoslovakia, and when she was a girl she learned baking at the
Archbishop's Castle, where the chef was the former cook for Emperor Franz
Josef. This is her favorite recipe from those days.

COOKIES

*4 large eggs, separated, at
room temperature*

*12 tablespoons unsalted
butter, softened to room
temperature*

*6 ounces confectioner's
sugar*

1 teaspoon vanilla extract

Grated zest of ½ lemon

*6 ounces bittersweet
chocolate, melted*

*1½ cups all-purpose flour,
sifted*

ICING

Juice of ½ lemon

1 egg white

*2 cups sifted confectioner's
sugar (more if needed)*

Makes 4 dozen.

Preheat oven to 350° F. Butter and flour a cookie sheet with sides at least ½ inch high.

Beat the egg whites to stiff peaks and set aside.

Beat the butter, egg yolks, sugar, vanilla, and lemon zest until fluffy and doubled. Add the chocolate and mix until it is well incorporated into the batter. Add the egg whites and the flour and fold in gently.

Spread the batter onto the cookie sheet evenly and bake for 20 minutes, until it is light brown on top and the edges begin to pull away from the pan. If a toothpick inserted in the center of the pan comes out clean, the cookies are ready.

Take the pan out of the oven, cover with tea towels for 10 minutes, and meanwhile prepare the icing.

Beat all icing ingredients in a small bowl until smooth and spreadable—you may need more sugar. Spread the icing on the cookie dough, let dry, and with a cookie cutter cut half-moons.

These cookies freeze well.

LIZZIES

◆◆◆◆◆◆◆◆◆◆◆◆◆◆◆◆◆◆◆◆◆◆◆

Barbara Rowe   Pollok, Texas An excellent cookie, reminiscent of fruit-
◆◆◆◆◆◆◆◆◆◆◆◆◆◆◆◆◆◆◆◆◆◆◆ cake but with a rich chewy consistency.
Barbara Rowe got the recipe many years ago from an elderly friend. Lizzies
are extremely colorful and would make especially good gifts.

1 pound golden raisins

1 pint whiskey

1 cup dark brown sugar,
    packed

8 tablespoons butter,
    softened to room
    temperature

4 eggs

3 cups all-purpose flour,
    sifted

1 teaspoon baking soda

1/2 teaspoon nutmeg,
    preferably freshly grated

1/2 teaspoon ground cloves

1 pound candied cherries,
    halved

1 1/2 pounds candied
    pineapple, cut into 1/4-
    inch pieces

2 pounds pecans, coarsely
    chopped

3 tablespoons buttermilk

1 teaspoon vanilla extract

Makes about 300.

S oak the raisins in the whiskey overnight.

Preheat oven to 350° F. Butter 2 cookie sheets and
set aside.

Cream together the brown sugar and butter. Gradually beat
in the eggs, 1 at a time.

Sift together 2¾ cups of the flour, the baking soda, nutmeg,
and cloves, and add to the egg mixture. Mix well.

By hand, add the raisins and whiskey. Mix well. Toss the
cherries with the remaining ¼ cup flour. Add the fruits, nuts,
buttermilk, and vanilla. Mix well.

Drop the mixture by generous teaspoonfuls onto the prepared
cookie sheets, leaving 1 inch between the cookies. Bake for
20 minutes, remove from the oven, and cool on racks.

AUER "FAMILY SECRET" SUGAR COOKIES

◆◆◆◆◆◆◆◆◆◆◆◆◆◆◆◆◆◆◆◆◆◆◆◆

Denise Auer   Wichita, Kansas Lovely sugar cookies—of all the recipes
◆◆◆◆◆◆◆◆◆◆◆◆◆◆◆◆◆◆◆◆◆◆◆◆ we received, we had the most submissions of sugar cookies, which seem to be particularly beloved. This previously secret recipe is one of the best.

1½ cups all-purpose flour
½ teaspoon baking powder
½ teaspoon baking soda
½ teaspoon salt
8 tablespoons butter
½ cup sugar
1 egg
2 tablespoons milk
1 teaspoon lemon extract
Makes 1½ dozen.

Sift together the flour, baking powder, baking soda, and salt. Cream together the butter and sugar; mix in the egg. Add the dry ingredients alternately with the milk and lemon extract. Blend well. Chill the dough overnight in a flattened rectangle, wrapped in plastic wrap.

Preheat oven to 400° F. Butter a cookie sheet and set aside.

On a floured surface, roll the dough out to ⅝ inch thick. Cut with cookie cutters.

Transfer the cookies to the prepared cookie sheet and bake 7 to 10 minutes, or until lightly colored. Remove the cookies from the pan and let them cool on a rack.

AUNT IRENE'S COOKIES

◆◆◆◆◆◆◆◆◆◆◆◆◆◆◆◆◆◆◆◆◆◆◆◆◆◆◆◆◆◆

Betsey Crampe   Charlotte, North Carolina These especially delicious cookies are a little
◆◆◆◆◆◆◆◆◆◆◆◆◆◆◆◆◆◆◆◆◆◆◆◆◆◆◆
difficult to make—not for the inexperienced baker, but well worth the trouble.

2 envelopes active dry
   yeast

6 tablespoons milk, heated
   to warm, plus ⅓ cup
   for glaze

5 cups all-purpose flour

5 eggs, beaten, plus 1
   more for glaze

½ teaspoon salt

2 cups butter, melted

1 jar apricot preserves or
   baker's filling (apricot
   or nut)

Makes 7 dozen.

Mix the yeast with the 6 tablespoons warm milk and set aside.

Combine half of the flour and half of the beaten eggs, salt, and melted butter. Mix well. Add the proven yeast.

Combine the other half of the flour and the other half of the beaten eggs, salt, and butter. Mix well. Form both mixtures into 1 ball, and wrap in plastic wrap.

Chill the dough at least 4 hours.

Preheat oven to 350° F.

To roll out, divide dough into quarters. Sprinkle the work surface with flour and sugar. Roll out dough ⅜ inch thick and divide into 3-inch squares. Drop a teaspoon of apricot preserves or prepared filling on one corner. Roll from the corner to the opposite corner.

Mix the remaining egg and ⅓ cup milk to make a glaze. Brush the glaze over the rolled cookies.

Grease 2 cookie sheets and place cookies on them. Bake for 15 to 17 minutes, or until golden. Remove to racks for cooling.

Thanksgiving and Christmas

GREEN TOMATO MINCEMEAT

◆◆◆◆◆◆◆◆◆◆◆◆◆◆◆◆◆◆◆◆◆◆◆◆◆◆

Gene L. Cain   Fairfax, Vermont A rich, unusual chutney-like mince-
◆◆◆◆◆◆◆◆◆◆◆◆◆◆◆◆◆◆◆◆◆◆◆◆ meat from a very old family recipe.
The original specifies lard; the family uses margarine; we suggest butter.

*3 cups green tomatoes,
    washed and chopped*

*3 cups apples, peeled,
    cored, and chopped*

*2 cups dark brown sugar,
    firmly packed*

*½ cup white vinegar or
    juice from sweet pickles*

½ teaspoon cinnamon

¼ teaspoon ground cloves

*¼ teaspoon nutmeg,
    preferably freshly grated*

¼ teaspoon salt

1½ cups seedless raisins

*¼ cup lard, margarine,
    or butter*

**Makes enough mincement
    for 1 (8- or 9-inch) pie.**

Place the tomatoes in a colander to drain. Discard the juice.

In a large saucepan, combine the tomatoes and apples with the brown sugar and vinegar. Stir well, and heat slowly to the boiling point, stirring often. Add the spices and salt.

Reduce heat and simmer 2 to 3 hours, until mixture thickens, adding raisins after 1½ hours.

Stir in the shortening and remove from the heat. Allow to cool before using as a pie filling. Keeps well either canned or frozen.*

Note: A few drops of brandy added just before baking will enhance the flavor.

*See page 294 for instructions on standard canning procedures.

UNCOOKED MINCEMEAT

◆◆◆

Margaret McCain Florenceville, New Brunswick A particularly
◆◆◆◆◆◆◆◆◆◆◆◆◆◆◆◆◆◆◆◆◆◆◆◆◆◆◆◆◆◆◆◆◆◆◆◆◆◆◆ delicious easy
recipe that has been in Mrs. McCain's family for more than two hundred years.

1 pound ground beef

1 pound ground suet

1 pound seedless raisins

2 pounds muscat raisins,
  seeded

2½ pounds brown sugar

5 pounds apples, peeled,
  cored, and chopped

Juice of 3 oranges

Juice of 2 lemons

Grated zest of 2 oranges

Grated zest of 1 lemon

1 tablespoon salt

3 teaspoons cinnamon

3 teaspoons nutmeg,
  preferably freshly grated

1 teaspoon ground cloves

¾–1 cup apricot brandy
  (optional)

½ cup strawberry jam
  (optional)

*Makes enough mincemeat
for 2 (8- or 9-inch)
pies.*

Mix together all ingredients except the brandy and jam. Add the brandy, if desired; this will keep the mincemeat up to 6 months in the refrigerator; without brandy, the mincemeat should be used within the week or processed, in which case it will keep indefinitely.* There will be enough mincement for 2 double-crust pies.

To bake: Before putting the top crust on the pie, spread the mincemeat with the strawberry jam, if you wish. Bake pies at 425° F. for 10 minutes, then lower heat to 375° F. and bake 40 minutes.

*See note on page 294 for instructions on processing mincemeat.

PUMPKIN CHUNK PIE

◆◆◆◆◆◆◆◆◆◆◆◆◆◆◆◆◆◆◆◆◆◆◆◆◆◆◆◆◆◆◆◆◆

Catherine Oettinger Port Jefferson, New York The chunky tex-
◆◆◆◆◆◆◆◆◆◆◆◆◆◆◆◆◆◆◆◆◆◆◆◆◆◆◆◆◆◆ ture of this pie is a
pleasant surprise. It was a nice earthy spiciness, and it stands up very well to
vanilla or cinnamon ice cream.

1 (4½-pound) sugar
  pumpkin or 5 cups
  pumpkin cubes

⅔ cup golden raisins

¾–1 cup dark brown
  sugar, to taste

3 tablespoons flour

2 teaspoons freshly
  squeezed lemon juice

½ teaspoon ground ginger

¼ teaspoon nutmeg,
  preferably freshly grated

¼ teaspoon ground cloves

1 (9-inch) unbaked pie
  shell

1 (9-inch) unbaked top
  crust

1 egg beaten with ⅓ cup
  milk for egg wash
  (optional)

Serves 8 to 10.

Cut the pumpkin in half and remove the seeds. Cut each half into ¾-inch strips. Peel the strips and cut into cubes the size of caramels. You will need 5 cups; plan on at least 45 minutes to prepare pumpkin.

Preheat oven to 350° F.

Combine all ingredients except pastry and mix thoroughly until blended. (If you like a less sweet pie, use ¾ cup brown sugar instead of 1 cup.) Pour the pumpkin into the pie shell and cover with the top crust. Slash steam holes into top crust—a cut-out Halloween face works well—and brush with an egg wash, if desired.

Bake for 1 hour, or until pumpkin is tender—test it through the steam holes.

FRESH PUMPKIN PIE

◆◆◆◆◆◆◆◆◆◆◆◆◆◆◆◆◆◆◆◆◆◆◆◆◆◆◆◆◆◆

Linda Cantoni   Brooklyn, New York This creamy, spicy pie has a
◆◆◆◆◆◆◆◆◆◆◆◆◆◆◆◆◆◆◆◆◆◆◆◆◆◆◆◆ wonderful depth of flavor. It's
definitely worth the trouble to use fresh pumpkin—but it does take a long time,
more than an hour. If you must substitute, use frozen pumpkin squash rather
than the canned pumpkin, which has very little flavor.

This pie looks particularly appealing covered with rosettes of whipped cream.

*1 tablespoon all-purpose
 flour*

¾ cup sugar

½ teaspoon salt

1 teaspoon cinnamon

1 teaspoon ground allspice

1 teaspoon ground ginger

*¼ cup unsulfured
 molasses*

2 cups cooked pumpkin

3 eggs, beaten

1 cup evaporated milk

*1 (10-inch) deep-dish pie
 shell*

Serves 8 to 10.

Choose a firm 3–4-pound pumpkin. Peel, seed, and remove fibers. Cut the pumpkin into 1½-inch chunks and place in a saucepan with 2 inches of water. Cover and bring to a boil. Lower heat and simmer 20 minutes, or until tender.

Remove cover and cook briefly, shaking the pan, until pumpkin is dry. Puree in a blender or food processor. The puree will keep in the refrigerator for 1 week or in the freezer for 3 months.

Preheat oven to 400° F.

Combine the flour, sugar, salt, and spices. Add the molasses—be sure to measure correctly, since it's easy to spill it over, and too much is overwhelming—and pumpkin, mixing well. Add the eggs and milk and mix well. Pour into the crust. Place the pie on a foil-lined cookie sheet and bake 40 minutes, or until center is set.

Cool, then chill until ready to serve.

CRANBERRY PECAN PIE

◆◆◆◆◆◆◆◆◆◆◆◆◆◆◆◆◆◆◆◆◆◆◆◆◆◆◆◆◆◆

Virginia Stalder   Nokesville, Virginia   A truly unusual pie, perfect for
◆◆◆◆◆◆◆◆◆◆◆◆◆◆◆◆◆◆◆◆◆◆◆◆◆◆◆◆◆ the winter holidays. Cranberries peep through the crisp pecan topping, and their tartness cuts the richness of the traditional pecan pie. This pie also looks gorgeous.

3 eggs

1 cup dark corn syrup

⅔ cup sugar

4 tablespoons butter, melted

⅛ teaspoon salt

1 cup fresh cranberries, chopped

1 (9-inch) unbaked pie shell

1 cup pecan halves

Serves 8.

Preheat oven to 325° F.

In a large bowl, beat the eggs with a fork just until blended. Stir in the corn syrup, sugar, butter, and salt.

Sprinkle the cranberries in the pastry shell. Arrange the pecan halves on top of the cranberries. Pour the syrup mixture carefully over the pecans.

Bake for 50 to 55 minutes, or until a knife inserted halfway between the center and the edge of the pie comes out clean. Cool on a rack before serving.

If the edge of the pie seems to be browning too quickly, cover it with a strip of foil.

PUMPKIN PIE

Priscilla Van de Workeen Dudley, Massachusetts This knockout of a pie comes from Mrs. Van de Workeen's husband's great-grandmother. If you can't use the real thing, use frozen pumpkin squash, *not* canned pumpkin.

1 cup flour

¼ teaspoon sugar

1 teaspoon grated lemon
    or orange zest

8 tablespoons butter

1 egg yolk, lightly beaten

¼ teaspoon vanilla extract

FILLING

3 cups pumpkin puree (see
    page 197)

2 eggs plus 1 egg white,
    beaten

¼ cup molasses

1¼ teaspoons vegetable oil

11 ounces evaporated milk

2 tablespoons cornstarch

1½ teaspoons cinnamon

1½ teaspoons ground
    ginger

1 teaspoon nutmeg,
    preferably freshly grated

¼ teaspoon ground cloves

1 cup sugar

Cinnamon whipped cream
    (optional, for garnish)

Serves 8.

Have ready a 9-inch springform pan. Preheat oven to 400° F.

Combine the flour, sugar, and citrus zest. Cut in the butter until the mixture is crumbly. Add the egg yolk and vanilla and mix.

Pat a third of the dough over the bottom of the pan (with side removed). Bake about 6 minutes, or until golden. Cool.

Attach side to bottom of pan. Pat the remaining dough around side of pan to height of about 1¾ inches.

Preheat oven to 425° F. Combine all filling ingredients until smooth and well blended. Pour into the prepared crust and bake for 10 minutes; then lower heat to 350° F. for 50 minutes, or until pie is firm and set.

Serve on a plate garnished with a rosette of cinnamon whipped cream, if you wish.

Note: Mrs. Van de Workeen's favorite pumpkin for this pie is the small sugar pumpkin, very fleshy and aromatic. She freezes the puree in 3-cup batches at harvest time. A 4-pound pumpkin will produce 3 cups of puree.

WHITE CHRISTMAS PIE

Joanie Lingle Fairview, Oregon This unusual recipe involves a little extra work—but its flavor is exceptional and it's very pretty. We decorated it with red and green candied cherries, and it looked beautifully festive.

1 envelope unflavored gelatin

4 tablespoons all-purpose flour

1 cup sugar

½ teaspoon salt

1½ cups milk

¾ teaspoon vanilla extract

¼ teaspoon almond extract

½ cup heavy cream, whipped to peaks

3 large egg whites, at room temperature

¼ teaspoon cream of tartar

1½ cups moist shredded coconut

1 (9-inch) baked pie shell

Candied cherries (optional)

Serves 8.

Soften the gelatin in ¼ cup cold water and set aside.

Mix together the flour, ½ cup of the sugar, and the salt in a medium saucepan. Stir in the milk gradually. Bring to a boil over medium-low heat, stirring constantly to prevent scorching. Boil for 1 minute. Remove from the heat and stir in the gelatin. Stir until dissolved. Set aside to cool.

When the mixture is partially set, beat with a rotary beater until smooth. Blend in the vanilla and almond extracts. Gently fold in the whipped cream.

In a medium mixing bowl, beat the egg whites and cream of tartar until frothy. Gradually beat in the remaining ½ cup sugar until the mixture is stiff and glossy. Fold into filling mixture. Fold in 1 cup of the coconut.

Pile the filling into the cooled baked pie shell. Sprinkle the remaining ½ cup coconut over the top. Chill for at least 2 hours to set. Take pie out of refrigerator 20 minutes before serving. Decorate with candied cherries, if desired.

GRANDMOTHER COX'S CHRISTMAS CAKE

◆◆◆◆◆◆◆◆◆◆◆◆◆◆◆◆◆◆◆◆◆◆◆◆

Norma Duer   Fletcher, Ohio   A very old recipe from Mrs. Duer's hus-
◆◆◆◆◆◆◆◆◆◆◆◆◆◆◆◆◆◆◆◆◆   band's great-grandmother. It's an old-fashioned, wonderfully satisfying cake that's a refreshing change from the usual
fruitcake.

¾ cup butter

2 cups sugar

3 eggs, separated, at room
    temperature

3 cups plus 1 tablespoon
    all-purpose flour

3 teaspoons baking
    powder

½ teaspoon salt

1 cup milk

1 cup raisins

½ cup currants

1 teaspoon cinnamon

½ teaspoon ground cloves

1 teaspoon nutmeg,
    preferably freshly grated

1 tablespoon molasses

*Makes 1 (9-inch) layer
    cake; serves 8 to 10.*

Preheat oven to 350° F. Grease 3 (9-inch) cake pans. Cream the butter and sugar. Add the egg yolks.

Sift the 3 cups flour with the baking powder and salt. Add the flour mixture and milk to the batter alternately.

Beat the egg whites to stiff peaks and fold into the batter. In a bowl, toss the dried fruit with the remaining tablespoon flour. Remove a third of the batter and mix it with the fruit, adding the spices and molasses. Pour into 1 cake pan.

Divide the remaining batter between the 2 remaining cake pans and bake all 3 for 30 minutes.

To assemble the cooled layers, stack the fruited layer in the middle and frost with your favorite white icing. (Mrs. Duer specifies Seven Minute Icing.)

YULE LOG

◆◆◆◆◆◆◆◆◆◆◆◆◆◆◆◆◆◆◆◆◆◆◆◆◆◆◆◆◆

Muriel Watson Hamersville, Ohio A truly stunning dessert, this is
◆◆◆◆◆◆◆◆◆◆◆◆◆◆◆◆◆◆◆◆◆◆◆◆ both gorgeous—the centerpiece of
any Christmas dinner—and perfectly delicious. Be warned, however: it's a
labor-intensive project requiring several hours of concentrated work, well
rewarded though it is.

LOG

*4 eggs, separated, at room
    temperature*

¾ cup sugar

¾ cup all-purpose flour

½ teaspoon baking powder

ICING

*2 cups unsalted butter,
    cut into pieces*

*1 (1-pound) package
    confectioner's sugar,
    sifted*

*2 egg yolks (reserve egg
    whites for meringue)*

*3 heaping teaspoons
    granulated instant
    coffee*

*4 ounces unsweetened
    chocolate, chopped*

CAKE SYRUP

1 cup sugar

*½ cup rum, whiskey, or
    Cognac*

Preheat oven to 350° F. Generously butter the sides and
bottom of a 12 × 18-inch sheet pan.

Beat the egg whites until stiff but not dry. Set aside.

Beat together the sugar and egg yolks until light lemon in
color.

Sift the flour together with the baking powder and add to
egg mixture. Beat about 2 minutes. Remove from mixer and
carefully fold in the beaten egg whites.

Pour the mixture into the prepared sheet pan and smooth
out with a spatula to an even thickness over entire pan.

Bake for 15 to 20 minutes, or until a toothpick inserted in
the center comes out dry.

On the work surface, spread out a long piece of aluminum
foil slightly longer than the sheet pan. Put a damp tea towel
over the aluminum foil. Immediately turn the cake upside
down onto the foil and carefully remove the pan. Quickly roll
up the cake from a long side into a moderately tight jelly roll.

Let the log cool while preparing icing.

Cream the butter until soft. Add the confectioner's sugar, a
little at a time, until well incorporated (the entire package
may not be required). Continue beating until quite smooth,
about 2 minutes.

HOLLY LEAVES AND BERRIES

½ (1-pound) package confectioner's sugar, sifted

2 tablespoons milk, heated

½ teaspoon lemon extract

Green and red food coloring

MERINGUE MUSHROOMS

2 egg whites, reserved from the icing, at room temperature

6 tablespoons sugar

2 tablespoons cocoa powder

4 tablespoons reserved chocolate icing

Serves 12.

Add the egg yolks and beat 1 minute. Scrape down and beat another minute. Divide mixture in half, using 2 mixing bowls.

For mocha icing, dissolve the instant coffee in ¼ cup boiling water. Let cool. Add to half the icing mixture and mix well.

For chocolate icing, melt the chocolate in a double boiler over medium-low heat, or in a saucepan in a preheated 200° F. oven for 25 minutes. Let cool to room temperature and combine with remaining icing. Set both icings aside in a cool place while preparing cake syrup. Do not place in refrigerator or icing will become too hard to spread.

In a saucepan, combine the sugar and 1 cup cold water. Bring to a boil and cook over high heat for about 2 minutes. Remove from heat, cool slightly, and add the liquor.

To assemble the yule log: Carefully unroll the cake and generously brush the cake syrup over the entire inside area— use ⅓ to ½ cup syrup, depending on dryness of cake.

With a pastry spatula, spread mocha icing over entire inside area about ⅛ inch thick. Reroll cake and spread chocolate icing over entire outside area, making sure to cover the bottom and sides. Reserve 4 tablespoons of chocolate icing for meringue shell assembly.

With a fork, create a rough bark-grain texture over surface of log.

Cover lightly with plastic wrap and freeze for about 2 hours before serving. Just before serving, lightly dust with confectioner's sugar and decorate with holly leaves and berries and meringue mushrooms.

Mix the sugar, hot milk, and lemon extract together, beating slowly, until well incorporated, about 2 minutes.
(Continued on next page.)

(Continued from previous page.)

Divide the mixture into 1 large batch—about three quarters of the mixture—and 1 small batch.

Mix the large batch with about 2 to 3 drops of green food coloring and combine well.

Mix the small batch with 1 drop of red food coloring and combine well.

With a rolling pin, roll out the green sugar dough on a board to ⅛ inch thick. Cut out holly leaves with a pointed paring knife.

Roll out holly berries from the red dough by making little balls between the fingers and palms of your hands. Assemble the berries next to the holly leaves and place on the top and sides of the yule log.

Beat the egg whites to soft peaks. Slowly add the sugar by tablespoonfuls, taking about 5 minutes. Place the meringue mixture in a pastry bag fitted with a ½-inch-wide tip.

Preheat the oven to 225° F.

Line a 12 × 18-inch sheet pan with parchment paper or grease with a generous amount of butter.

Holding the pastry bag at a 90° angle, pipe out 10 wide, slightly rounded mushroom caps about 1 inch in diameter.

At the same angle, pipe out 10 tapered mushroom stems about 1 inch high and ¼ inch thick.

Bake for 30 minutes; they should be dry and white. Sprinkle cocoa powder on the mushrooms. Attach the stems with a little chocolate icing and arrange around log.

CRANBERRY APPLE CRUNCH

◆◆◆◆◆◆◆◆◆◆◆◆◆◆◆◆◆◆◆◆◆◆◆◆◆◆◆◆◆◆◆◆

Cathy Power   Medfield, Massachusetts This especially delicious rec-
◆◆◆◆◆◆◆◆◆◆◆◆◆◆◆◆◆◆◆◆◆◆◆◆◆◆◆◆ ipe seems to turn up at almost
any meal. Cathy Power's family loves it with turkey, chicken, pork, and pot
roast; they also eat it at brunch. We thought it was perfect as a dessert, served
with the Old-fashioned Christmas Custard on page 221. In any case, it's certainly
very good and easy to make.

3 cups peeled and cored
apples, in bite-size
pieces

2 cups whole cranberries,
washed and picked over

½ cup raisins

½ cup granulated sugar

1½ cups uncooked quick
oats

½ cup firmly packed dark
brown sugar

1 teaspoon cinnamon

¼ teaspoon nutmeg,
preferably freshly grated

⅓ cup all-purpose flour

⅓ cup chopped pecans or
walnuts

8 tablespoons butter,
melted

Serves 8.

Preheat oven to 300° F. Butter a 2-quart casserole and
set aside.

Combine the apples, cranberries, raisins, and granulated
sugar. Mix well and pour into the casserole. Smooth out to
an even thickness.

Mix together the oats, brown sugar, cinnamon, nutmeg,
flour, nuts, and butter. Combine well and spread evenly over
cranberry-apple mixture.

Bake uncovered for 1 hour, or until bubbly and slightly
browned.

HOLIDAY FRUITCAKE

◆◆◆◆◆◆◆◆◆◆◆◆◆◆◆◆◆◆◆◆◆◆◆◆◆◆◆◆◆◆◆◆◆◆◆

Adah M. Dingeldine   Waukesha, Wisconsin A superb fruitcake that's
◆◆◆◆◆◆◆◆◆◆◆◆◆◆◆◆◆◆◆◆◆◆◆◆◆◆◆◆◆◆◆◆ also very easy to make.
It's moist, chewy, spicy, and fragrant—and it also looks gorgeous.

2½ cups all-purpose flour

1 teaspoon baking soda

2 eggs, lightly beaten

2⅔ cups mincemeat (28-ounce jar or homemade)

1 (14-ounce) can sweetened condensed milk

2 cups mixed candied fruit

1 cup coarsely chopped walnuts

Preheat oven to 325° F. Butter a 9-inch springform or bundt pan. Line the bottom with wax paper and butter the paper as well.

Sift together the flour and baking soda. Combine the eggs, mincemeat, condensed milk, fruit, and nuts. Fold in the dry ingredients.

Pour into the papered pan and bake until center springs back when pressed with a finger. Cool in pan and remove paper.

Note: For a particularly attractive presentation, make a lattice design of sifted confectioner's sugar with bits of green and yellow candied fruit tucked in the lattice corners.

WHITE FRUITCAKE

◆◆◆◆◆◆◆◆◆◆◆◆◆◆◆◆◆◆◆◆◆◆◆◆◆◆◆◆

Anita Bassett   San Antonio, Texas This delicately flavored classic
◆◆◆◆◆◆◆◆◆◆◆◆◆◆◆◆◆◆◆◆◆◆◆◆◆ fruitcake was made by Anita Bassett's mother when the family lived in Honolulu in the 1920s. Her father wouldn't allow liquor of any kind in the house, but her mother kept a bottle of Okolehau (roughly translated: Ironbottom) hidden away upstairs for the fruitcake. One of the three girls would have to put on a large apron and sneak upstairs to fetch it. When Mrs. Bassett makes the cake now, she uses brandy.

*4 cups sifted all-purpose
  flour*

1 teaspoon baking powder

½ teaspoon baking soda

¼ teaspoon salt

1 pound golden raisins

*1 pound blanched
  almonds, chopped*

½ cup citron, cut fine

*½ pound candied orange
  peel*

*½ pound candied lemon
  peel*

*½ pound candied
  pineapple*

*½ pound candied red
  cherries*

1 cup butter

½ cup sugar

*1 tablespoon freshly
  squeezed lemon juice*

10 egg whites, stiffly beaten

Brandy

Makes 2 (3-pound) cakes.

Preheat oven to 250° F. Grease 2 tube pans or 6 small bread pans and line with wax paper.

Combine the flour, baking powder, baking soda, and salt. Sift together 5 times. Put all the fruits and nuts into a large bowl, sift 1 cup of the flour mixture over them, and mix thoroughly.

Cream the butter until light and fluffy, add the sugar gradually, and cream together. Add the remaining flour mixture to the creamed butter and sugar, a small amount at a time. Mix well together after each addition of flour until smooth.

Add the lemon juice and fruit and nuts. Fold in the egg whites. Pour into the prepared pans and bake for about 2½ hours, then increase heat to 300° F. for 15 minutes.

When the cake is done, poke holes in it with a skewer and douse it with brandy before wrapping in a tea towel or cheesecloth that's also brandied. Store the cake covered with foil in a tin.

TENNESSEE FRUITCAKE

◆◆◆◆◆◆◆◆◆◆◆◆◆◆◆◆◆◆◆◆◆◆◆◆◆◆◆◆◆◆◆◆◆

Eileen Steward   Traverse City, Michigan   Here is a particularly deli-
◆◆◆◆◆◆◆◆◆◆◆◆◆◆◆◆◆◆◆◆◆◆◆◆◆◆◆◆◆   cious fruitcake—crunchy
outside, moist and chewy inside—with a light, breadlike texture. It also looks
beautiful sliced. Don't be daunted by the long ingredients list; it's really worth
the effort.

1 pound (2 cups) candied
   pineapple

1¾ pounds (4 cups) pitted
   dates

1 pound (2 cups) shelled
   pecans

15 ounces (2½ cups)
   currants

15 ounces (2½ cups) dark
   seedless raisins

1 pound (2 cups) candied
   cherries

1 pound blanched
   almonds

½ pound (1 cup) candied
   citron, sliced

½ pound (1 cup) candied
   orange peel

½ pound (1 cup) candied
   lemon peel

6 cups all-purpose flour

1 tablespoon cinnamon

2 tablespoons nutmeg,
   preferably freshly grated

2 teaspoons ground
   allspice

Preheat oven to 300° F. Heavily butter a 9-inch bundt
pan or 2 (9 × 5-inch) loaf pans or 16 (5 × 3-inch) mini-
loaf pans. Set aside.

Dice the pineapple and dates. Roughly chop the nuts. In a
very large bowl, toss the fruits, nuts, and peels together.
Sift the flour, spices, and baking soda over the bowl and toss
until thoroughly coated.

In another very large bowl, cream the butter. Gradually beat
in the sugar, eggs, and melted chocolate. Stir in the fruits
and nuts alternately with the grape juice and honey.

Spoon into the prepared pans. Bake 45 minutes to 1¾ hours
(the shorter time is for the mini-loaves), until golden and a
tester inserted in the center of the cakes comes out clean.

Cool overnight. Remove from pans, place the cakes on sheets
of plastic wrap, and pour brandy over them—1 tablespoon

1 teaspoon baking soda

2 cups butter

2 cups sugar

1 dozen eggs, beaten

2 (1-ounce) squares
    semisweet chocolate,
    melted

1 cup grape juice

1 cup honey

Brandy or good port wine

Assorted candied fruit for
    decoration

*Makes 1 large fruitcake, 2
    small ones, or 16 mini-
    loaves.*

for the smaller cakes, 2 tablespoons for the loaf cakes, 4 tablespoons for the large cake. Decorate with candied fruit, wrap well, and store in tins or in the freezer. The cakes will slice more easily if they're chilled.

FRUITY FRUITCAKE

◆◆◆◆◆◆◆◆◆◆◆◆◆◆◆◆◆◆◆◆◆◆◆◆◆◆◆◆◆◆◆◆◆◆◆◆

Dinny McAllister Hampton, Virginia Mrs. McAllister searched for
◆◆◆◆◆◆◆◆◆◆◆◆◆◆◆◆◆◆◆◆◆◆◆◆◆◆◆◆◆◆◆◆◆ years to find the perfect fruitcake—nearly all fruits and nuts and very little batter. She's produced an
especially delicious cake that's very moist and not too sweet. She serves it
barely warmed, with her grandmother's hard sauce. Because the McAllisters
are originally from Kentucky, they use only bourbon whiskey on the cake, but
brandy or rum is fine if you prefer. The earlier in the season this cake is made,
the better—it only improves with age and another dollop of bourbon every now
and then to keep it moist.

1 pound dates, chopped

*1 pound candied cherries,
    halved*

1 pound pecan pieces

*1 pound candied
    pineapple, chopped*

Pinch of salt

6 eggs

*4½ tablespoons vanilla
    extract*

1½ cups all-purpose flour

1½ cups sugar

Bourbon

Serves 16.

Preheat oven to 250° F. Butter a 10-inch tube pan and
set aside.

Mix together the dates, cherries, pecans, pineapple,
and salt. Set aside. Beat the eggs until foamy. Add the
vanilla, flour, and sugar, and mix well.

Add the batter to the fruit mixture and stir well to coat the
fruit.

Pour into the prepared pan, set in a roasting pan filled with
hot water, and bake for 2 to 3 hours, or until a toothpick
inserted in the center comes out clean.

Cool the cake; run a knife around the sides and bottom of
the pan and remove the cake. Douse with bourbon and wrap
in cheesecloth to store. Put the cake in an airtight tin and
check often to make sure the cake is moist—a little bourbon
every now and then will help.

HARD SAUCE

*8 tablespoons butter,
    softened to room
    temperature*

Sifted confectioner's sugar

*1 teaspoon Kentucky
    bourbon*

Makes about 1 cup.

Cream the butter and sugar—as much sugar as you like, depending on how sweet you like it—until the sauce is thick. Add the bourbon, and keep the hard sauce at room temperature until ready to serve.

MOLASSES FRUITCAKE

◆◆◆◆◆◆◆◆◆◆◆◆◆◆◆◆◆◆◆◆◆◆◆◆◆◆◆◆◆◆◆

Mary Dye   New Matamoras, Ohio An extremely unusual fruitcake with
◆◆◆◆◆◆◆◆◆◆◆◆◆◆◆◆◆◆◆◆◆◆◆◆◆◆◆◆ a rustic appearance—it's delicious,
moist, and spicy. The finished cake makes a stack of fruitcake "pancakes" held
together with layers of delicately spiced applesauce.

CAKE

1 egg

1½ teaspoons baking soda

1 cup buttermilk

*½ cup butter, softened to
    room temperature*

1 cup sugar

½ cup dark molasses

½ teaspoon salt

*1½ teaspoons ground
    ginger*

*4½–5 cups all-purpose
    flour*

FILLING

*2½–3 cups thick
    applesauce*

1 teaspoon ground allspice

*¼ teaspoon nutmeg,
    preferably freshly grated*

Confectioner's sugar

Makes 1 (8-inch) cake.

P reheat oven to 400° F. Oil a medium #6 cast-iron skillet
and set aside.

Beat the egg and baking soda into the buttermilk and
set aside. Cream the butter and sugar. Beat in the molasses,
salt, and ginger.

Add the buttermilk mixture gradually until well blended. Add
enough flour to make a soft dough. Divide the dough into 6
parts, and roll to approximate size of the skillet.

Press 1 circle of dough into the skillet, fluting the edges.
Bake for 5 to 7 minutes, until the dough is set. Turn out
onto wax paper to cool. Bake the remaining 5 parts of dough
in the same way, oiling the skillet before each new cake is
baked.

Combine the applesauce and spices. Layer the cake rounds—
they will be about ½ inch thick—adding ½ cup of applesauce
between each layer. Press the layers together as you stack
them.

This cake can be baked up to 3 days in advance; it will stay
very moist. Dust it with sieved confectioner's sugar before
serving.

DARK SUET PUDDING

◆◆◆◆◆◆◆◆◆◆◆◆◆◆◆◆◆◆◆◆◆◆◆◆◆◆◆◆◆◆◆◆◆◆◆◆

Elaine Sparkes   Clarkes Beach, Newfoundland This earthy pud-
◆◆◆◆◆◆◆◆◆◆◆◆◆◆◆◆◆◆◆◆◆◆◆◆◆◆◆◆◆◆◆◆ ding comes from an
old Newfoundland recipe. It's old-fashioned and absolutely delicious.

½ cup suet

1½ cups all-purpose flour

½ teaspoon salt

¾ teaspoon baking powder

1 teaspoon baking soda

2 teaspoons ground
  allspice

½ cup molasses

½ cup milk

½ cup raisins or currants

2 tablespoons brandy

Serves 10 to 12.

SAUCE

½ cup brown sugar

2 teaspoons all-purpose
  flour

1 tablespoon butter

1 teaspoon vanilla extract
  or lemon flavoring

Have ready a 1½-quart pudding basin (or soufflé dish),
buttered, and a buttered piece of wax paper to put
over the basin.

Cut up the suet into very small pieces—a food processor
will do this effectively. Rub the suet through the flour. Add
the dry ingredients to the suet-flour mixture. Blend in the
molasses and milk, and stir until well mixed. Add the fruit
and brandy.

Pour into the greased pudding basin and steam for 2½ hours
(see directions on page 216). Store if not serving immediately.

To serve: Steam again for 1 hour, then serve hot with sauce
below.

Combine the sugar and flour thoroughly in a small saucepan.
Add the butter and stir in 1½ cups boiling water.

Place over heat and boil for a few minutes. Add the vanilla
or lemon flavoring and serve warm.

CHRISTMAS PLUM PUDDING

Janet Kinnicutt Harwichport, Massachusetts Janet Kinnicutt's mother and grandmother made this pudding, which goes back to the 1920s, every year. Now she makes it for herself and her husband and a pudding each for the families of her four children. It's a glorious light-textured festive dessert with a first-class hard sauce on the side.

1 cup suet

1 pound raisins

½ pound currants

¼ pound candied citron

½ cup walnuts or pecans, chopped

1 cup soft bread crumbs

1 cup brown sugar

1 teaspoon salt

1 cup all-purpose flour

1 teaspoon cinnamon

1 teaspoon nutmeg, preferably freshly grated

½ teaspoon ground cloves

1 cup milk

4 egg yolks

4 egg whites, beaten to soft peaks

HARD SAUCE

8 tablespoons butter

1 cup confectioner's sugar, sifted

Grease and flour a 2-quart pudding mold.

Put the suet, raisins, currants, and citron through a food grinder or chop in a food processor.

Combine with the nuts, bread crumbs, brown sugar, salt, flour, cinnamon, nutmeg, cloves, milk, and egg yolks. Mix well, and gently stir in the egg whites.

Pour the mixture into the prepared pudding mold, filling it two-thirds full. Cover and place on a rack in a kettle. Add boiling water to come up 2 inches above the bottom of the mold. Steam covered for 5 hours.

Invert on rack to cool, and pudding will fall free from mold. Wrap in plastic wrap and return to mold to store. It will keep several months.

When ready to use, reheat by steaming again for 1 hour.

To prepare the hard sauce, beat the butter and confectioner's sugar together until light and fluffy. Add the flavoring gradually while beating. Beat long enough to make the hard sauce fluffy and light.

½ teaspoon vanilla extract or 1 tablespoon brandy

1 cup brandy (for flaming)

Serves 16 to 20.

To serve: Place the pudding on a flameproof platter. Heat the brandy, pour over the pudding, and light with a match. The pudding will burn beautifully as you spoon brandy back over it.

ENGLISH PLUM PUDDING

◆◆◆◆◆◆◆◆◆◆◆◆◆◆◆◆◆◆◆◆◆◆◆◆◆◆◆◆◆◆◆◆◆◆◆◆◆◆

Anne Richard Norby Pittsburgh, Pennsylvania Here is a classic
◆◆◆◆◆◆◆◆◆◆◆◆◆◆◆◆◆◆◆◆◆◆◆◆◆◆◆◆◆◆◆◆◆◆◆◆◆◆ British plum pudding that Anne Norby's grandfather remembers his grandmother making. It's
dense, rich, intense, and memorable, with a superb sauce that packs a punch.
As Mrs. Norby's grandfather would say, "No more pudding, but pass the
sauce."

Be sure to make the pudding well in advance—Mrs. Norby makes it every
other year—but a couple of months ahead is ideal.

PUDDING

*¼ pound candied citron,
sliced thin*

2 pounds raisins

2 pounds currants

*1 pound dark brown
sugar*

*1 pound suet, ground or
chopped fine*

*1 heaping quart dry bread
crumbs, fine or grated
(measure after grating)*

2 eggs, well beaten

*⅓ cup all-purpose flour,
sifted*

*1 heaping teaspoon
nutmeg, preferably
freshly grated*

Have ready new, unbleached 100 percent cotton muslin;
thread, needle, scissors; 2 large (6-cup) and 2 small
(3-cup) pudding basins or heavy plastic bowls (margarine bowls work very well)—the important thing is that they
have at least a small lip.

Combine the fruit, sugar, and suet. Mix thoroughly with your
hands or a wooden spoon, cover bowl tightly, and leave out
overnight.

The next day, add the remaining ingredients and mix well.
Pack into pudding basins or plastic tubs. Pack the bowls very
full, tamp them down, and leave a mound in the center.

Cut squares of muslin* about ½ inch larger than the tops of
the bowls. Butter the squares and lay them, buttered side
down, on top of the puddings. Tuck in the edges.

Next cut large squares of muslin, take a square, and place
it on top of the bowl over the original piece of muslin. Using
string or heavy thread, tie the muslin on by tying under the

* If finding muslin is out of the question, use wax paper secured tightly
with string—it tested perfectly for us. Then wrap the puddings in foil to
store.

6 tablespoons liquor (½
wine/½ bourbon or
brandy)

**Serves 12 to 14 (the 2
large puddings) and 6
to 8 (the small ones).**

lip of the bowl—make sure it's tight. Excess material will
hang down. Bring up the 4 corners back over the rim and
fasten them together, sewing them securely so that the
pudding can be lifted out of boiling water by this handle.

Place the puddings in a large pot of boiling water, cover the
pot, and boil for 4 hours. The boiling water should come halfway up the sides of the puddings. Be sure to keep the water
boiling, adding boiling water as necessary.

Drain the puddings, let them dry, and store in a cool, dry
place—or freeze them.

To serve: Boil 1 more hour. Serve hot, flaming with brandy,
accompanied by the sauce (below).

SAUCE

1 cup sugar

8 tablespoons butter

2 egg yolks, beaten

3 egg whites, stiffly beaten

Rum, brandy, or bourbon

Put the sugar, butter, and egg yolks in the top of a double
boiler and cook over low heat until thickened, stirring from
time to time.

Stir in the egg whites. Chill. When cold, flavor with judicious
amounts of rum, brandy, or bourbon.

NOËL PUDDING

◆◆◆◆◆◆◆◆◆◆◆◆◆◆◆◆◆◆◆◆◆◆◆◆◆◆◆◆◆◆◆

Jo Lynn Berens   Hazen, North Dakota   This pudding tastes very good
◆◆◆◆◆◆◆◆◆◆◆◆◆◆◆◆◆◆◆◆◆◆◆◆◆◆◆◆   indeed and is fragrant, rich,
and satisfying. Unlike most Christmas puddings, it can be made on the day you
plan to serve it. Serve it on a platter with whipped cream.

1 cup grated carrots

1 cup grated potatoes

1 cup sugar

1 cup all-purpose flour

*8 tablespoons butter,
softened to room
temperature*

1 teaspoon baking soda

1 teaspoon cinnamon

*1 teaspoon nutmeg,
preferably freshly grated*

1 teaspoon ground cloves

1 teaspoon salt

½ cup raisins

½ cup currants

Serves 10 to 12.

Grease a 1½-quart pudding basin (or soufflé dish) and set aside. Mix the ingredients together well in the order given.

Pour the pudding into the basin and set the basin in the top of the steamer pot. Steam covered for 3 hours.

PLUM PUDDING

◆◆◆◆◆◆◆◆◆◆◆◆◆◆◆◆◆◆◆◆◆◆◆◆◆◆◆

Dale Ann Aitken   Calgary, Canada A first-rate old-fashioned plum
◆◆◆◆◆◆◆◆◆◆◆◆◆◆◆◆◆◆◆◆◆◆◆◆◆ pudding that has been in Dale Ann
Aitken's family since her childhood. The pudding should ripen 2 to 3 months.

1 cup seedless raisins

1 cup dates, chopped

½ cup candied citron or chopped candied orange and lemon peel

1 cup all-purpose flour

1 teaspoon baking powder

¼ teaspoon baking soda

¼ teaspoon salt

½ teaspoon cinnamon

¼ teaspoon nutmeg, preferably freshly grated

¼ teaspoon ground cloves

¼ teaspoon ground allspice

8 tablespoons butter

½ cup brown sugar

2 eggs

⅓ cup molasses

1 cup milk

2 teaspoons rum

2 teaspoons brandy

½ cup chopped walnuts

1 cup soft bread crumbs

Brandy for flaming

Serves 10 to 12.

Grease 1 (1½-quart) pudding bowl well and set aside. Put the fruit in a large bowl and dust with 1 tablespoon of the flour. Set aside. Combine the remaining flour, baking powder, baking soda, salt, and spices.

In a large bowl, cream the butter and sugar together. Make a well and add the eggs 1 at a time. Blend in the molasses, milk, rum, and brandy.

Add the dry ingredients, fruit, nuts, and bread crumbs. Turn into the greased bowl, cover tightly, and steam for 3 hours. Cover the bowl with wax paper and store in refrigerator until serving day.

To serve: Steam pudding again, tightly covered, for 3 hours. Check the boiling water from time to time and replenish with fresh boiling water as necessary. Flame with brandy, garnish with holly, and serve with a good hard sauce.

CARROT PUDDING

◆◆◆◆◆◆◆◆◆◆◆◆◆◆◆◆◆◆◆◆◆◆◆◆◆◆◆◆

Georgia Smith   Dover, New Jersey This especially good carrot pudding recipe, handed down in Georgia Smith's family, was particularly enjoyed during the Depression on the prairies of western Canada, where she grew up—the traditional ingredients for plum pudding weren't available, and carrot pudding reigned.

1 cup ground suet

1 cup grated carrot

1 cup grated potato

1½ cups all-purpose flour

1 teaspoon baking soda

*1 teaspoon nutmeg,
  preferably freshly grated*

1 teaspoon cinnamon

1 cup sugar

2 teaspoons salt

2 eggs

1 tablespoon molasses

1 cup raisins

1 cup currants

Serves 10 to 12.

SAUCE

8 tablespoons butter

1 cup brown sugar

2 eggs

*½ tablespoon vanilla
  extract*

Combine the ingredients in the order listed and beat until well blended. Place in a buttered 1½-quart pudding basin. Cover the basin with a sheet of wax paper, buttered on the pudding side; tie the paper securely onto the bowl with kitchen string.

Place in a large kettle of boiling water, enough to reach halfway up the side of the mold, and steam covered for 3 hours. The pudding can be stored for many months in the refrigerator.

To serve: Steam again in the same way for 1½ hours. Serve unmolded with sauce below. Garnish with holly for Christmas.

Cream the butter. Gradually add the sugar and beat well. Add the eggs and beat to a froth. Stir in ¼ cup boiling water and continue to beat until foamy. Beat in the vanilla.

Chill and serve over hot carrot pudding.

OLD-FASHIONED CHRISTMAS CUSTARD

◆◆◆◆◆◆◆◆◆◆◆◆◆◆◆◆◆◆◆◆◆◆◆◆◆◆◆◆◆◆◆◆

Joyce Sanders   Harrodsburg, Kentucky A superb custard to be ea-
◆◆◆◆◆◆◆◆◆◆◆◆◆◆◆◆◆◆◆◆◆◆◆◆◆◆◆◆◆◆◆◆ ten from a punch cup with
a spoon, as the locals do, or served on the side with fruitcake, jam cake, or
Christmas cookies. An old family recipe that comes from Joyce Sanders's
grandmother, it seems to taste best as the older generation likes it, with a
couple of tablespoons of good Kentucky bourbon.

1 quart milk

1½ tablespoons cornstarch

½ cup sugar

Dash of salt

*4 eggs, separated, at room
temperature*

*1 scant teaspoon vanilla
extract*

*2 tablespoons good
Kentucky bourbon
(optional)*

*Makes 1½ quarts or
serves 12 as dessert.*

In a double boiler, heat the milk to just below boiling. Meanwhile, in a medium bowl, combine the cornstarch with the sugar and salt and blend well. Add the egg yolks to the sugar mixture and mix well. Add the mixture to the heated milk in the double boiler, stirring well and fairly often, making sure that the mixture does not boil, or it will curdle.

Beat the egg whites until frothy. When the egg-milk mixture begins to coat the side of the pan or the spoon, whisk in the egg whites a little at a time. Continue cooking about 10 to 15 minutes, stirring frequently. The mixture will get frothy and thicken slightly.

Remove from the heat and add the vanilla and bourbon, if using.

Strain the mixture and place a covering of plastic wrap directly on top of the custard to prevent a skin from forming.

AUNT PAULINE'S FAMOUS PLUM PUDDING

◆◆◆◆◆◆◆◆◆◆◆◆◆◆◆◆◆◆◆◆◆◆◆◆◆◆◆◆◆◆◆◆◆◆◆

Mary Angela Welsh   Trumbull, Connecticut A gloriously simple tra-
◆◆◆◆◆◆◆◆◆◆◆◆◆◆◆◆◆◆◆◆◆◆◆◆◆◆◆◆◆◆◆◆◆◆◆ ditional suet pudding,
handed down from Mary Angela Welsh's Aunt Pauline, who was born on
Christmas in 1895. The recipe originated in County Cork, Ireland. Unlike most
plum puddings, this one is easy to make—the recipe makes two, one to give
away.

1 cup suet, finely chopped
1 cup buttermilk
1 cup light brown sugar
1 teaspoon baking soda
½ teaspoon salt
1 cup raisins
1 cup all-purpose flour
*Brandy (optional, for
    flaming)*

Serves 20 to 24.

Have ready 2 well-buttered coffee cans or pudding basins. For steaming the puddings, you'll need a large pot with a lid and a kettle full of boiling water on the side. Mix all the ingredients and place in the cans or basins. Place the puddings in the pot, add boiling water to come halfway up the sides of the puddings, and cover the pot. Boil the puddings for 3 hours, replenishing the boiling water frequently. Be attentive: if the water drops below a boil, the puddings will be sodden, the great plague of plum puddings.

To store: Cut circles of wax paper to fit the cans or basins, butter them heavily, and place over the puddings. Secure these either in the traditional way, with pudding covers or towels tied with string on the outside, or simply cover tightly with aluminum foil.

To serve: Steam again, in the same way, for about 1½ hours. Remove covers and serve with the sauce below. If you like, you can serve the pudding flaming: heat a little brandy or rum in a saucepan, remove from the heat, and light with a match, quickly pouring the flaming liquid over the pudding.

FOAMY SAUCE
6 tablespoons butter
1 cup sugar
*3 eggs, separated, at room
    temperature*

Cream the butter and slowly add the sugar. Beat well.

Beat the egg yolks until lemon-colored, add the butter-sugar mixture, and stir. Add 2 tablespoons boiling water and the

½ teaspoon salt

1 teaspoon vanilla extract

2 tablespoons bourbon
   (optional)

salt and mix thoroughly. Beat the egg whites until stiff and fold into the mixture.

Cook in a double boiler 5 minutes. Add the vanilla and, if desired, bourbon. Serve over the warm plum pudding.

CHRISTMAS STOLLEN

◆◆◆◆◆◆◆◆◆◆◆◆◆◆◆◆◆◆◆◆◆◆◆◆◆◆◆

Joyce Bryan   Colfax, Washington

◆◆◆◆◆◆◆◆◆◆◆◆◆◆◆◆◆◆◆◆◆◆◆◆◆◆◆

When she was growing up in Buffalo, New York, Joyce Bryan had a neighbor, Mrs. Schnitzel, who was famous for her delicious baked goods. Stollen was Joyce's favorite, and Mrs. Schnitzel brought it unfailingly on Christmas Eve. Making a stollen is a bit of a fuss, but this one is truly outstanding, worth the effort once a year.

1 cup plus 2 teaspoons granulated sugar

2 envelopes active dry yeast

1 cup scalded milk

8 tablespoons unsalted butter, softened to room temperature and cut into pieces

4 large eggs

6 cups all-purpose flour, sifted

1½ teaspoons salt

1½ teaspoons nutmeg, preferably freshly grated

2 teaspoons grated lemon zest

¼ cup candied citron, cut into ¼-inch dice

¼ cup candied cherries, cut into ¼-inch dice

1½ cups seedless raisins

1 cup blanched whole almonds, chopped into ¼-inch dice

In a large mixing bowl, combine ½ cup warm water (110°–115° F.) and 2 teaspoons of the sugar; let the yeast soften in this and rise about 5 minutes.

Meanwhile, cool the scalded milk to lukewarm. Add the cooled milk, ½ cup of the sugar, and the 8 tablespoons softened butter to the yeast mixture. Mix well. Lightly beat 2 of the eggs and beat in. Stir in 3 cups of the sifted flour, the salt, nutmeg, and grated lemon zest. Beat until the batter drops in ribbons from a spoon.

Stir in the remaining 3 cups flour, citron, cherries, raisins, and chopped nuts. Turn the mixture out onto a lightly floured surface and knead the dough until smooth and satiny.

Put the dough into a greased bowl, turning to bring greased side to the top. Cover and let rise in a warm place—80°–85° F.—for 1 hour, or until dough has doubled in size.

Punch down the dough, re-cover, and let rest for 10 minutes.

Divide the dough in half and roll each ball out on a lightly floured board to an oval approximately 12 × 10 inches.

Combine the ground almonds, remaining ½ cup sugar, the dates, remaining 2 eggs, and the almond extract. Mix well and divide into 2 batches.

2 cups blanched almonds, ground to a powder in food processor

1 cup pitted dates, cut into ¼-inch pieces

1 teaspoon almond extract

4 tablespoons unsalted butter, melted

1 cup confectioner's sugar

Additional candied citron and candied cherries for garnish

Makes 2 stollen; serves 12 each.

Spread each batch evenly on top of each oval, leaving a ½-inch margin all around.

Fold over the dough ovals the long way and tightly press the edges closed to seal. Form into a crescent shape with the fold on the inside.

Brush the tops with the 4 tablespoons melted butter. Cover with a tea towel and let rise in a warm place for 45 minutes, or until doubled.

Meanwhile, preheat the oven to 350° F.

Bake for 30 minutes, until browned on the outside but not burned on the bottom.

Place on racks and cool slightly.

Meanwhile, prepare a glaze of the confectioner's sugar combined with ¼ cup hot water. Mix well and brush on top of the stollen while still warm. Decorate with candied citron and cherries cut into attractive shapes.

CRANBERRY NUT BREAD

Dorothy Applegate   Carlsbad, California A satisfyingly tasty bread that would be good for breakfast, lunch, or tea—or anytime with coffee or tea. The bread is easily made and keeps well.

2 cups all-purpose flour

1 cup sugar

1½ teaspoons baking powder

1½ teaspoons baking soda

½ teaspoon salt

1 egg, well beaten

1 juice orange

1 cup cranberries, chopped

1 cup walnuts or pecans, chopped

Makes 1 loaf.

Preheat oven to 350° F. Butter a 9 × 5 × 3-inch loaf pan and set aside.

Sift the dry ingredients together and add the egg. Stir well. Grate the zest from the orange and juice it. Put the zest and juice into a glass measuring cup and fill with boiling water to make ¾ cup altogether.

Add the orange liquid to the egg-flour mixture and fold in the cranberries and nuts. Pour the batter into the prepared pan and bake for 1 hour, or until golden.

ORANGE-CRANBERRY SAUCE

◆◆◆◆◆◆◆◆◆◆◆◆◆◆◆◆◆◆◆◆◆◆◆◆◆◆◆◆◆◆◆◆◆

Judy Fairless Bridgewater, New Jersey An excellent recipe with a
◆◆◆◆◆◆◆◆◆◆◆◆◆◆◆◆◆◆◆◆◆◆◆◆◆◆◆◆◆ wonderful citrus flavor and
a great texture. Judy Fairless evolved this recipe over the years until she got
it just right.

*1 pound fresh cranberries,
sorted and rinsed*

*2 cups apples, peeled and
diced*

Grated zest of 1 orange

*1 cup orange segments,
seeded and diced*

3½ cups sugar

Makes 5 cups.

In a large saucepan, bring the cranberries and 1 cup water to a boil. Cook over high heat for about 5 minutes, until the skins have popped.

Add the apples, orange zest, orange segments, and sugar. Simmer uncovered for 30 minutes.

Store in the refrigerator or freeze.

CRANBERRY PORT WINE SALAD

◆◆◆◆◆◆◆◆◆◆◆◆◆◆◆◆◆◆◆◆◆◆◆◆◆◆◆

Rosemary Marvel Tucson, Arizona A good gelatin salad without the

◆◆◆◆◆◆◆◆◆◆◆◆◆◆◆◆◆◆◆◆◆◆◆◆◆ sweet, sweet taste of many in

this genre. The port makes a big difference; don't omit it.

1 (6-ounce) package
   raspberry gelatin
   dessert

2 cups fresh cooked
   cranberries, lightly
   sweetened

1 (20-ounce) can crushed
   pineapple, with juice

1 envelope unflavored
   gelatin

1 cup port wine

1 cup walnuts, chopped

1 (8-ounce) container
   sour cream

1 (3-ounce) package
   cream cheese

1 tablespoon mayonnaise

1 tablespoon sugar

Serves 10 to 12.

Oil well a 9 × 13-inch Pyrex dish or gelatin mold.

Dissolve the raspberry gelatin in 1 cup boiling water and pour into a large bowl. Add the cranberries. Drain the pineapple and reserve the juice. Add the pineapple and refrigerate mixture until cool.

Dissolve the unflavored gelatin in the reserved pineapple juice, add the port, and add this to the fruit mixture along with the nuts.

Pour into the prepared dish or mold and chill until set.

When ready to serve, mix the sour cream, cream cheese, mayonnaise, and sugar and serve as a sauce on the side.

CRANBERRY MOLD

◆◆◆◆◆◆◆◆◆◆◆◆◆◆◆◆◆◆◆◆◆◆◆◆◆◆◆◆◆◆◆

Norma Marshall Brooklyn, New York In a world of sticky-sweet,
◆◆◆◆◆◆◆◆◆◆◆◆◆◆◆◆◆◆◆◆◆◆◆◆◆◆◆◆◆◆◆ bizarre gelatin salads, this one
is different—not very sweet to begin with, it has the tartness of fresh cranberries
and the zest of oranges, as well as the pleasant texture of pecans and celery.

1 (3-ounce) package wild
 cherry gelatin dessert

1 scant cup sugar

Dash of salt

1 (8-ounce) can crushed
 pineapple, with juice

1 cup raw cranberries

1 cup chopped celery

1 navel orange, ground,
 with peel on

½ cup pecans, coarsely
 chopped

1 tablespoon freshly
 squeezed lemon juice,
 or more to taste

Serves 12.

SAUCE

1 cup mayonnaise

1 cup sour cream

Oil an 8-inch ring mold and set aside.

Dissolve the gelatin in 1 cup boiling water and stir until all the granules disappear.

Add the sugar and salt. Then add the pineapple with its juice, cranberries, celery, ground orange, pecans, and lemon juice.

Pour the mixture into the prepared mold and refrigerate until set.

Unmold and serve with the sauce below on a bed of lettuce or watercress.

Mix ingredients together thoroughly and serve with the cranberry mold.

OLD-FASHIONED CRANBERRY JELLY

◆◆◆◆◆◆◆◆◆◆◆◆◆◆◆◆◆◆◆◆◆◆◆◆◆◆◆◆◆◆

Mary Lepp   Yankton, South Dakota A very tasty cranberry jelly that's
◆◆◆◆◆◆◆◆◆◆◆◆◆◆◆◆◆◆◆◆◆◆◆◆◆◆◆◆◆◆ been in Mary Lepp's family for
many years; the Lepps always have it for Thanksgiving dinner. The consistency
is more like a jam than a jelly, and we liked it best with bread or muffins.

*4 cups fresh cranberries,
sorted and washed*

*2 tablespoons freshly
squeezed lemon juice*

2 cups sugar

***Makes a little more than
2 cups.***

In a large saucepan, combine the cranberries, 2 cups water, and the lemon juice. Bring to a boil and continue to boil until the skins have popped. Remove from heat and force mixture through a food mill.

Place the pulp in a saucepan, stir in the sugar, and bring to a boil, stirring constantly till the sugar is dissolved. Keep boiling 3 to 5 minutes, or until the mixture falls off the spoon in ribbons. Skim the mixture and turn into a quart container. Refrigerate until set.

MAPLE-CRANBERRY SAUCE

◆◆◆◆◆◆◆◆◆◆◆◆◆◆◆◆◆◆◆◆◆◆◆◆◆◆◆◆◆◆◆◆◆◆◆◆◆◆◆

Bonnie Holbrook-Chatfield Fair Oaks, California This is one of
◆◆◆◆◆◆◆◆◆◆◆◆◆◆◆◆◆◆◆◆◆◆◆◆◆◆◆◆◆◆◆◆◆◆◆◆◆ those great "idiot's delight" recipes—it's so delicious that it seems impossible it could have been so mindlessly easy to prepare.

*1 (12-ounce) package
 fresh whole cranberries*

*1 cup fancy-grade maple
 syrup**

Makes 1½ cups.

In a medium saucepan, combine the cranberries and the maple syrup. Bring to a boil, stirring occasionally. Reduce heat and simmer till all the cranberries have popped. Continue to simmer 5 more minutes.

Remove from heat and let cool. Refrigerate.

* It's important to use the fancy-grade syrup; otherwise you'll get a cloying cranberry sauce with none of the finesse this recipe offers.

HOLIDAY SALAD RING

◆◆◆◆◆◆◆◆◆◆◆◆◆◆◆◆◆◆◆◆◆◆◆◆◆◆◆◆◆◆

Shirley Baker   La Grange, Georgia This unusual jellied salad comes
from the Women's Exchange Tea
Room in Memphis. Mrs. Baker serves it filled with curried chicken salad—a
perfect accompaniment. It makes a light refreshing lunch in the middle of the
rich holiday eating season. Since it can be made the day before, it's on the table
in moments.

2 (3-ounce) packages
  lemon gelatin dessert

2 cups apple juice

2 cups mincemeat

½ cup walnuts or pecans,
  chopped

Watercress

Serves 12.

Oil an 8-inch ring mold. Dissolve the gelatin in 1½ cups
hot water; add the apple juice and chill until slightly
thickened. Stir in the mincemeat and nuts. Pour into
the ring mold and chill until firm.

Unmold and fill with curried chicken salad (see page 38).

Decorate with watercress.

Condiments
and Candies

BREAD AND BUTTER PICKLES

◆◆◆◆◆◆◆◆◆◆◆◆◆◆◆◆◆◆◆◆◆

Elaine Lindsay   Hamilton, Ohio These are first-rate pickles, the sort
◆◆◆◆◆◆◆◆◆◆◆◆◆◆◆◆◆◆◆◆ you can't quite seem to get enough of
no matter how many you eat. They're crunchy and sweet, perfect for any meal
from picnics to the big holiday feasts.

1 gallon cucumbers, sliced

6 medium onions, sliced

2 green peppers, cored,
   seeded, and chopped

3 cloves garlic, minced

⅓ cup salt

3 cups white vinegar

5 cups sugar

1 tablespoon mustard seed

2 teaspoons celery seed

2 teaspoons ground
   turmeric

*Makes 4 quarts or 8
pints.*

Mix the cucumbers, onions, peppers, and garlic in a large bowl. Sprinkle the salt over the vegetables and mix in 2 trays of ice cubes. Let stand for 3 hours. Drain well.

In a separate bowl, mix the vinegar, sugar, mustard seed, celery seed, and turmeric. Pour the mixture over the drained cucumbers.

Put the cucumbers in a large pot and bring to a boil. As soon as they've come to a boil, pack them into sterile jars, so that they don't lose their crunchiness. Seal the jars and process 5 minutes.*

*See page 294 for instructions on standard canning procedures.

GARLIC DILL PICKLES

Jeanne Boyle   Hewitt, New Jersey These pickles are truly superior and amazingly easy to make. Mrs. Boyle and her husband have been making them every year for the past eight years.

2 pounds small pickling
    cucumbers
5 cloves garlic, crushed
¼ cup salt
1 quart white vinegar
2 tablespoons mixed
    pickling spices
1 bunch fresh dill
1 slice day-old Jewish rye
    bread

Makes 1 gallon or 4
    quarts.

Have ready a clean stoneware crock or 4 quart jars—you'll need a gallon capacity.

Wash the cucumbers and arrange them and the garlic in the jars or crock. Combine the salt, 1 quart water, the vinegar, and spices in a pan. Bring to a boil and pour over the cucumbers. Put the dill in and add the slice of rye bread (in pieces if you're using quart jars) on top. Cover. Let stand at room temperature 3 days; refrigerate for 5 days before serving.

DILLED SMALL CARROTS

◆◆◆◆◆◆◆◆◆◆◆◆◆◆◆◆◆◆◆◆◆◆◆◆◆◆◆◆

Lois Creith   La Riviere, Manitoba These zippy little carrots would be
◆◆◆◆◆◆◆◆◆◆◆◆◆◆◆◆◆◆◆◆◆◆◆◆◆◆ a refreshing change from the usual
carrot sticks on the crudités platter.

5 pounds little carrots,
    peeled and stemmed

6 sprigs fresh dill

6 cloves garlic

2 cups white vinegar

½ cup pickling salt or
    kosher salt

Makes 6 pints.

Have ready 6 pint jars, sterilized.

Divide the carrots among the jars and add a sprig of dill and a clove of garlic to each.

Mix the vinegar, pickling salt, and 4 cups water and bring to a boil in a saucepan. Pour the brine over the carrots. Seal the jars and process for 5 minutes.*

*See page 294 for instructions on standard canning procedures.

DILLED CUCUMBERS

◆◆◆◆◆◆◆◆◆◆◆◆◆◆◆◆◆◆◆◆◆◆◆◆◆◆◆◆◆◆◆

Janet Pomeroy **Anaheim, California** These cucumbers are more like

◆◆◆◆◆◆◆◆◆◆◆◆◆◆◆◆◆◆◆◆◆◆◆◆◆◆◆◆◆ a relish than a pickle, and re-

freshing like a salad. A good choice for a picnic or buffet table.

½ cup white vinegar

½ cup sugar

1 teaspoon salt

½ teaspoon snipped fresh
   dill

3 large cucumbers

Makes 1 quart or 2 pints.

Mix together in a saucepan the vinegar, sugar, ¼ cup water, the salt, and dill. Bring the mixture to a boil, stirring constantly.

Pare the cucumbers, score them with a fork lengthwise, and slice them. Put them in a jar with a tight-fitting lid. Pour the liquid over the cucumbers and seal. Chill in the refrigerator for 24 hours. The cucumbers will keep almost indefinitely.

SWEET PICKLES

◆◆◆◆◆◆◆◆◆◆◆◆◆◆◆◆◆◆◆◆◆◆◆◆◆◆◆◆◆◆◆◆◆◆

Shirley Koehler   Long Beach, California   These pickles are very crisp
◆◆◆◆◆◆◆◆◆◆◆◆◆◆◆◆◆◆◆◆◆◆◆◆◆◆◆◆◆◆◆◆   and tasty, and easy to make,
though the process takes several days. They have a great old-fashioned flavor.

*15 medium unblemished
   cucumbers*

4 cups cider vinegar

5 teaspoons salt

*2 tablespoons mixed
   pickling spices*

8 cups sugar

***Makes about 3 quarts or
   6 pints.***

Wash the cucumbers and place in a container large
enough to hold them plus enough boiling water to
cover them completely. Add the boiling water and
let the cucumbers stand uncovered overnight.

Drain the cucumbers, boil fresh water, and pour over the
cucumbers. Let stand uncovered overnight again, and repeat
the process for the next 3 days—5 days altogether.

Drain the cucumbers, and slice them ½ inch thick. During
the soaking process, some of them may have become soft
and started to disintegrate—discard these. The good ones
will still be firm and will "fizzle" when they are cut.

Combine the vinegar, salt, spices, and sugar and pour the
mixture over the cucumbers. Let stand covered for 2 days.
On the third day, bring the pickles to a boil and pack in hot
sterile jars. Seal and process 5 minutes for long-term storage*
or refrigerate if you plan to use within several weeks.

*See page 294 for instructions on standard canning procedures.

PICKLED MUSTARD BEANS

Bettylu Reeves   New Ross, Nova Scotia   An old-fashioned yellow string bean pickle that's sweet and sour. This recipe makes about 6 quarts—these homey pickles make wonderful gifts.

7½ quarts yellow wax beans

½ cup coarse salt

6 cups cider vinegar

5 cups sugar

1 cup all-purpose flour

1 cup dry mustard

1 teaspoon ground turmeric

2 teaspoons celery seed

Makes 6 quarts or 12 pints.

Have sterilized and ready 6 quart jars or 12 pint jars.

Top and tail the beans, wash them, and break into 2-inch pieces. Put the beans in a large pot, add the salt, cover with hot water, and let them boil 30 minutes. Drain.

Add 4½ cups of the vinegar and the sugar and bring to a boil. Mix the flour, mustard, turmeric, and celery seed with the remaining 1½ cups vinegar and add this mixture to the boiling beans. Simmer for 5 minutes at 180–185° F.

Distribute the beans among the jars and seal with paraffin.

PICCALILLI

◆◆◆◆◆◆◆◆◆◆◆◆◆◆◆◆◆◆◆◆◆◆◆◆◆◆◆◆◆

Eleanor Sullivan   New York, New York One of Eleanor Sullivan's
◆◆◆◆◆◆◆◆◆◆◆◆◆◆◆◆◆◆◆◆◆◆◆◆◆◆◆ earliest memories is of pic-
calilli stewing away in the kitchen. It was the first recipe she asked her mother
for—perfect for barbecues and picnics and buffets. This makes a great deal of
piccalilli; unless you have a 12-quart pot available and a strong appetite for
piccalilli, you may want to cut the recipe in half.

14 pounds green tomatoes

1 cup salt

4 green peppers

2 hot peppers (serranos)

8 medium to large onions

1 quart cider vinegar

1 pint white vinegar

*1 pound dark brown
  sugar*

1 pound granulated sugar

*¾ pound small white
  onions, peeled*

*¼ cup mixed pickling
  spices, tied in a cloth
  bag*

Dash of ground allspice

Dash of cinnamon

**Makes 6 quarts or 12
  pints.**

Cut the tomatoes into quarters and remove stems. Pour
the salt over them and let stand covered overnight.

Have ready 6 sterile quart jars. Rinse the tomatoes and
put them through a food grinder or a food processor with
the 6 peppers and the medium to large onions.

Pour both vinegars and both sugars into a 12-quart pot. Add
the vegetables, including the white onions, and simmer with
the pickling spices for 3 hours, or until the piccalilli is thick
like a relish and most of the liquid is reduced. Add the allspice
and cinnamon at the end and remove the bag of spices.

Pack in sterile jars and seal. Process 5 minutes for long-
term storage* or refrigerate if you plan to use within several
weeks.

*See page 294 for instructions on standard canning procedures.

SWEET HOT MUSTARD

◆◆◆◆◆◆◆◆◆◆◆◆◆◆◆◆◆◆◆◆◆◆◆◆◆◆

Nancy Hammel   Dufur, Oregon   A superb mustard sauce. Nancy Ham-

◆◆◆◆◆◆◆◆◆◆◆◆◆◆◆◆◆◆◆◆◆◆◆◆ mel likes to make up half-pints of this condiment around the holidays and take it to friends on a platter with various smoked meats.

1 cup malt vinegar

1 (4-ounce) can Colman's dry mustard

½ cup sugar

6 eggs

Makes about 1 quart.

In the top of a double boiler, add the vinegar to the mustard slowly, thoroughly beating the mustard to break up any lumps. Let sit 2 hours.

Stir in the sugar, and add the eggs 1 at a time, beating the mixture after each addition. Place the pan over cold water and begin to cook. Stir with a whisk constantly until desired consistency is reached. When the water in the bottom of the double boiler begins to simmer, reduce heat.

Take care to whisk the sides and bottom of the pan so you do not end up with scrambled eggs. When sauce is ready, in just a few minutes, pack into jars and refrigerate.

WHIPPED HORSERADISH SAUCE

◆◆◆◆◆◆◆◆◆◆◆◆◆◆◆◆◆◆◆◆◆◆◆◆◆◆◆◆◆

Mary Lepp   Yankton, South Dakota This is a first-rate spread, wonderful with ham or roast beef. If you thin it a bit with milk, it makes an excellent dip, particularly for shrimp. We tried it on cold roast beef sandwiches and as a cracker spread with ham, and in both cases it was splendid.

1 (8-ounce) package
   cream cheese, softened
   to room temperature

1 tablespoon confectioner's
   sugar

1 tablespoon freshly
   squeezed lemon juice

1 tablespoon
   Worcestershire sauce

2–3 tablespoons prepared
   horseradish, to taste

½ cup heavy cream,
   whipped

Makes about 1 cup.

Blend the cream cheese with the sugar, lemon juice, Worcestershire sauce, and horseradish. Fold in the whipped cream. Refrigerate until ready to serve.

LABOR DAY BARBECUE SAUCE

Rebecca Purro   New York, New York   An exhilarating barbecue sauce, perfect for chicken or fish.

½ cup freshly squeezed
  orange juice

¼ cup mushroom soy
  sauce (or regular soy
  sauce)

1 jigger (3 tablespoons)
  gin

2 tablespoons chopped
  pickled ginger

1 tablespoon Dijon
  mustard

½ cup honey

1 teaspoon freshly ground
  black pepper

1 clove garlic, minced

Makes 1½ cups.

Combine all ingredients. Marinate chicken or fish in the refrigerator for at least 4 hours and preferably overnight. Broil or barbecue, brushing additional sauce over the food after each turning.

UNCLE WALTER'S HAM SAUCE

◆◆◆◆◆◆◆◆◆◆◆◆◆◆◆◆◆◆◆◆◆◆◆◆◆◆◆◆◆◆◆

Lynn Church   Torrington, Connecticut   A superb mustard sauce that
◆◆◆◆◆◆◆◆◆◆◆◆◆◆◆◆◆◆◆◆◆◆◆◆◆◆◆◆◆ can be served hot or cold. It
keeps well and only improves as it ages.

½ cup sugar

4 tablespoons dry mustard

Salt (optional, to taste)

2 eggs, beaten

½ cup milk

½ cup cider vinegar

4 tablespoons butter

Makes about 1 cup.

Combine the sugar, mustard, and salt, if using. Add the eggs and milk. Cook in the top of a double boiler for 5 minutes. Add the vinegar and cook over medium heat, until thick.

Remove from the heat, add the butter, and beat until smooth. Serve hot or cold.

TOMATO BUTTER

◆◆◆◆◆◆◆◆◆◆◆◆◆◆◆◆◆◆◆◆◆◆◆◆

Dot Toulson   Salem, New Jersey Southern New Jersey has been fa-
◆◆◆◆◆◆◆◆◆◆◆◆◆◆◆◆◆◆◆◆◆◆◆◆ mous for its tomatoes ever since
1820, when Colonel Robert Gibbon Johnson stood on the Salem City Courthouse
steps and ate a tomato while his doctor and the townspeople stood by awaiting
his demise—up until that day tomatoes were thought to be poisonous. This
very tasty conserve recipe has been in the Toulson family for years, and it's a
fine way to cope with a lavish harvest of innocent tomatoes.

½ bushel basket ripe
  tomatoes (about 24
  pounds)
6 pounds sugar
1 cup white vinegar
1 teaspoon cinnamon
½ teaspoon ground
  allspice
1½ lemons

Makes 8 half-pints.

Have ready 8 (½-pint) jars, sterilized.

Core the tomatoes and put them in a large nonaluminum kettle. Break them up with a wooden spoon and cook them down until they've begun to thicken.

Add the sugar, vinegar, and spices. Slice the lemons, including the peel, very thin, and cut them further into small bits. Add the lemons to the mixture, stir well, and cook slowly for about 2 hours, or until the mixture reaches the consistency of preserves. Stir often and watch carefully to be sure it doesn't burn. Pack into jars while hot.

CHRISTMAS CHUTNEY

◆◆◆◆◆◆◆◆◆◆◆◆◆◆◆◆◆◆◆◆◆◆◆◆◆◆◆◆◆◆◆◆◆◆◆◆

Leone Parker Powell River, British Columbia A spirited change
◆◆◆◆◆◆◆◆◆◆◆◆◆◆◆◆◆◆◆◆◆◆◆◆◆◆◆◆◆◆◆◆◆◆◆◆ from the usual cranberry relish. This was Leone Parker's mother's recipe—it's wonderful with
turkey or goose, and also with ham or pork. A jar of this chutney makes a
lovely present from your own kitchen.

1 pound cranberries

½ pound dried apricots

1 cup dark rum

1 cup freshly squeezed
    orange juice

½ cup chopped dates

½ cup chopped onion

½ cup chopped preserved
    ginger

½ cup white or cider
    vinegar

½ cup corn syrup

2 teaspoons salt

1 teaspoon mustard seed

4 drops Tabasco sauce

2 cloves garlic, crushed

Makes 4 pints.

Combine all ingredients and let stand 1 hour. Cook until thick, stirring often, about 1 hour. Pour into sterilized jars and seal. Process 5 minutes for long-term storage* or refrigerate if you plan to use within several weeks.

*See page 294 for instructions on standard canning procedures.

APPLE CHUTNEY

Mrs. J. Howard Henderson   Spartanburg, South Carolina   This very simple chutney tastes a bit like candied apples, with the zip of vinegar added. If you like yours spicy, add nutmeg, cinnamon, ginger, and mace to taste.

2 quarts peeled, diced tart apples

2 pounds (4 cups) sugar

2 cups raisins

½ cup vinegar

Freshly grated nutmeg, cinnamon, ground ginger, ground mace (optional, to taste)

Makes 4 to 6 half-pints.

Mix all ingredients in a large Dutch oven or heavy pan. Bring to a boil over low heat. Cook 1 to 1½ hours, until dark and thick. Stir occasionally, so the mixture does not stick and burn. If you wish, add spices to taste.

Remove from heat, cover, and let sit covered overnight.

The next day, bring to a boil, pack into hot sterilized jars, and seal. Process 5 minutes for long-term storage* or refrigerate if you plan to use within several weeks.

*See page 294 for instructions on standard canning procedures.

GINGER MARMALADE

◆◆◆◆◆◆◆◆◆◆◆◆◆◆◆◆◆◆◆◆◆◆◆

E. Kirt Walling   Ogden, Utah   The Wallings first tasted ginger marma-
◆◆◆◆◆◆◆◆◆◆◆◆◆◆◆◆◆◆◆◆◆◆ lade on a visit to Santa Cruz, California,
where it was served with cream cheese and crackers. They could never find a
recipe for it, so Mr. Walling decided to invent one. Through trial and error he
hit upon the scheme of using the pressure cooker. This is a delicious preserve
that's also excellent served with game or as a glaze for ham.

½ pound fresh gingerroot

*1½ tablespoons cream of
   tartar*

5½ cups sugar

*6 ounces (2 pouches)
   liquid pectin*

Makes about 5 half-pints.

Have ready 5 half-pint jars, sterilized.

Peel the ginger, cut into ½-inch slices, and place in a saucepan. Cover with water, bring to a boil, and boil for 10 minutes. Drain, reserving ginger liquid.

Place the ginger in a pressure cooker and cover with water. Pressure-cook for 1 hour. Bring pressure down quickly by running cold water over the cover.

Drain, once again saving the cooking liquid. Chop the ginger finely in a food processor.

Combine the ginger, reserved cooking liquid to measure 1½ cups (add water if necessary), and cream of tartar in a saucepan. Bring to a boil.

Add the sugar, bring to a boil, and simmer for 10 minutes. Add the pectin, boil 1 minute, and skim. Fill the prepared jars with the jelly. Cap with sterilized lids and rings. Turn the jars upside down for 10 minutes, then shake them and place them right side up—there should be a good seal. Store in a cool, dark place.

ORANGE MARMALADE

◆◆◆◆◆◆◆◆◆◆◆◆◆◆◆◆◆◆◆◆◆◆◆◆◆◆◆◆◆◆

Nancy Jackson   Waccabuc, New York   This bright-tasting, not-too-
◆◆◆◆◆◆◆◆◆◆◆◆◆◆◆◆◆◆◆◆◆◆◆◆◆◆◆◆◆   sweet marmalade has a lovely
old-fashioned flavor. It's especially good on breakfast toast and muffins. It takes
several days to make, but it's very easy.

*6 large or 8 medium
   navel oranges,
   unpeeled, sliced very
   fine*

Sugar

*1 cup freshly squeezed
   lemon juice*

Makes 8 pints.

Cover the oranges with water—about 1½ times as much water as fruit—and let them stand covered overnight.

The next day, boil the mixture for 45 minutes. Let stand overnight again.

The third day, sterilize 8 pint jars and set aside. Measure the mixture and add 1½ times as much sugar as fruit. Boil 45 minutes; before removing from the heat, add the lemon juice. Pour the preserves into the sterilized jars and seal.

HOMEMADE STRAWBERRY JAM

◆◆◆◆◆◆◆◆◆◆◆◆◆◆◆◆◆◆◆◆◆◆

Linda Brown   Medley, Alberta This jam is very easy to make, and for
◆◆◆◆◆◆◆◆◆◆◆◆◆◆◆◆◆◆◆◆◆◆◆ some reason the time it spends sitting
in its juices seems to intensify the flavor.

4–5 cups sugar

*4 cups halved clean
   strawberries*

*3 tablespoons freshly
   squeezed lemon juice*

Makes 6 pints.

Measure the sugar to your taste and mix with the strawberries. Let the mixture stand covered overnight.

The next day, bring the sweetened strawberries to a boil in a saucepan and simmer 15 minutes. Remove from the heat and add the lemon juice. Pour into sterilized jars and seal.

PEANUT CLUSTERS

◆◆◆◆◆◆◆◆◆◆◆◆◆◆◆◆◆◆◆◆◆◆◆◆◆◆◆◆

Leann Campbell Lamar, Missouri You have to be a lover of dark
◆◆◆◆◆◆◆◆◆◆◆◆◆◆◆◆◆◆◆◆◆◆◆◆◆ chocolate to truly appreciate this
candy, which is very easy to make. We preferred it with unsalted peanuts.

2 cups sugar

1 cup evaporated milk

28 caramels

2 (6-ounce) packages
 semisweet chocolate
 chips

3 cups salted peanuts

Makes about 60 candies.

Have ready a long sheet of wax paper. In a large heavy
saucepan, combine the sugar and milk and bring to a
boil. Add the caramels and stir to melt. When the
caramels are melted, boil for 1 minute.

Remove from the heat, stir in the chocolate chips, and stir
until melted. Stir in the peanuts. Drop from a teaspoon onto
wax paper and let cool.

GERMAN RUM TOPF

◆◆◆◆◆◆◆◆◆◆◆◆◆◆◆◆◆◆◆◆◆◆◆◆◆◆◆◆◆◆◆

Susie Hummer   Windermere, Florida In northern Germany, winter
◆◆◆◆◆◆◆◆◆◆◆◆◆◆◆◆◆◆◆◆◆◆◆◆◆◆◆ passes a little more happily when
there's a rum topf in the household. Putting it together begins with the first
strawberries of the season; it will be ready for ladling over vanilla ice cream
and puddings by Thanksgiving. A little of the juice makes a delicious after-
dinner drink.

*Strawberries (begin with 2
   pounds)*

Sugar

*Rum, light or dark
   (inexpensive rum is
   fine)*

*Peaches, peeled and cut
   in small pieces*

Raspberries

Blackberries

Cherries (sour if possible)

*Mangoes (not too ripe),
   peeled and cut in small
   pieces*

*Makes several pints,
   according to
   ingredients added.*

Begin with a large crock; a slow cooker or large porcelain
pot will do. If you live in a warm climate, you'll need
to refrigerate the rum topf; in Germany it's left in the
pantry.

Wash and dry the strawberries and remove the stems.
Measure them and put them in the crock. Add half as much
sugar as strawberries and cover them with rum.

Every time you add a new fruit, repeat the process with the
sugar and the rum. Cover the rum topf with plastic wrap and
secure it with a sturdy rubber band.

Important: Do not add apples, pears, plums, or grapes; they
are too mushy and will spoil the consistency.

CHOCOLATE FUDGE

◆◆◆◆◆◆◆◆◆◆◆◆◆◆◆◆◆◆◆◆◆◆◆◆◆◆◆◆◆◆◆◆◆

Mary Buckman San Lorenzo, California This smooth, creamy, de-
◆◆◆◆◆◆◆◆◆◆◆◆◆◆◆◆◆◆◆◆◆◆◆◆◆◆◆◆◆ licious fudge also happens
to be very easy to make. It makes a regular appearance at Mary Buckman's
house at Christmas, as it has for many years.

4½ cups sugar

1 (13-ounce) can
   evaporated milk

3 (6-ounce) packages
   semisweet chocolate
   chips

1 cup butter

1 (7-ounce) jar
   marshmallow cream

½ teaspoon vanilla extract

2 cups chopped walnuts or
   pecans

Makes about 5 pounds.

Butter a cookie sheet—one with sides—and set aside.

Combine the sugar and milk in a heavy saucepan. Bring to a boil. Boil for 10 minutes, stirring constantly. Reduce heat to a simmer and add remaining ingredients. Mix until well blended. Remove from heat.

Pour onto the cookie sheet and let cool. Cut into 1-inch squares.

ENGLISH TOFFEE

◆◆◆◆◆◆◆◆◆◆◆◆◆◆◆◆◆◆◆◆◆◆◆◆◆◆◆◆◆◆◆◆◆◆◆◆◆

Jane Rodenkirch   Fond du Lac, Wisconsin If you've never tried
◆◆◆◆◆◆◆◆◆◆◆◆◆◆◆◆◆◆◆◆◆◆◆◆◆◆◆◆◆◆◆◆ homemade toffee, you'll
be amazed at how utterly delicious it is, and how easy to make. It's nearly
impossible to keep away from it. And of course it makes a wonderful gift.

2 cups sugar

2 cups butter

Pinch of cinnamon

1 teaspoon vanilla extract

*1¼ pounds couverture
   chocolate*

*¼ pound almonds,
   chopped and toasted*

Makes 2 pounds.

Melt the sugar and butter together in a fairly heavy
medium saucepan. Add 10 tablespoons water and the
cinnamon, then the vanilla.

Using a candy thermometer, cook the toffee slowly, stirring
frequently, until it reaches the hard-crack stage. Meanwhile,
prepare a cookie sheet by covering it with heavy-duty foil;
then butter the foil well.

When the toffee has reached the hard-crack stage, pour it
at once into the prepared pan. Set aside to cool.

Melt the chocolate and pour half of it over the toffee. Sprinkle
with half the nuts. Cool. Turn over the toffee and repeat
with the rest of the chocolate and nuts.

When the toffee is completely cool, crack it with a hammer
into small pieces.

PEANUT BUTTER ICE CREAM TOPPING

◆◆◆◆◆◆◆◆◆◆◆◆◆◆◆◆◆◆◆◆◆◆◆◆◆◆◆◆◆◆◆◆◆◆◆◆◆

Linda Montaug-Martin   San Fernando, California   This very tasty
◆◆◆◆◆◆◆◆◆◆◆◆◆◆◆◆◆◆◆◆◆◆◆◆◆◆◆◆◆◆◆◆◆◆◆ topping is easy
to make, smooth and creamy, and a great hit with kids. We thought it tasted
best served slightly warm.

*1 cup firmly packed dark
     brown sugar*

⅓ cup milk

1 tablespoon butter

¼ cup light corn syrup

*½ cup chunky peanut
     butter*

Makes 1⅓ cups.

Combine the sugar, milk, butter, and corn syrup in a small saucepan. Heat until the butter just melts and the sugar is dissolved. Remove from the heat, add the peanut butter, and stir until smooth.

Serve warm or cool over ice cream. Keep refrigerated; the topping can also be frozen.

Breakfast

CINNAMON BUNS

◆◆◆◆◆◆◆◆◆◆◆◆◆◆◆◆◆◆◆◆◆◆◆◆◆◆◆◆◆◆◆◆◆◆◆◆◆

Virginia Rampton   Morden, Manitoba An excellent recipe, adapted
◆◆◆◆◆◆◆◆◆◆◆◆◆◆◆◆◆◆◆◆◆◆◆◆◆◆◆◆◆◆ from one that originally appeared in *Canadian Living* magazine. We liked these buns even better when
we made them with maple syrup.

4 tablespoons granulated
   sugar

1 envelope active dry yeast

1 cup milk

¼ cup vegetable oil

2 teaspoons salt

2 eggs, slightly beaten

Up to 6 cups all-purpose
   flour

1 cup butter, softened to
   room temperature

⅔ cup brown sugar,
   packed firmly

1½ cups raisins

4 tablespoons butter,
   melted

2–3 teaspoons cinnamon

1 cup corn or maple syrup

Makes 30.

In a large bowl, dissolve 2 tablespoons of the sugar in 1 cup lukewarm water. Sprinkle the yeast over this and let stand in a warm place 10 minutes, until bubbly.

In a small saucepan, scald the milk. Add the oil, the remaining 2 tablespoons sugar, and the salt. Stir until the sugar dissolves. Add the milk mixture and beaten eggs to the dissolved yeast. Gradually beat in 3 cups of the flour. Beat vigorously by hand or with an electric mixer until smooth. Stir in enough remaining flour to make a dough that is easy to handle.

Turn the dough out onto a floured board. Knead until smooth and elastic, about 5 minutes. Place in a greased bowl, turning the dough to coat all sides. Cover with a tea towel and let rise in a warm place for 1 to 1½ hours, or until doubled in bulk.

While the dough is rising, stir together the softened butter and brown sugar. Divide mixture evenly between 2 (13 × 9-inch) pans. Sprinkle ½ cup of the raisins over each pan.

When the dough has doubled, punch down and divide in half. Roll out each half on a lightly floured board to a 15 × 8-inch rectangle. Brush each with 2 tablespoons melted butter and sprinkle with 1 teaspoon cinnamon (or more to taste) and ¼ cup raisins.

Roll up the rectangles, as though you were making a jelly roll, beginning at the wide end. Pinch the edges of the dough together along the length of the roll. Slice each roll into 15 slices 1 inch thick. In each pan, arrange the slices slightly apart, with the cut side up. Cover and let rise until doubled in bulk, about 30 minutes.

Preheat oven to 400° F.

Bake 20 minutes. Pour ½ cup syrup over each pan and bake for an additional 5 minutes. Remove from the oven and let stand for 1 minute. Invert pans onto a large tray. Serve warm.

FRENCH DOUGHNUTS

◆◆◆◆◆◆◆◆◆◆◆◆◆◆◆◆◆◆◆◆◆◆◆◆◆◆◆◆◆◆

Erica Fitzpatrick Ottawa, Ontario These truly extraordinary muffin-
◆◆◆◆◆◆◆◆◆◆◆◆◆◆◆◆◆◆◆◆◆◆◆◆◆◆◆ tin "doughnuts" have been made
in Erica Fitzpatrick's family for years—her mother found the recipe in the New
Brunswick newspaper the *Daily Gleaner* in the 1960s. They are very addictive;
our testers couldn't stop eating them.

5 tablespoons butter

½ cup sugar

1 egg, beaten

1½ cups all-purpose flour, sifted

2½ teaspoons baking powder

¼ teaspoon nutmeg, preferably freshly grated

¼ teaspoon salt

½ cup milk

8 tablespoons butter, melted

Cinnamon sugar for rolling doughnuts

Makes 1 dozen.

Preheat oven to 350° F. Butter and flour a muffin tin and set aside.

Cream the 5 tablespoons butter and the sugar. Add the beaten egg and mix well. Mix together the sifted flour, baking powder, nutmeg, and salt, and add, alternating with the milk. Mix well.

Spoon into the muffin tin and bake 15 minutes, or until golden. While hot, dip in the 8 tablespoons melted butter and roll in cinnamon sugar.

PAIN PERDU

◆◆◆◆◆◆◆◆◆◆◆◆◆◆◆◆◆◆◆◆◆◆◆◆◆◆◆◆◆

Jeanne Boyle   Hewitt, New Jersey This very sophisticated French toast
◆◆◆◆◆◆◆◆◆◆◆◆◆◆◆◆◆◆◆◆◆◆◆◆◆ comes from Pierre Franey. It would
make an elegant New Year's Day champagne brunch, with sausages on the
side.

2 eggs

½ cup granulated sugar

1 cup milk

1 teaspoon vanilla extract

*½ teaspoon grated lemon
zest*

*8 (1-inch-thick) slices day-
old French bread*

8 tablespoons butter

*3 tablespoons orange
marmalade*

Confectioner's sugar

Freshly grated nutmeg

Serves 4.

Beat the eggs with the ½ cup sugar. Stir in the milk,
vanilla, and lemon zest. Arrange the bread in a single
layer in a shallow baking dish. Pour the egg mixture
over and let stand 30 minutes.

Heat 4 tablespoons of the butter in a large skillet and sauté
the bread until golden, about 6 minutes on each side.
Meantime, combine the marmalade with the remaining 4
tablespoons butter in a small saucepan and heat until the
butter melts.

Arrange the bread slices on a serving platter and sprinkle
with the confectioner's sugar and nutmeg. Serve with the
marmalade butter.

FILLED SWEET ROLL

◆◆◆◆◆◆◆◆◆◆◆◆◆◆◆◆◆◆◆◆◆◆◆◆◆◆◆◆◆◆

Ramona Davidson   Buhl, Idaho An especially delicious pastry that's a
◆◆◆◆◆◆◆◆◆◆◆◆◆◆◆◆◆◆◆◆◆◆◆◆◆◆◆ little tricky to make—it's definitely
worth the trouble, but if you're a beginning cook you may find it a bit too
challenging.

⅓ cup sugar

*6 envelopes (¼ cup) active
dry yeast*

*3 eggs, at room
temperature*

*1 tablespoon plus 1
teaspoon vanilla extract*

*8 tablespoons butter,
melted, plus 4
tablespoons, melted, for
brushing dough*

*12 cups all-purpose flour,
sifted*

2 tablespoons salt

*2 cups raspberry or
apricot preserves*

*1 cup confectioner's
sugar, sifted*

*½ teaspoon almond
extract*

*½ teaspoon freshly
squeezed lemon juice*

*½ cup walnuts, pecans,
or toasted almonds,
chopped*

*Makes 2 sweet rolls;
serves 12.*

In a large bowl, mix the sugar and 3 cups warm water
(105°–110° F.). Add the yeast and stir gently. Let stand
until the mixture is foamy.

Beat the eggs until foamy. Add 1 tablespoon of the vanilla
and the 8 tablespoons melted butter and mix into the yeast
mixture. Add 6 cups of the flour and beat 10 minutes, using
a mixer with a dough hook if possible.

Add the salt and the remaining 6 cups flour. Knead until the
dough is no longer sticky and is "earlobe" soft, approximately
10 to 15 minutes.

Put the dough in a lightly greased bowl. Turn to coat all
sides, cover with a tea towel, and let rise until doubled in
bulk, about 30 to 40 minutes.

Punch down the dough and knead it 6 to 10 times on a lightly
floured surface. Divide dough in half. Roll each half out into
a rectangle approximately the same size as a large baking
sheet. Grease the baking sheet and place a rectangle of
dough on it.

Brush the middle third of the dough with 1 tablespoon of the
remaining melted butter. Spread 1 cup of the preserves on
top of the butter, stopping within 1 inch of the top and bottom
of dough.

With a sharp knife or pizza cutter, cut dough on both sides (the part of the dough without the preserves) at ½-inch intervals on a 45° angle, stopping ½ inch from the edge of the preserves. You'll have a herringbone pattern; now fold the strips over, starting at the upper left, in an alternating pattern, lapping them over each other and the preserves all the way to the bottom.

Repeat with the second rectangle of dough.

Brush the finished rolls lightly with the remaining 2 tablespoons melted butter, cover with a tea towel, and let rise until doubled in bulk.

Preheat oven to 350° F.

Bake 20 to 25 minutes, or until golden brown. Cool.

To make a glaze, combine the confectioner's sugar, the remaining 1 teaspoon vanilla, the almond extract, and lemon juice. Add enough warm water to make the glaze runny. Brush on the cooled rolls, and while still wet, sprinkle on the chopped nuts.

BUBBE'S BABKE

◆◆◆◆◆◆◆◆◆◆◆◆◆◆◆◆◆◆◆◆◆◆◆◆◆◆◆

Joyce Landes   Sunnyvale, California *Bubbe* is the Yiddish word for
◆◆◆◆◆◆◆◆◆◆◆◆◆◆◆◆◆◆◆◆◆◆◆◆◆ "grandmother"—the source of
this wonderful babke. Joyce Landes's *bubbe* was born in Lithuania in the late
1800s and came to America in 1912. Each year her family would observe the
fast on the holiest day of the Jewish year, Yom Kippur; at sundown they would
break the fast with this delicious sweet bread. Although her grandmother is
gone now, Joyce Landes continues the tradition.

*Up to 8 cups all-purpose
    flour*

2 teaspoons salt

1 cup granulated sugar

*3 envelopes active dry
    yeast*

2 cups milk

1 cup butter

2 tablespoons vegetable oil

3 eggs

Melted butter

1 cup dark brown sugar

4 tablespoons cinnamon

1 cup raisins

1 egg, slightly beaten

Serves 10 to 12.

Combine 3 cups of the flour, the salt, sugar, and yeast
in a large bowl. In a medium saucepan, heat the milk,
butter, and oil to a temperature between 120° and
130° F.—it should feel warm to the touch. Add this mixture
to the dry ingredients and whisk for 3 minutes.

Add the eggs and beat with the whisk 3 more minutes. Add
enough of the remaining 5 cups flour, in small amounts, to
make a soft dough. Knead until smooth and elastic. Grease
a large bowl with butter, put the ball of dough in it, turn to
grease both sides, and let rise, covered, in a warm place.

Let rise until doubled in bulk. Punch down the dough and
divide into 3 parts. Let it rest, covered with a tea towel, for
15 to 20 minutes.

Roll the dough into rectangles 10 × 15 inches. Brush them
with melted butter. Mix together the brown sugar, cinnamon,
and raisins and sprinkle the dough with the mixture. Preheat
oven to 350° F.

Roll the dough as though you were making a jelly roll, and
form into rings. Place the rings on a buttered cookie sheet
and let rise till doubled in bulk. Mix the beaten egg and 1
tablespoon water and brush the rings with the egg wash.
Bake babke for 40 minutes; remove to a rack to cool.

CINNAMON MARBLE CAKE

◆◆◆◆◆◆◆◆◆◆◆◆◆◆◆◆◆◆◆◆◆◆◆◆◆◆◆◆◆◆◆

Colleen Cross   San Mateo, California A good breakfast cake. The
◆◆◆◆◆◆◆◆◆◆◆◆◆◆◆◆◆◆◆◆◆◆◆◆◆◆◆◆ original source was an old newspaper clipping, identifying the cake as the favorite of Ralph Paiewonsky,
governor of the Virgin Islands—a man of good taste, apparently.

1 cup sour cream

1 teaspoon baking soda

8 tablespoons butter

8 tablespoons sugar

*1½ cups sifted cake flour
(or 1½ cups plus 3
tablespoons sifted all-
purpose flour)*

¼ teaspoon baking powder

¼ teaspoon salt

2 eggs

*1½ teaspoons vanilla
extract*

⅓ cup sliced pecans

2 tablespoons cinnamon

Serves 8 to 10.

Preheat oven to 350° F. Butter and flour a square
8 × 8-inch pan and set aside.

Mix the sour cream and baking soda and set aside.
Cream the butter and ¾ cup of the sugar until light. Sift the
flour, baking powder, and salt and set aside. Add the eggs
and vanilla to the butter mixture; beat to mix. Add the sour
cream and stir well to mix. Add the flour mixture, then the
pecans. Pour the batter into the prepared pan.

Mix the remaining ¼ cup sugar and the cinnamon and sprinkle
evenly over the cake. Cut the topping into the batter for a
marbled effect.

Bake for 30 minutes, or until a tester inserted in the center
of the cake comes out clean. Cool in the pan on a rack for
10 minutes, then remove cake to the rack to cool further.

DANISH COFFEE CAKE

◆◆◆◆◆◆◆◆◆◆◆◆◆◆◆◆◆◆◆◆◆◆◆◆◆◆◆◆◆◆◆

Lena Cammon Tacoma, Washington A very good coffee cake that
◆◆◆◆◆◆◆◆◆◆◆◆◆◆◆◆◆◆◆◆◆◆◆◆◆◆◆ smells wonderful while it's baking. It's best served right out of the oven.

CAKE
8 tablespoons butter
1 cup sugar
2 eggs
1 cup milk
2½ cups all-purpose flour
1 teaspoon baking powder
1 teaspoon vanilla extract
½ teaspoon salt

FILLING
1 cup dark brown sugar
1 tablespoon butter
*2 tablespoons all-purpose
   flour*
1 cup chopped walnuts
1 teaspoon cinnamon

Serves 8 to 10.

Preheat oven to 350° F. Grease a 9 × 13-inch pan and set aside.

Mix the cake ingredients together in a large bowl in the order given. Spread half the batter in the pan.

Mix the filling ingredients in a bowl and spread half the filling over the batter in the pan. Using a wet spatula, spread the remaining batter over the mixture in the pan. Spread the remaining filling on top.

Bake the cake 30 to 45 minutes, or until a tester inserted in the center of the cake comes out clean.

FEATHERY BRUNCH PANCAKES

◆◆◆◆◆◆◆◆◆◆◆◆◆◆◆◆◆◆◆◆◆◆◆◆◆◆◆◆◆◆◆◆◆◆◆◆◆◆

Patricia Pannone   Havelock, North Carolina These delicious pan-
◆◆◆◆◆◆◆◆◆◆◆◆◆◆◆◆◆◆◆◆◆◆◆◆◆◆◆◆◆◆◆◆◆◆◆◆ cakes are a specialty
of Patricia Pannone's father, Al. They're on the sweet side, so they should be
served with syrup and bacon or sausage.

2 tablespoons vegetable oil
   or melted butter

1 egg

1 cup milk

1 teaspoon vanilla extract

1¼ cups all-purpose flour

½ teaspoon salt

2 tablespoons baking
   powder

5 tablespoons sugar

Makes 10 small pancakes.

Put the oil, egg, milk, and vanilla into a blender jar and blend for 5 seconds. Add remaining ingredients and blend 20 seconds.

Heat a greased griddle until a drop of water hisses on it. Cook the pancakes on one side until golden, and turn; when the second side is golden, they're done. Serve at once or keep warm under foil in a slow oven.

DAVID'S PANCAKE

◆◆◆◆◆◆◆◆◆◆◆◆◆◆◆◆◆◆◆◆◆◆◆◆◆◆◆◆◆◆◆◆

Arthur Randall   New York, New York This dramatically puffed, very
◆◆◆◆◆◆◆◆◆◆◆◆◆◆◆◆◆◆◆◆◆◆◆◆◆◆◆◆◆◆◆ savory pancake works on the
same principle as Yorkshire pudding. The recipe may first have appeared in the
New York Times, though Scandinavians will recognize it as a very old recipe.
It makes a lovely breakfast dish, made in a moment.

4 tablespoons butter

½ cup all-purpose flour

½ cup milk

2 eggs, lightly beaten

*Pinch of nutmeg,
    preferably freshly grated*

*Freshly squeezed lemon
    juice*

Confectioner's sugar

Serves 2 to 4.

Preheat oven to 425° F.

In an ovenproof skillet, melt the butter in the oven. Combine the flour, milk, eggs, and nutmeg and beat lightly, leaving a little lumpy. Pour the batter into the skillet when the butter is hot.

Bake 15 to 20 minutes, until lightly brown. Serve at once, with a dash of lemon juice and a dusting of confectioner's sugar.

PITMAN BLINTZES

◆◆◆◆◆◆◆◆◆◆◆◆◆◆◆◆◆◆◆◆◆◆◆◆◆◆◆◆◆

Amy Wasserman Chicago, Illinois These very tasty blintzes also have
◆◆◆◆◆◆◆◆◆◆◆◆◆◆◆◆◆◆◆◆◆◆◆◆◆◆◆◆◆ a good texture. They're another
example of the grandmother tradition—in this case, Amy Wasserman's family
stood over their grandmother's shoulder and measured the ingredients as she
worked. The blintzes can be frozen before their last browning and heated before
serving, or browned then frozen to be reheated in a microwave oven.

DOUGH

6 eggs

1½ cups all-purpose flour

3 cups milk

Pinch of sugar

Pinch of salt

FILLING

*2 (8-ounce) containers pot
    cheese*

*1 (8-ounce) package
    cream cheese*

1 egg

Sugar to taste

½ teaspoon salt

Serves 6.

Mix all the dough ingredients—a blender works perfectly. Grease a frying pan with butter; set it over
medium heat. When the pan is hot, put a tablespoon
of batter in the pan to make a very thin pancake. Cook on
one side only until lightly browned. Dump the pancake out
onto a clean tea towel and repeat the process until all the
batter is used.

Mix all the filling ingredients together.

Place a pancake brown side up, spread it with about 2
tablespoons of the filling, and roll it, turning the ends in.
Repeat with all the pancakes.

Brown the rolled blintzes again in the greased pan, and serve.

Note: When strawberries are in season, they make a lovely
topping for the blintzes; they can also be mixed in with the
filling.

FINNISH PANCAKES

◆◆◆◆◆◆◆◆◆◆◆◆◆◆◆◆◆◆◆◆◆◆◆◆◆◆◆◆

Marguerite Re   Elmhurst, Illinois If you have one of those lovely
◆◆◆◆◆◆◆◆◆◆◆◆◆◆◆◆◆◆◆◆◆◆◆◆◆◆◆◆ Scandinavian iron skillets with a design on the bottom, this is the recipe you've been looking for. You can also
make these pancakes in a regular iron skillet or on a griddle—in that case you'll
probably want to make very small circles. These are delicious in any guise.
Scandinavians serve these pancakes with lingonberries and sour cream, but
they're also excellent with maple syrup, jam, or, for the sybarite, Nutella, the
hazelnut-chocolate spread.

4 eggs

2 cups milk

5 tablespoons butter,
   melted

¾ cup all-purpose flour,
   sifted

Salt to taste

Serves 2 to 6.

Beat the eggs thoroughly. While beating, add the milk,
butter, and, gradually, the flour and salt. Keep the
mixture thin; lightness of touch is essential. (You can
make the batter the night before and store it covered in the
refrigerator; stir thoroughly before proceeding.)

Have the skillet or griddle very hot. Grease it lightly with
butter before the first batch goes in. Spoon the batter into
the indentations of the pancake pan and brown quickly on
both sides. Or make tiny pancakes on the griddle and turn
over as soon as they brown on the first side.

CREPES FOR MARDI GRAS

◆◆◆◆◆◆◆◆◆◆◆◆◆◆◆◆◆◆◆◆◆◆◆◆◆◆◆◆◆◆◆

Eugenie Licalzi Southfield, Michigan Mrs. Licalzi is from New
◆◆◆◆◆◆◆◆◆◆◆◆◆◆◆◆◆◆◆◆◆◆◆◆◆◆◆ Orleans, and her great-
grandmother used to make hundreds of these crepes at a time, cooking in 3 or
4 pans simultaneously. On Mardi Gras the whole family would gather at her
house, go out for the parades, and come back for the buffet she kept well
stocked all day long for the revelers.

Those with a low tolerance for orange flower water may want to cut it to 2
tablespoons; sweet tooths may like a tablespoon or two of sugar in the batter.
However you put them together, these aromatic crepes are addictive.

4 cups all-purpose flour

*¾ teaspoon nutmeg,
  preferably freshly grated*

1 teaspoon salt

*Juice and grated zest of 1
  lemon*

1½ ounces whiskey

*2–5 tablespoons orange
  flower water*

8 eggs

1 quart milk

*1–2 tablespoons sugar
  (optional)*

*Melted butter for cooking
  crepes*

Sugar for filling crepes

Makes 50 to 60.

Sift the flour with the nutmeg and salt into a mixing bowl
and add the lemon juice and zest, whiskey, and orange
flower water.

Beat the eggs and combine with the milk and 1 cup water.
Gradually beat this mixture into the flour mixture until you
have a very thin batter. Cook the crepes in a 5- to 6-inch
crepe pan, lightly buttered, using 1½ to 2 tablespoons batter
per crepe. Cook about 1 minute on the first side, or until
golden, and about 30 seconds on the other side. As each
crepe is cooked, butter the second side lightly and sprinkle
with a little sugar before rolling.

LIGHT CRISP WAFFLES

Frances Fouche Hastings-on-Hudson, New York These airy but very satisfying waffles appeared in a magazine sometime in the 1950s. They're relatively healthful, with their oats, eggs, cornmeal, and buttermilk. The amount of baking powder is not an error but the secret of the crisp, tender result.

1 cup all-purpose flour

½ cup yellow cornmeal

1 cup rolled oats

2 tablespoons baking powder

½ teaspoon salt

2 eggs

½ cup melted bacon drippings or other shortening

3 cups buttermilk

Makes 12 waffles.

Put all the dry ingredients into a bowl, break in the eggs, add the shortening—not too hot—and then stir in the buttermilk.

The batter will be of a thick, pouring consistency. Let stand 15 to 30 minutes to allow baking powder to work. The batter will almost double. Bake waffles to a light golden brown.

HEARTY WAFFLES

◆◆◆◆◆◆◆◆◆◆◆◆◆◆◆◆◆◆◆◆◆◆◆◆◆◆◆◆◆◆◆◆◆

Jim Monson   Claremont, California These old-fashioned waffles are a
◆◆◆◆◆◆◆◆◆◆◆◆◆◆◆◆◆◆◆◆◆◆◆◆◆◆◆◆ long-time Sunday morning tradition in the Monson family, particularly appealing when they're made with
blueberries folded into the batter.

1 cup all-purpose flour

1 cup cornmeal

1 cup whole wheat flour

2 teaspoons salt

1 tablespoon sugar

*1 tablespoon baking
  powder*

½ cup vegetable oil

*1 cup blueberries
  (optional)*

Makes 12 waffles.

Mix all the ingredients together, including the blueberries, if using. Bake in a waffle iron until golden brown.

FRIED TOMATOES

◆◆◆◆◆◆◆◆◆◆◆◆◆◆◆◆◆◆◆◆◆◆◆◆

Lee Harmer   Atlanta, Georgia Here is one of those incredibly simple,
◆◆◆◆◆◆◆◆◆◆◆◆◆◆◆◆◆◆◆◆◆◆◆◆ simply delicious recipes that seem to
epitomize the best of home cooking. On Saturday mornings, Lee Harmer and
her father would wake up before the rest of the household, and by the time
she got to the kitchen her father would be at the stove, making bacon, fried
tomatoes, and grits. Then they'd take their plates out to the porch and watch
the rest of the world wake up.

*3 very firm tomatoes (not
    necessarily fully ripe)*

*Salt and freshly ground
    black pepper to taste*

Flour

Bacon drippings

Serves 2.

Stem the tomatoes and cut into thick slices—not more
than ½ inch thick. Season with salt and pepper, then
dredge with flour. Fry in hot bacon drippings until crisp,
turning only once, so as not to break up the slices. Drain on
paper towels.

Drinks

RHUBARB DRINK

◆◆◆◆◆◆◆◆◆◆◆◆◆◆◆◆◆◆◆◆◆◆◆◆◆◆◆

Karen Dodds   Braeside, Ontario Rhubarb drinks are old-fashioned and
◆◆◆◆◆◆◆◆◆◆◆◆◆◆◆◆◆◆◆◆◆◆◆◆◆ rare on anyone's menu—but they're
refreshing in a particularly reviving way; this one would make a great impression
at, say, a Fourth of July picnic.

4 cups chopped rhubarb

2 cups sugar

*½ cup frozen orange juice
   concentrate*

Juice and zest of 1 lemon

About 3 quarts ginger ale

*Makes 4½ quarts,
   including ginger ale.*

Bring the rhubarb and 4 cups water to a boil in a large saucepan over medium heat. Strain the mixture through a tea towel laid inside a sieve, then add the sugar, orange juice concentrate, and lemon juice and zest. Heat briefly to dissolve the sugar and the concentrate. The juice can then be frozen or stored in jars in the refrigerator. To serve, mix with 2 parts ginger ale to 1 part juice.

PENNSYLVANIA DUTCH TOMATO JUICE

◆◆◆◆◆◆◆◆◆◆◆◆◆◆◆◆◆◆◆◆◆◆◆

J. C. Musser   Baldwin, New York Captain Musser inherited a rather
◆◆◆◆◆◆◆◆◆◆◆◆◆◆◆◆◆◆◆◆◆◆◆ sketchy recipe for homemade to-
mato juice from his mother, who lived all her ninety-six years in the Pennsylvania
Dutch country. He's modified it to a more precise and less voluminous recipe.
Homemade tomato juice is our idea of a real treat.

2½ pounds ripe tomatoes

*2½ pounds ripe plum
tomatoes*

3 pounds medium onions

*2 large green peppers,
cored and seeded*

2 large stalks celery

2 cloves garlic (optional)

1 bunch Italian parsley

1 cup sugar

Juice of ½ lemon

*Salt and coarsely ground
black pepper to taste*

Makes 3 to 3½ quarts.

Coarsely chop the tomatoes and plum tomatoes, onions, green peppers, celery, and garlic; the food processor does this very well.

Place the vegetables in a large pot, add 2½ quarts water and the parsley and simmer over moderate heat until the vegetables are soft, about 2 hours.

Push the vegetables and their juice through a sieve, with pressure, to extract the maximum amount of juice. Strain, return to the stove, and bring to a boil, adding the sugar as the juice heats.

When boiling, add the lemon juice and salt and pepper to taste. Cool in the refrigerator before serving, or preserve in sterile glass jars, using standard canning procedures.*

*See page 294 for instructions on standard canning procedures.

CHAMPAGNE PUNCH

◆◆◆◆◆◆◆◆◆◆◆◆◆◆◆◆◆◆◆◆◆◆◆◆◆◆◆◆◆◆◆◆◆

Rebecca Dabrowski   Indialantic, Florida   The Dabrowski family has
◆◆◆◆◆◆◆◆◆◆◆◆◆◆◆◆◆◆◆◆◆◆◆◆◆◆◆◆◆ served this punch every
holiday season for thirty years. It's very light and, they warn, quite deceptively
strong.

*Juice of 9 oranges and 9
   lemons*
3 fifths apricot brandy
3 fifths vodka
6 bottles champagne
Fresh fruit for garnish
Serves 50.

Squeeze the fresh citrus juice into a punch bowl and add the brandy and vodka. Add the champagne and, just before serving, ice. Stir gently and decorate with bits of fresh fruit.

PEACH PUNCH

◆◆◆◆◆◆◆◆◆◆◆◆◆◆◆◆◆◆◆◆◆◆◆◆◆◆◆◆◆◆◆◆◆◆

Ursula Vedder   Mission, British Columbia   This punch recipe comes
◆◆◆◆◆◆◆◆◆◆◆◆◆◆◆◆◆◆◆◆◆◆◆◆◆◆◆◆◆◆◆◆ from Germany, where it's
traditionally served on New Year's Eve. It can be very powerful, especially if
you nibble on the fruit.

*1 large (29-ounce) can
  peaches, with their
  juice, or 1 quart fresh
  strawberries*

3–4 tablespoons sugar

*1 small (½-liter) bottle
  Cognac*

4 bottles dry white wine

*1 bottle champagne or
  carbonated water*

Serves 36.

Cut the peaches into bite-size pieces, and place them in a large bowl— the punch bowl itself is fine—along with their juice, the sugar, and Cognac. Cover and let sit for several hours.

Add the wine, stir, and shortly before serving add the champagne.

SWEDISH GOLDEN WASSAIL

◆◆◆

Mrs. Sherwin Palmer Cumberland, Wisconsin The Palmers cre-
◆◆◆◆◆◆◆◆◆◆◆◆◆◆◆◆◆◆◆◆◆◆◆◆◆◆◆◆◆◆◆◆◆◆◆◆◆◆ ated this nonalco-
holic punch for Christmas Eve—since so many people don't drink alcohol, it makes a good festive substitute for the more traditional spirits.

4 cups pineapple juice

1½ cups apricot nectar

4 cups apple cider or apple juice

1 cup orange juice

2 (3-inch) sticks cinnamon

1 teaspoon whole cloves

¼ teaspoon whole cardamom seeds, crushed

Orange slices for a garnish

Serves 16.

Combine all the ingredients except the orange slices in a large saucepan. Heat to a boil; reduce heat and simmer 15 to 20 minutes. Remove from heat and strain.

Serve the punch hot in mugs; garnish with thin orange slices.

PRALINE EGGNOG

◆◆◆◆◆◆◆◆◆◆◆◆◆◆◆◆◆◆◆◆◆◆◆◆◆◆◆◆◆◆◆◆◆◆◆

Deborah Tuosto Watsonville, California A rich, glorious eggnog with
◆◆◆◆◆◆◆◆◆◆◆◆◆◆◆◆◆◆◆◆◆◆◆◆◆◆◆◆◆◆◆◆◆ the surprise of caramel flavoring. If you'd prefer a less sumptuous eggnog, use all the milk specified.

1¼ cups sugar

3–6 cups milk

*3 (3-inch) sticks
cinnamon*

*1 vanilla bean, split in
half lengthwise*

2 cups heavy cream

*12 eggs, at room
temperature*

*Nutmeg, preferably freshly
grated*

Serves 16 to 21.

In a 4-quart pan, melt half of the sugar over high heat,
stirring constantly until golden; lumps will melt. Remove
from the heat and immediately add 3 cups milk (or all the
milk, if you're making the less rich version), the cinnamon
sticks, and vanilla bean. Be careful; the mixture will sputter
a bit.

Return the pan to medium heat and stir until the caramelized
sugar is dissolved. Cover and chill until cold, at least 4 hours
or overnight.

Remove the spices. Rinse the vanilla bean and let dry; it can
be used later in other recipes.

Whip the cream until soft peaks hold; set aside. Whip the
eggs with the remaining sugar until about tripled in volume.
Whisk the eggs and half the cream into the caramelized milk.

Pour the eggnog into a 5-quart punch bowl, top with the
remaining whipped cream, and grate nutmeg on top. Serve
cold.

EGGNOG

◆◆◆◆◆◆◆◆◆◆◆◆◆◆◆◆◆◆◆◆◆◆◆◆◆◆◆◆◆

Marguerite Buderus   Kingwood, Texas A traditional eggnog, wildly
◆◆◆◆◆◆◆◆◆◆◆◆◆◆◆◆◆◆◆◆◆◆◆◆◆◆◆◆◆ rich with cream. The stirring
and tasting have always been a solemn ritual with Marguerite Buderus's father—
this was the essential drink for both Thanksgiving and Christmas at their house.

*6 eggs, separated, at room
temperature*

1 cup sugar

1½ cups brandy

½ cup dark rum

1½ quarts milk

*3 cups heavy cream,
whipped*

*Nutmeg, preferably freshly
grated*

Serves 20.

Beat the egg yolks until very thick and light. Gradually add the sugar, beating constantly. While still beating, add the brandy and rum gradually. Chill for 1 hour, stirring occasionally.

Add the milk slowly, then fold in the whipped cream. Beat the egg whites until stiff and fold in until blended. Store in covered jars 24 hours before serving. Serve in punch glasses with a sprinkle of grated nutmeg.

GLÜHWEIN

◆◆◆◆◆◆◆◆◆◆◆◆◆◆◆◆◆◆◆◆◆◆◆◆◆◆◆◆◆◆

Monika Paradi Mississauga, Ontario This traditional recipe origi-
◆◆◆◆◆◆◆◆◆◆◆◆◆◆◆◆◆◆◆◆◆◆◆◆◆◆◆◆ nated with Monika Paradi's
grandmother, who grew up in Germany. Even the children in the family toasted
the New Year with this brew, which also doubled as a cold remedy—you drink
it as hot as possible, then retire to sweat out your cold.

¾ *cup sugar*

3 whole cloves

1 (5-inch) stick cinnamon

3 cups dry red wine

1 lemon, sliced

Serves 8.

In a saucepan, bring 1 cup water, the sugar, cloves, and cinnamon to a boil. Add the wine and return to the boil. Remove from the heat.

Put the lemon slices into a large heatproof punch bowl or pitcher and pour the hot wine over them. Serve hot.

CONTRIBUTORS

Dale Ann Aitken, Plum Pudding, 219

Laurey Andreas, Chestnut Tart, 59

Dorothy Applegate, Cranberry Nut Bread, 226

Christine Jean Appleyard, Aunt Mary's New York Cheesecake, 164

Denise Auer, Auer "Family Secret" Sugar Cookies, 190

Janet Bailey, Leslie Newman's Coleslaw, 51

Shirley Baker
Holiday Salad Ring, 223
Orange Bread, 112

Megan Balterman, Coconut Cheesecake, 162

Anita Bassett, White Fruitcake, 207

Barbara Belew, Lemon Tea Bread with Black Walnuts, 114

Jo Lynn Berens, Noël Pudding, 218

Charyl Borgwald-Lawrence, Sarah's Persimmon Pudding, 157

Jeanne Boyle
Clams Bordelaise, 13
Garlic Dill Pickles, 235
Italian Salad, 48
Pain Perdu, 261

Rochelle Bray, Koprova (Potato Soup with Dill), 31

Katherine Brower, Pecan Tarts, 184

Linda Brown, Homemade Strawberry Jam, 250

Joyce Bryan, Christmas Stollen, 224–25

Fay Buckley, Stella's Lemon Cake, 153

Mary Buckman, Chocolate Fudge, 253

Marguerite Buderus
Eggnog, 282
Molasses Sugar Cookies, 183

Pat Burt, Pat's Chili Roast, 100

Mrs. David Butler
Aunt Ash's Fresh Corn Pudding, 72
Authentic Old-Fashioned Sweet Potato Pudding, 69
Fried Black-Eyed Peas, 4

Ruth Butler, Butter Tarts, 173

Gene L. Cain, Green Tomato Mincemeat, 194

Lena Cammon, Danish Coffee Cake, 266

Leann Campbell, Peanut Clusters, 251

Linda Cantoni, Fresh Pumpkin Pie, 197

Linda Carlson, Oatmeal Buns, 122

Sabrina Charbonneau, Gurkensalat, 49

Annamarie Childers, Grandma Khoury's Raisin Cake, 143

Pat Chopin, New Orleans Red Beans and Rice, 93

Lynn Church, Uncle Walter's Ham Sauce, 244

Fleurette Clough, Squash Rolls, 121

Paula Collins, Wisconsin Three-Cheese Ball, 19

Seretta Corl, Brown Bread, 108

Debbie Cox, Buttermilk Pie, 130

Betsy Crampe
Aunt Irene's Cookies, 191
Betsy's Peach Cobbler, 137

Lois Creith, Dilled Small Carrots, 236

Colleen Cross, Cinnamon Marble Cake, 265

Rebecca Dabrowski, Champagne Punch, 278

Sharon West DaRe, Cheesecake Cookies, 181

Conway Davenport, Steamed Hard-Shell Crabs, 90

Ramona Davidson, Filled Sweet Roll, 262–63

Frances Davis, Soft Sugar Cookies, 178

Mrs. George Davis, Pecan Balls, 168

Barbara Dehner, Oyster Stuffing, 58

Deborah DeMarco, Tutta, 78

Adah M. Dingeldine, Holiday Fruit Cake, 206

Louise Dodd, Talmadge Country Cured Ham, 94

Karen Dodds, Rhubarb Drink, 276

Dorothy Dorrance
Old-Fashioned Cooked Dressing, 53
Strawberry Salad, 43

Crescent Dragonwagon, Dairy Hollow House Gingerbread Muffins, 107

Rose Drinkwater, Onion Pie, 79

Norma Duer, Grandmother Cox's Christmas Cake, 201

Mary Dye, Molasses Fruitcake, 212

Judy Fairless, Orange-Cranberry Sauce, 227

Erica Fitzpatrick, French Doughnuts, 260

Brenda Flasowski, Spicy Pumpkin Bread, 105

Jim Fobel, Pumpkin Seed Dip, 20

Eleanor Forbes, Ginger Spice Cake, 146

Fouche, Frances
Light Crisp Waffles, 272
St. David's Day Leeks, 65

Carole Fuller, Chocolate Marie Cake, 138

Linda Gay, Annie's Pickled Shrimp, 14

Sage German, Arctic Salmon Cooked in a Dishwasher, 91

Sibley Gillis
Curried Brussels Sprouts in Cream, 73
Goat Cheese with Garlic and Herbs, 18
Santa Fe Pecans, 22

Tracy Gilmore, Momma G's Applesauce Cake, 148–49

Kathleen Gordon, Triple Meat Marinade, 92

Phyllis Gore, Tater Pie, 131

Nini Guidotti, Icebox Cookies, 187

Nancy Hammel, Sweet Hot Mustard, 241

Susie Hammer, German Rum Topf, 252

Lee Harmer
Cheese Grits, 74
Fried Tomatoes, 274

Bertram Heckel, Blue Cheese Mousse, 21

Marguerite Re
Finnish Pancakes, 279
Finnish Sour Rye Bread, 106
Bettylu Reeves, Pickled Mustard
Beans, 239
Beverly Reid, Alaskan Blueberry
Buckle, 136
Marie Edna Reynolds, Blueberry
Muffins, 123
Anita Roberts, Tostadas with Sun-
Dried Tomatoes, Goat Cheese, and
Thyme, 15
Shelagh Robinson, Home-Smoked
Fish, 11
Susan Robyn, Jellied Consommé
Madrilène, 33
Jane Rodenkirch, English Toffee, 254
Barbara Rowe, Lizzies, 189
Donna Russell, The Easiest Pie
Crust, 128
Charlotte St. Germain, Red Cabbage
Salad, 52
Joyce Sanders, Old-Fashioned
Christmas Custard, 221
Sandra Schifferle, Curried Chicken
Salad, 39
Linda Schwerin
Fruit Soup, 36
Lazy Daisy Cake, 147
Martha Sgriccia, Phil's Favorite
Molasses Cookies, 177
Mary Ann Shivers, Hyer's Drugstore
Pound Cake, 142

Liz Sirois, Orange Cheesecake,
160–61
Linda Sloan, Pumpkin Cheesecake,
159
Del Smith, Oakwood Feed Store Chili,
98–99
Georgia Smith, Carrot Pudding, 220
Elaine Sparkes, Dark Suet Pudding,
213
Virginia Stalder
Cranberry Pecan Pie, 198
Fruited Stuffed Goose, 86
Stuffed Crown Roast of Pork, 83
Lynn Stallworth, Lime Gelatin Salad,
41
Norma Stealy, Stibbles Scottish
Shortbread, 154
Billie Steele, Reunion Tomato Salad,
45
Mairi Stevenson, Two-Hundred
Dollar Carrot Cake, 144
Eileen Steward, Tennessee
Fruitcake, 208–9
Gysilla Stuckey, Grandmother
Watson's Tea Cookies, 174
Eleanor Sullivan, Piccalilli, 240
Joyce Sykes, Old English Almond
Tarts, 186
Judith Thorn, Spinach Balls, 6
Dot Toulson, Tomato Butter, 245
Deborah Tuosto
Autumn Squash Soup, 30
Praline Eggnog, 281
Whole Grain Pumpkin Muffins, 104

Donia Tyner, Barbecued Corned Beef,
87
Elena Ugarte, Ensaimada Filipina, 111
Clare Urion
Bril's V.I.P. Pecan Pie, 135
Raw Mushroom Salad, 46
Priscilla Van de Workeen, Pumpkin
Pie, 199
Greg Varrati, Clams Casino à la
Varrati, 12
Ursula Vedder, Peach Punch, 279
E. Kirt Walling, Ginger Marmalade,
248
Amy Wasserman, Pitman Blintzes,
269
Muriel Watson, Yule Log, 202–4
Donald Weaving, Escargots
Prosciutto, 7
Mary Angela Welsh, Aunt Pauline's
Famous Plum Pudding, 222–23
George Wertke, Cherry Nut Cake,
152
Peggy Whiter
Apricot Bread, 113
Roy's Dressing, 57
Barb Williams, Pumpkin Bread, 102
Mary Williams, Gram's Blue Ribbon
Date Nut Bread, 119
Judy Wolfe, Sweet Potatoes with
Apples and Chestnuts, 68
Sandra Wong, Turkey with Chinese
Rice Stuffing, 84–85
Janis Zarkowsky, Buttermilk Walnut
Cake, 139

INDEX

Several of the recipes for canning and pickling call for processing the food for a specific amount of time. The timing must be followed exactly to ensure safe results. In the case of fruits or high-acid vegetables, as found in these recipes, processing means to submerge the canning jars in a boiling water bath of 212° F. for the amount of time indicated in each recipe. In order to further ensure safe canning, please bear in mind the following instructions:

Sterilize all equipment including jars, screwbands and lids by immersing them in boiling water for 10 minutes. Keep them submerged in hot water until you are ready to use them.

Bring the water in the processing container to a full, rolling boil before adding canning jars, and make sure that at least 3 inches of water cover the jars during the entire processing procedure.

Make sure the processing container has a rack on which to place the canning jars that rests at least 3/4″ from the bottom of the container.

When pickling, make sure the brine covers the food in the canning jars completely.

Fill the jars completely and remove any air bubbles by running a spatula around the inside of the jar.

Note: If you choose to process Uncooked Mincemeat (page 195), do so in a pressure cooker, not in a boiling water bath as described above. The standard instructions for this type of recipe call for 10 pounds of pressure (240° F.) for 20 minutes, but because altitude and type of cooker can affect the amount of time and pressure needed for safe results, you should consult a canning equipment manufacturer's instructions before proceeding with this recipe.

MP9R